Witches'
Spell-A-Day
Almanac

Holidays & Lore • *Spells & Recipes*
Rituals & Meditations

You can order Llewellyn books and annuals from *New Worlds*, Llewellyn's magazine catalog. To request a free copy of the catalog, call toll-free 1-877-NEW WRLD, or visit our website at http://subscriptions.llewellyn.com.

ISBN 0-7387-0229-3
Llewellyn Worldwide
PO Box 64383, Dept. 0-7387-0229-3
St. Paul, MN 55164

Table of Contents

About the Authors

Elizabeth Barrette serves as the managing editor of *PanGaia* and assistant editor of *SageWoman*. She has been involved with the Pagan community for more than fifteen years, and in 2003 earned ordination as a priestess through Sanctuary of the Silver Moon. She lives in central Illinois and enjoys herbal landscaping and gardening for wildlife. Visit her website at: http://www.worthlink.net/~ysabet/index.html.

Stephanie Rose Bird enjoys a rich life as an artist, writer, herbalist, healer, mother, and companion. Her art work is included in several significant art collections around the world, and she is a faculty member at the School of the Art Institute of Chicago. Currently, she leads herb craft workshops at the Chicago Botanic Gardens and writes a column for *SageWoman* magazine.

Denise Dumars is cofounder of the Iseum of Isis Paedusis, an Egyptian religion study group chartered by the Fellowship of Isis. Her book *The Dark Archetype: Exploring the Shadow Side of the Divine,* coauthored with Lori Nyx, was published in 2003. Denise also teaches college English and classes on Isian religion, aromatherapy, and magic at various southern California New Age shops.

Ember is a poet and freelance writer inspired by a path of nature-centered spirituality. She enjoys listening to music, reading, gardening, camping, and hiking. Her writing has appeared in *PanGaia, newWitch,* and various Llewellyn annuals. She lives in the Midwest with her husband and two feline companions.

Emely Flak has been a practicing solitary witch for ten years. She is a freelance writer based in Daylesford, Australia, who is also employed as a learning and development professional. Much of her work is dedicated to embracing the ancient wisdom of Wicca for the personal empowerment of women in the competitive work environment.

Karen Follett has been a practitioner of witchcraft for over thirty years. Initiated in the Georgian tradition, she currently practices as a solitary. She is also a psychic, empath, energy intuitive, and educator in the metaphysical arts. By profession, she is a registered nurse, specializing in maternal and child health and teaches childbirth classes with a local hospital.

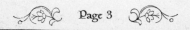

Lily Gardner-Butts has studied folklore and mythology since she learned to read. In addition to her contributions to the Llewellyn annuals, her short stories are beginning to show up in literary journals. Lily lives in Portland, Oregon, and is a member of the Power of Three coven.

James Kambos is a writer and folk artist. He holds a degree in history and has had a lifelong interest in folk magic. He has authored numerous articles on the folk magic traditions of Greece, the Near East, and the Appalachian region of the United States. The beautiful hill country of southern Ohio is where he calls home.

Ruby Lavender is a singer, herbalist, perfumer, poet, and freelance writer who teaches creative writing and film studies. She is also a Romano-Celtic Witch practicing with an Alexandrian-derived Hellenistic coven founded in 1974.

Kristin Madden is a homeschooling mom raised in a shamanic home. She is the dean of Ardantane's School of Shamanic Studies and the founder of Pathfinder Nature School. A Druid and tutor in the Order of Bards, Ovates, and Druids, Kristin also writes books and rehabilitates wild birds. Visit her online at http://www.kristinmadden.com.

Edain McCoy has practiced Witchcraft for more than twenty years and is listed in *Who's Who In America* and *Contemporary Authors*. When the economy began to slow in 2001, Edain made the difficult decision to leave her career as a stockbroker in order to write full time. She the author of nineteen Llewellyn books and has written for numerous Llewellyn annuals.

Paniteowl, simply known as "Owl" in the Pagan community, lives in the foothills of the Appalachian Mountains in northeastern Pennsylvania. She and her husband Will have fifty-six acres of natural woodland on which they are in the process of developing a private retreat for spiritual awareness.

Laurel Reufner has been a solitary Pagan for over a decade now. She is active in the local CUUPS chapter, Circle of Gaia Dreaming, and is often attracted to bright and shiny ideas. Southeastern Ohio has always been home, where she currently lives in lovely Athens County with her wonderful husband and two adorable heathens, er, daughters. Her website may be found at www.spiritrealm.com/Melinda/paganism.html.

Tammy Sullivan writes from her home in the beautiful foothills of the Great Smoky Mountains. She has been a practicing solitary Witch for over a decade. The mother of four teenagers, she is currently writing a spell book for teens.

S. Y. Zenith is three-quarters Chinese, one tad Irish, and a full solitary Pagan with an interest in both Eastern and Western traditions. Over the past two decades, she has lived and traveled to countries such as India, Nepal, Thailand, Malaysia, Singapore, Borneo, and Japan. She is now based in Australia where her time is divided between writing, experimenting with alternative remedies, and teaching the use of gems, holy beads, and religious objects from India and the Himalayas. She is also a member of the Australian Society of Authors.

Introduction

A Note on Magic and Spells

The spells in the *Witches' Spell-A-Day Almanac* evoke everyday magic designed to improve our lives and homes. You needn't be an expert on magic to follow these simple rites and spells; as you will see if you use these spells through the year, magic, once mastered, is easy to perform. The only advanced technique required of you is the art of visualization.

Visualization is an act of controlled imagination. If you can call up in your mind a picture of your best friend's face or a flag flapping in the breeze, you can visualize. In magic, visualizations are used to direct and control magical energies. Basically, the spell-caster creates a visual image of the spell's desired goal, whether it be perfect health, a safe house, or a protected pet.

Visualization is the basis of all good spells, and as such it is a tool that should be properly used. Visualization must be real in the mind of the spell-caster so that it allows him or her to raise, concentrate, and send forth energy to accomplish the spell.

Perhaps when visualizing, you'll find that you're doing everything right, but you don't feel anything. This is common, for we haven't been trained to acknowledge—let alone utilize—our magical abilities. Keep practicing, however, for your spells can "take" even if you're not the most experienced natural magician.

You will notice also that many spells in this collection have a some-what "light" tone. They are seemingly fun and frivolous, filled with rhyme and colloquial speech. This is not to diminish the seriousness of the purpose, but rather to create a relaxed atmosphere for the practitioner. Lightness of spirit helps focus energy; rhyme and common language help the spell-caster remember the words and train the mind where it is needed. The intent of this magic is indeed very serious at times; and magic is never to be trifled with.

Even when your spells are effective, magic won't usually sparkle before your very eyes. The test of magic's success is time, not immediate eye-popping results. But you can feel magic's energy for yourself by rubbing

your palms together briskly for ten seconds, then holding them a few inches apart. Sense the energy passing through them, the warm tingle in your palms. This is the power raised and used in magic. It comes from within and is perfectly natural.

Among the features of the *Witches' Spell-A-Day Almanac* are an easy-to-use "book of days" format; new spells specifically tailored for each day of the year (and its particular magical, astrological, and historical energies); and additional tips and lore for various days throughout the year—including color correspondences based on planetary influences, obscure and forgotten holidays and festivals, and an incense-of-the-day to help you waft magical energies from the ether into your space.

In creating this product, we were inspired by the ancient almanac traditions and the layout of the classic nineteenth-century almanac *Chamber's Book of Days*, which is subtitled *A Miscellany of Popular Antiquities in connection with the Calendar.* As you will see, our fifteen authors this year made history a theme of their spells, and we hope that by knowing something of the magic of past years we may make our current year all the better.

Enjoy your days, and have a magical year!

2005
Year of Spells

January

January is the first month of the year of the Gregorian calendar, and a time of beginnings. Its astrological sign is Capricorn, the goat (Dec. 20–Jan. 19), a cardinal earth sign ruled by Saturn. The name of the month itself comes from the two-faced Roman god Janus, who rules over gates and doorways. This wintry month is marked by icicles, hoarfrost, and snowdrifts, and by the warmth of the home hearth. Traditionally, handicrafts such as wool-spinning were practiced in January, and the spinning wheel has become a symbol of the season. According to Pagan traditions, even in this frozen time there are signs of new life. The days, for instance, are now slowly growing longer, and a few early flowers, such as the paper-white narcissus and white hellebore, begin blooming. The Full Moon of January is called the Storm Moon. The main holiday of the month is, of course, New Year's Day, a day that calls for safeguards, augurs, and charms. All over the world, people are eager to see what the new year will bring; they kiss strangers, shoot guns in the air, toll bells, and exchange gifts. In Scotland, people watch the threshold to see what the "firstfooter," or first visitor, augurs for the year. People who make visits on New Year's Day therefore should be sure to bring gifts of herring, bread, and wood for the fire along with them.

January 1
Saturday

New Year's Day – Kwanzaa ends

 3rd ♏

Color of the day: Black
Incense of the day: Lavender

Runic Spell for the New Year

At this time of new beginnings, adorn your altar with an orange cloth, a sapphire, and a vase of flowers. These symbols honor Odin, the god who gave the human race the runic alphabet. Place the following runes in front of you left to right: Mann (ᛗ), for the self; Beorc (ᛒ), for growth; Eh (ᛖ), for transformation; and Ing (ᛜ), for fertility. As you meditate on the runes, say: "As I live so I manifest." Ing represents the completion of beginnings. It is important to remain centered now. Finally, place the rune Feoh (ᚠ), the rune of fulfillment, in front of you. Remember to share your good fortune with others.

Lily Gardner-Butts

Notes:

Holiday lore: New Year's Day calls for safeguards, augurs, charms, and proclamations. All over the world on this day, people kiss strangers, shoot guns into the air, toll bells, and exchange gifts. Preferred gifts are herring, bread, and fuel for the fire.

January 2
Sunday

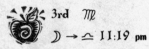 3rd ♏
☽ → ♎ 11:19 pm

Color of the day: Yellow
Incense of the day: Poplar

New Year Affirmation

We constantly hear of the benefits of positive thinking and keeping an optimistic attitude. These intentions are also behind the power of magic, so affirmations and visualizations can give your spells personal power to guarantee success. Try this exercise for positive thinking: Focus on an area of your life that needs improvement. You must convince your unconscious mind to believe you will get what you need. After all, you deserve it. Write an affirmation in support of this need. For example, write something like: "I am a strong and healthy person." Be as specific as possible about your situation. "I deserve a raise so I can pay my rent." "I will find true love in my life." "I will lose fifteen pounds

before spring." Write several sentences if necessary. Repeat this activity several times a day, and speak the sentences aloud to yourself if possible. Memorize the words. Believe in them. Picture yourself in the situation you desire.

Ember

Notes:

names of your family nine times on a piece of paper. Fold the paper three times, and place it on the center of your altar. Weight the paper with a piece of coral or topaz. Pray to Saint Genevieve to keep you and yours safe from harm.

Lily Gardner-Butts

Notes:

January 3
Monday

 3rd ♎
Fourth Quarter 12:46 pm

Color of the day: Gray
Incense of the day: Maple

Spell to Avert Disaster

Saint Genevieve, whose feast day is celebrated today, saved Paris from both the Franks and Attila the Hun. Parisians continue to invoke her in troubled times. Begin this spell by fasting for twenty-four hours, then eat a meal of beans and barley bread, nothing more. Anoint two candles—one green, one gold—with a mixture of four drops of basil, four drops of geranium, two drops of pine, and six of clove. Write your name and the

January 4
Tuesday

 4th ♎
☽ → ♏ 7:00 pm

Color of the day: Red
Incense of the day: Gardenia

Return to Stress Protection Spell

At this time of year, many of us return to work after the festive holiday season break. For most of us, it's been an exhausting or exhilarating few days celebrating with friends and family. Because of the return after a long pause, you risk returning to an environment of job-related negativity and conflict. This can threaten your holiday happiness and spiritual harmony. Protect yourself from this unnecessary disruption to your personal bliss. Here are some tips to reduce stress and to bring magic and inspiration to your workplace or office:

> Start the year fresh by removing clutter from your desk and in trays.
>
> Place a crystal on your desk to absorb any excess energy from your computer.
>
> Keep a bowl of water in your work area to take in negative vibrations. Change the water daily.
>
> Display your favorite inspirational quotations around your desk.

Emely Flak

Notes:

Two Months Till Spring Spell

We miss the Sun in January. To overcome seasonal affective disorder, try this simple spell. Turn on all the lights in your home. In your favorite room, light at least seven candles. Burn incense with a spring aroma, such as hyacinth or lavender, then relax and meditate. Envision a spring garden with buds bursting through the earth. Speak the following in a soft chant: "I am the Sun; the Sun is within me. My joy will increase, by my will mote it be." Repeat at least three times. When you are finished, fix yourself a cup of herbal tea and begin planning a garden. Picture your home as it will be when the plants are established.

Paniteowl

Notes:

January 5
Wednesday

4th ♏

Color of the day: Brown
Incense of the day: Cedar

January 6
Thursday

4th ♏
☽ → ♐ 10:44 pm

Color of the day: Green
Incense of the day: Evergreen

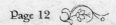

Make a Wish Spell

Today is Epiphany, or the Twelfth Night of Christmas. This holiday is considered to be a night of great power and is honored worldwide. In Greece, the homeland of my grandparents, it was believed this was the night wishes could come true. Many cultures hold celebrations and feasts on this night. Gather family and friends at your home. For dessert serve rich cakes, pastries, and plenty of chocolate. Top off the meal with coffee and a new bottle of sweet white wine. Then have your guests write one wish on a small piece of white paper. Ask them to wish for something they would like to see occur in the coming year. Place all the wishes in a roaring fire, and let each person visualize their wish merging with the rising smoke and being answered by the divine.

James Kambos

Notes:

Holiday lore: Twelfth night and the night following it are when wassailing used to take place. The word "wassail" comes from the Anglo-Saxon words *waes heil*, meaning "to

be whole or healthy." People drank to each other's health from a large bowl filled with drink such as "lamb's wool," which was made of hot ale or cider, nutmeg, and sugar with roasted crab apples. In some parts of Britain, trees and bees are still wassailed to ensure a healthy crop. Having drunk to the tree's health, people fire shotguns into the branches. Different regions sing different wassail songs to the tree. Here's one from Worcestershire:

> Here's to thee, old apple tree,
> Whence thou mayest bud,
> Whence thou mayest blow,
> Whence thou mayest bear
>   apples enow.

January 7
Friday

 4♌ ♐

Color of the day: White
Incense of the day: Ginger

Feast of Aphrodite Ritual

Today is a good day to celebrate the goddess Aphrodite's many blessings. Prepare a feast in honor of Aphrodite's loving sensuality and warmth. Decorate your house with pink carnations, the flowers of friendship. Burn yellow sandalwood-scented candles. Sandalwood helps loosen inhibitions. Put symbols of love, such as pomegranates, apples, and seashells in blue ceramic or crystal bowls, and

invite friends to bring an aphrodisiac food for sharing (cherries, oysters, papaya, chocolate, and red wine are appropriate). Open a window or door slightly, and join hands around the dinner table, reciting thrice:

> Aphrodite,
> Goddess of friendship,
>   love, and life,
> Come join us.
> Bring peace, and
>   eliminate all strife.
>
> We welcome you with
>   fruit, flowers, fire, and
>   fresh air.
> Release us from anxiety,
>   stress, and despair.
>
> Come down, be with us.
> Visit on this special day.
> We call you with love.
> We hope you will stay.

Stephanie Rose Bird

Notes:

Color of the day: Indigo
Incense of the day: Jasmine

Weight Loss Spell

To lose a bit of weight, take a black candle and carve the number of pounds you wish to lose into it. Take a red candle and carve the words "weight loss" lengthwise into it. Light the red candle and let it drip onto the black candle. Charge the black candle by visualizing how you will look with the extra weight gone. Light the black candle and say: "Extra weight melts away from me. I am healed and harmonized. My body is beautiful." Repeat the chant until the black candle has burned down completely. Carry the hardened wax chips with you until you reach your desired weight. Repeat this spell as needed.

Tammy Sullivan

Notes:

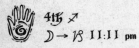

January 8
Saturday

4th ♐
☽ → ♑ 11:11 pm

January 9
Sunday

4th ♑

Color of the day: Orange
Incense of the day: Cinnamon

Using Ginseng Spell

For guarding health and drawing strength and courage, ginseng is very useful. It's not for nothing that ginseng is called the "wonder of the world" root. Carry the root with you, in pieces or whole, wrapped in a piece of red cloth and secured with gold or orange thread. Or else keep a ginseng pouch in your living room or on your altar. Ginseng when burnt and used as a fumigant is potent for breaking hexes. For purifying home interiors, place ginseng root on your altar for three days. Then soak it in a bowl of warm water and leave it to stand overnight. Sprinkle the water from the bowl around the rooms of your home, or on the windows and doors. Sprinkle the water in the four corners of the property for protection against entities. Store the ginseng water in a spray bottle. Before you dress each morning, lightly spritz your body from head to foot. The ginseng spritz is especially helpful for those engaged in healing and psychic work.

S. Y. Zenith

Notes:

January 10
Monday

4th ♑

New Moon 7:03 am

☽ → ♒ 9:37 pm

Color of the day: Lavender
Incense of the day: Lilac

Crone Power Spell

The New Moon on the Moon's day in the dark of winter is a perfect time to access the power of the Crone. The Goddess as Crone is not to be feared; she is the loving grandmother, the powerful mentor, and the wise elder. Place black and silver candles and oak leaves if possible on your altar. Burn a flowery incense as the Crone is feminine as well as strong. Place a statue of your favorite Crone goddess on the altar if you wish. Offer a libation of a liqueur such as Strega. Call quarters or cast a simple circle. Meditate on the Crone as goddess, then say:

> Lady of night,
> Wise counsel and brave
> elder,
> Touch my life,
> Touch my heart.

Now you may ask the Crone for the guidance you seek. Once the candles and incense have burned, dispose of them, if possible, in a receptacle near a crossroads.

Denise Dumars

January 11
Tuesday

 1st ≈

Color of the day: Black

Incense of the day: Honeysuckle

Carmenta's Blessings

Today is the day of the Carmenta, the Roman childbirth goddess. Seek Carmenta's blessings of good health and safe delivery in your own pregnancy. Find some quiet time when you will not be disturbed. Light a white candle, and focus on your body's good health and the good health of your unborn child. Ask Carmenta to continue watching over both of you during the duration of your pregnancy and to offer you safe delivery. Try to repeat the quiet meditation every Tuesday thereafter until your baby is delivered. Find time afterwards to light the candle once more and thank Carmenta for her protection.

Laurel Reufner

January 12
Wednesday

1st ≈

☽ → ♓ 9:50 pm

Color of the day: White

Incense of the day: Maple

More Offerings to Carmenta

The Roman holiday of Carmentalia honors the goddess Carmenta, who oversees pregnancy and childbirth. Pregnant women made offerings of rice to Carmenta to ensure an easy delivery. People also hung straw dolls to propitiate Mania, the mother of ghosts, since the door of life swings both ways. Carmenta's feast foods include long cream-filled and triangular raspberry-filled pastries to represent the genitalia from which all life springs. Bake or buy a batch of these to share with friends. If you or someone you know is pregnant, today is perfect for a baby shower. Or you can babysit for friends who have small children, or

donate baby clothes to a charity. Here is a verse for working with Carmenta:

> Mother, sister, daughter, wife,
> hinge that hangs the door of life,
> Pour your blessings on the earth,
> healthy baby, gentle birth.

Elizabeth Barrette

Notes:

amount of nutmeg in the center of the dollar, and fold it up tightly. Seal it with a paper clip or a gold string. Hold the dollar packet with both hands at forehead level. Visualize this dollar attracting other bills of all denominations. Now hold the packet in front of your heart and feel how wonderful it is to have money. Call up a belief that your dollar has become a money magnet and will always attract what you need. Carry your money magnet in your wallet at all times, and trust that it is working.

Kristin Madden

Notes:

January 13
Thursday

 1st ♓

Color of the day: Turquoise
Incense of the day: Vanilla

Money Magnet Spell

With three planets in Capricorn, this is a wonderful day to do success and money magic. And with the Moon in Pisces, an emotional investment adds power to your spells. Purify a clean dollar bill with the smoke of burning sage. Place a small

January 14
Friday

 1st ♎

Color of the day: Pink
Incense of the day: Parsley

Resting Season Spell

All species have their resting season. Humans too have cycles, even though they are the only species that looks upon inactivity as being "bad." So let's honor our cycles, and embrace our natural behaviors by turning off all the lights in our homes some time today. Light a green votive candle, and burn incense such as patchouli or pine. Relax, and play soothing music or nature sounds. Breathe deeply, and imagine you are a bear deep in its winter cave, or a seed buried deep in the earth. Speak the following words:

> I am of the earth. I am one with all things. I will care for myself. I will allow myself to rest.

When you are ready, turn on the lights and let the candle burn out. As you go through your busy days, remember the joy of allowing yourself the luxury of doing nothing.

Paniteowl

Notes:

Preparing for Blooms Spell

January can be deceiving. On the surface, all may appear to be frozen in stillness. Under this quiet surface, however, a flurry of soil-nourishing activity is occurring. Such activity assures healthy growth in spring and the eventual bounty of the harvest. Focus now on your desires for personal growth and eventual harvest. Focus on the mental or emotional attributes that need to be nourished in order to sustain your growth. Sit in front of a mirror that reflects your face. Light candles and incense that are attuned to the attributes you desire, and place them between you and the mirror. As the incense and candles burn, visualize this attribute being nourished inside of you. Document how these attributes are nourishing you. Be aware of any changes that you see manifesting in your life. When you feel that your soil is nourished, seek your bounty.

Karen Follett

Notes:

January 15
Saturday

1st ♓

☽ → ♈ 12:27 am

Color of the day: Gray
Incense of the day: Violet

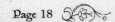

January 16
Sunday

 1st ♈

Color of the day: Gold
Incense of the day: Sage

Fire Spell for Change

On this day, Buddhist monks pay homage to Betora Bromo, the Indonesian god of fire. Fire is the element of change, so write down the intentions you made for the New Year. Have flowers and small gifts of food prepared for the gods of fire. If you have a fireplace, start a new fire in it. If you don't, pour sand in the bottom of your cauldron to a height that will hold a candle. Burn your gifts and thank the powers of fire. When the gifts are burned, meditate on the changes that you need to make in order to realize your New Year's resolutions. When you feel ready to burn your intentions, say:

> I wish for this, this wish
> to be. I wish this wish,
> this wish for me.

Lily Gardner-Butts

Notes:

January 17
Monday

Birthday of Martin Luther King, Jr.
(observed)

 1st ♈

Second Quarter 1:57 am

☽ → ♉ 7:06 am

Color of the day: White
Incense of the day: Coriander

Benjamin Franklin's Birthday Spell

Benjamin Franklin is one of America's most famous statesmen. He was also a creator, a thinker, and a doer. Franklin loved two simple yet joyful activities almost more than life itself—reading and air baths. We can then use his example to honor his memory. Find some time today for a ritual inspired by Benjamin Franklin's love for books and air. Start by pulling a comfortable chair to a spot near a window. Open the window just enough to let in some cool air. Grab an interesting book, the newspaper, or some of your favorite magazines. Take off your clothes. Sit down and relax in the chair. Feel the gentle element of winter air interact with your body. Read. When it becomes too cold, simply close the window—but always continue to read and enjoy the fresh air that you've let inside your home.

Stephanie Rose Bird

Notes:

deities to be with me in all things. I trust I can change those things that are harmful to me. I trust that I can achieve my goals." Do this as often as you like.

Paniteowl

Notes:

January 18
Tuesday

2nd ♉

Color of the day: Maroon
Incense of the day: Poplar

Change You Spell

The first thing any spell changes is you. Words have power, and as you weave a spell, you must be aware of what you are saying. "I will do something" is a very different statement from "I will try to do something." A friend once told me his tribe teaches never to say "try"; instead, always say "I trust I can do this." This advice is in fact very invaluable in spellworking. If there is an area in your life you'd like to improve, try this simple affirmation. First, gaze into your mirror. Light a pink votive candle, and turn off the lights in the room. Say this affirmation three times: "I trust that I am an honorable person. I trust my

January 19
Wednesday

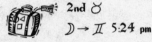 2nd ♉

☽ → ♊ 5:24 pm

☉ → ♒ 6:22 pm

Color of the day: Yellow
Incense of the day: Pine

Breaking Winter Doldrums Spell

January is rough. It's cold and dark, and winter doldrums can set in. This is just the right time for a spell of creativity enhancement. Everyone is creative. Some can sing and dance, others have a green thumb or a way with animals. Some are wordsmiths or good cooks; others are good at magic. Begin by drawing a symbolic picture of yourself with some images representing the talents you'd like to develop. Draw yourself writing in your journal, or taking photos, or

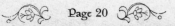

working in your garden. Next, create a small altar in a place that you see every day. Place the drawing on your altar with some other items symbolizing the talents you wish to enhance. Be creative with this—use a packet of seeds, a paintbrush, or a favorite CD as symbols. Wednesday is Mercury's day, of new beginnings and creativity. Light a yellow candle, visualizing yourself doing what you love. Each day take some time, even if only a few minutes, to practice your talent. Place offerings on the altar—flowers, fruit, wine, stones—that further symbolize your resolve to nurture your burgeoning talents.

Ruby Lavender

Notes:

negative associations. Visualize a world where money is available to everyone. Imagine that money will be there when you need it. Take the coin or bill and place it on your altar or other personal space. Surround it with a circle of stones and crystals, and imagine this as a protective barrier to keep the funds safe. Sprinkle dried basil over the circle and chant:

> There is no need that
>   can't be met,
> I have the means to pay
>   all debts.
> The funds will come, and
>   bring no harm.
> In love and trust, I bless
>   this charm.

After one entire moon cycle, put the coin or bill away in a safe place.

Ember

Notes:

January 20
Thursday
Inauguration Day

 2nd ♊

Color of the day: Purple
Incense of the day: Sandalwood

Money Smoke Spell

Pass a coin or bill through smoke of burning sage to clear it of all

January 21
Friday

 2nd ♊

Color of the day: Rose
Incense of the day: Rose

Marigold Spell for Love's Longevity

The marigold (*Calendula officinalis*), as a symbol of endurance, was in the old days referred to as "husband's dial" and "summer's bride" in Britain. It was often used in a wedding garland. Obtain some earth from your partner's footprints and mix it with fertile soil enough to fill a terra cotta pot. Plant a handful of marigold seeds in the pot, and place it in a sunny spot. Water and nurture the pot with care so that the marigolds will self-seed for many years, drawing influences of stability, constancy, and fidelity. Marigold petals added to bathwater helps regain affection and respect from a loved one after a tiff or separation. When planning romantic evenings at home, light pink candles and place marigold flowers together with roses in a vase. Decorate the base of the vase by surrounding it with rose quartz stones. Relax and enjoy.

S. Y. Zenith

Notes:

Holiday lore: Feast Day of Saint Agnes of Rome. Since the fourth century, the primitive church held Saint Agnes in high honor above all the other virgin martyrs of Rome. Church Fathers and Christian poets sang her praises, and they extolled her virginity and heroism under torture. The feast day for Saint Agnes was assigned to January 21. Early records gave the same date for her feast and the Catholic Church continues to keep her memory sacred.

January 22
Saturday

2nd ♊

☽ → ♋ 5:42 am

Color of the day: Black
Incense of the day: Cedar

Brain Power Spell

For this spell you need a yellow candle, some rosemary oil, and a carving instrument. Carve the word "clarity" lengthwise on one side of the candle, and on the other side carve the word "logic." Repeat with the words "memory" and "concentration." Anoint the candle with rosemary oil. Hold the candle to your mouth and whisper:

> I set your task
> To bring forth what I
> ask:
> Improved memory,

And perfect clarity.
I concentrate longer,
My logic is stronger,
With goodwill to all
And harm to none.
As I speak it
So it is done!

Repeat the chant nine times. Allow the candle to burn out. Save some of the hardened wax drippings for use in sachets.

Tammy Sullivan

Notes:

of Alexandria, he was known for his generosity to those less fortunate, regardless of their religion. Today would be a good time to perform a spell that would focus your energy on giving. On your altar place one white candle, a small new house-plant, and one penny. Light the candle and say: "This candle burns for the ill, the poor, and the lonely. Let this flame lead me to those in need. So mote it be." Thank the earth for what you have by pressing the penny into the plant's soil. As you care for the plant let it remind you of the spell, and as the plant grows know that so does your spirit of giving.

James Kambos

Notes:

January 23
Sunday

 2nd ☽

Color of the day: Amber
Incense of the day: Basil

Charity-Giving Spell

Sometimes life gets so hectic we fail to take time to give our aid to charity. This is the feast day of St. John the Almsgiver; as patriarch

January 24
Monday

 2nd ♋

☽ → ♌ 6:21 pm

Color of the day: Silver
Incense of the day: Myrrh

Abundance of Alasitas Spell

Today marks the beginning of the annual seven-day Alasitas Fair in Bolivia. This celebration is dedicated to Ekeko, the Bolivian god of the household. Bolivians celebrate Alasitas as a festival of abundance. In agrarian times, the fair celebrated a plentiful harvest. Today, it's a time to invoke abundance in your life in the form of success in all your endeavors and more general happiness in your personal life. And this year, this festival is ideally positioned just before a Full Moon. So, to take advantage of the Alasitas energy of abundance, write your desire or something you wish to attract on a yellow piece of paper. Make sure that your wish is a positive one, and ideally make it a wish that is achievable and realistic. Fold up the paper along with a small magnet to enhance the force of attraction. Tie or tape the folded paper to secure it. Keep it with you in your bag or pocket, or at least close to you.

Emely Flak

Notes:

January 25
Tuesday
Burns' Night in Scotland

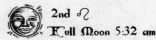 2nd ♌

🌕 **Full Moon** 5:32 am

Color of the day: Scarlet
Incense of the day: Juniper

Let Sekhmet Roar Spell

This is an excellent day to show leadership ability. Wear an article of red clothing today such as a red "power" tie, and, if you wear jewelry, wear gold. Call on Sekhmet, the Egyptian lioness goddess, to help you gain the strength you need to succeed. Today you will have both the Sun and the Moon shining on your endeavors; make good use of their blessings. On your altar place a small statue of Sekhmet or of a lioness, a red rose, and a libation of red ale. In the morning, step outside, greet the Sun, and say:

Solar lioness,
Shine on me!
Amplify my light,

Let me lead!
Sa sekhem,
Sa sekhem,
Great lady Sekhmet.

Repeat this under the Full Moon as it rises. Toast Sekhmet at cocktail hour with a red ale, saying: "Sa sekhem, sa sekhem." Any success sought today will bring rich rewards.

Denise Dumars

Notes:

Holiday lore: Burns' Night is a key event in Scotland that has been observed for about 200 years in honor of Robert Burns, who was born on this day. One of Scotland's most beloved bards, Burns immortalized haggis in a famous poem. This a Scottish dish of animal organs boiled in a sheep's stomach with suet and oatmeal. "Burns' Suppers" are celebrated not only in Scotland but wherever patriotic Scots or those of Scottish descent live.

January 26
Wednesday

 3rd ♌

Color of the day: Topaz
Incense of the day: Neroli

Protection from Aggressive Business Competitors

Is business competition starting to harm your company? Try this spell to lessen the effects of aggressive competitors. Light a black candle. On a piece of paper either write or draw a general description of whatever business you and your competition are engaged in. Mentally picture customers or clients standing before both of your businesses and then making the choice to enter yours instead of your competition's. Please be careful what you wish for. This spell isn't intended to destroy your competition, merely to lessen the impact they have on your business. When you are satisfied with the amount of energy you've poured into your drawing, rip it in half and light it on fire with the candle while chanting repeatedly:

Mercury, hear my plea.
Bring more customers to
me.

Make sure there's a fire-proof container nearby so you can drop the flaming paper into it. Scatter the ashes.

Laurel Reufner

Notes:

Set us both free.
As swords into
plowshares,
So mote it be.

Keep the folded images with you as a reminder of peace.

Elizabeth Barrette

Notes:

January 27
Thursday

 3rd ♌

☽ → ♏ 6:24 am

Color of the day: White
Incense of the day: Carnation

All Work Together Spell

We all get into arguments sometimes. This spell helps set aside past animosity so that people can work together again. To start, sort out the sword and coin suits from a tarot deck. Choose the sword card that closely represents your current situation, and pick out the coin card that represents your desired goals. Photocopy each and cut them out. Hold the sword copy and say: "Here is where I am." Switch to the coin copy and say: "Here is where I want to be." Now fold the two copies together so that the coin completely encloses the sword, and say:

Symbols of power,
Do as you see
Past grievances settle,

January 28
Friday

 1st ♈

Color of the day: Coral
Incense of the day: Dill

Banana Split Celebration Spell

Indulge yourself today in a joyous celebration of all the healthy, loving relationships you now have and that you have had in the past. Create a magical banana split! Begin by first charging a small bowl of chopped nuts. Holding your palms open over the bowl, send the feeling of being in a healthy, happy relationship into the nuts. Tell yourself that you will continue to create these experiences throughout your life. Slice a banana in half, and lay it in the bottom of a bowl. Top it with a generous scoop of your favorite ice cream. Add fresh whipped cream, the nuts, strawberries, and blackberries. Top it off with three cherries. With each bite give thanks for each moment you have with a special person. Bless that person and yourself, knowing that you will continue to experience many beautiful memories and loving relationships.

Kristin Madden

Notes:

January 29
Saturday

 3rd ♏

☽ → ♎ 5:13 pm

Color of the day: Blue
Incense of the day: Patchouli

Stay at home Time Spell

In the Gaulish Coligny calendar, this time is marked as Anagantiros, or "stay at home time," because bad weather keeps people in. January's Full Moon is also called the Storm Moon. Try doing a spell now to bless your hearth. If you do not have a fireplace, your stove or kitchen table will do. Light a green candle for abundance and calm energy. Make a small charm

bag by taking a square of fabric of about four or five inches, and placing some dried herbs inside it sacred to Hestia, goddess of the hearth. These include rose petals, pennyroyal, acorns, rosemary, cinnamon, and lavender. Tie the bag with a green ribbon. Place it near your hearth, saying:

> Goddess hestia, I honor
> you with these herbs, and
> ask you to preside over
> my hearth and my home,
> blessing it with good will,
> abundance, and hospitality
> from within and without.

On nights when the weather is not too harsh, ask Hestia's help with blessing a small gathering of friends. Have a potluck, a dinner party, or just some pizza and beer.

Ruby Lavender

Notes:

January 30
Sunday

 3rd ♎

Color of the day: Orange
Incense of the day: Coriander

Festival of Janus Dedication

The month of January is named after Janus, the two-headed god who faces both the future and the past. His symbol is the threshold. For this spell, you will need a small cake, a goblet of wine, and a sheet of fine paper. Fold the paper in half lengthwise. On one half of the paper, write the things you learned and accomplished from the prior year. On the other half, write your goals for the new year. Cast your circle. Offer the cake and say:

> Great god Janus, with
> this offering of cake, I
> pray thee.
> Be generous to me, my
> household, and my family.

Offer the wine and say:

> O Father Janus, as I
> have prayed thee good
> prayers in offering these
> gifts.
> For the same object let this
> offering of wine succeed.

Burn the paper with your past and future.

Lily Gardner-Butts

Notes:

January 31
Monday

3rd ♎

Color of the day: Ivory
Incense of the day: Chrysanthemum

Light of higher Self Spell

I love watching cartoon characters get ideas. Each time a revelation occurs, a literal light bulb lights up over their heads. Wouldn't it be great if we had such light bulbs to signal revelations? Then again, we do have them—we call them spirit guides. We may not always recognize the signals, but their light is there. Using a guided meditation, visualize a stream of reciprocal energy flowing between you and your guide. Request a signal that indicates an incoming message. Focus on any sensations, words, or visions that follow. Document any perceived messages, your response, and the outcome until you feel comfortable discerning the voice of your guide from the voice of your ego.

Karen Follett

Notes:

February

February is the second month of the Gregorian calendar, and the year's shortest month. Its astrological sign is Aquarius, the water-bearer (Jan 19-Feb 18), a fixed air sign ruled by unpredictable Uranus. The month itself is named for Februa, an ancient festival of purification. As days slowly lengthen, people begin to emerge from their inward state and look outward toward the planting season. There are signs of life as snow begins to recede, buds begin to appear, and some herbs such as thyme and witch hazel begin to grow. February is traditionally a good time for foretelling the future and for purifying oneself. The Full Moon of the month is appropriately called the Chaste Moon. February is also the time for banishing winter, and the main holiday of the month, Imbolc or Candlemas, is a time to gather the greenery used to adorn the house during Yuletide and use it to feed a sabbat fire. A ritual of the season is known as the Bride's Bed, in which a bundle of corn from the harvest is dressed in ribbons and becomes the Corn Bride. At midmonth, we celebrate Valentine's Day, named for the legendary patron saint of love. Images of Cupid, Venus, and the heart are common on this day. Medieval people believed February 14 was the day wild birds chose to couple in order to begin their spring mating.

February 1
Tuesday

3rd ♎
☽ → ♏ 1:51 am

Color of the day: Black
Incense of the day: Poplar

Magical Talisman Spell

Have you ever made a magical talisman? A talisman is a symbol, unique to you, that establishes a subtle yet powerful connection to your goal. To do this, on a piece of paper write your desired wish. Cross out the vowels and any letters that are repeated. Ideally, you are left with a list of meaningless letters. They are, however, of great significance. Using your creativity, make use of color, paper, and any writing implements you wish, and arrange these letters to make a design. You can overlap, decorate, and interlace letters. When you are happy with the final result, put your talisman, now charged with your own energy, away in a safe place. Hold the image you created in your mind's eye to charge your talisman and your goal continually.

Emely Flak

Notes:

February 2
Wednesday
Imbolc – Groundhog Day

3rd ♏
Fourth Quarter 2:27 am
Color of the day: Brown
Incense of the day: Sandalwood

Eternal Flame Within Spell

With the coming of February comes the Sun. It is growing stronger with each day. We also now honor the Irish goddess Brigid who holds the eternal flame of inspiration, transformation, and personal sovereignty. To ignite Brigid's eternal flame within yourself, you will need a white candle, preferably a large one with a firm foundation. You'll also need matches and an item that reminds you of a specific goal you want to achieve in the coming spring and summer. Sit on a chair or on the floor, placing the unlit candle in front of you. Take time to center yourself, focusing on connecting with Brigid's powers, while you also visualize her fire rising within you. When you are ready, light the candle and say:

> Blessed Brigid of the
> golden flame,
> hear me as I call your
> name:
> I invoke your spirit to
> burn in me,

**All I will, precious Lady,
so it must be.**

Keep your eyes open and gaze into the hazy yellow color of the flame's aura. (If you're sitting too close to the candle, gazing into the flame itself can harm your eyes.) Visualize the powers of inspiration, transformation, and personal sovereignty burning within you. When you feel you've been successful, offer your thanks to Brigid and extinguish the candle. Keep it covered and in a safe place so you can enact this spell whenever you feel you need the power of Brigid in your life.

Edain McCoy

Notes:

Holiday lore: On Imbolc, a bundle of corn from the harvest is dressed in ribbons and becomes the Corn Bride. On February 2, the Corn Bride is placed on the hearth or hung on the door to bring prosperity, fertility, and protection to the home.

February 3
Thursday

 4th ♏

☽ → ♐ 7:21 am

Color of the day: Green
Incense of the day: Carnation

Prayer Stick Spell

For this spell, find an appropriate stick—it should be about twelve inches long and a half inch in diameter. Ideally, find a twig that has fallen from a tree. If you must cut one, be sure to give thanks to the tree for the gift. Bless the stick with each of the four elements. Pass it through incense smoke for air, through a candle flame for fire, and sprinkle it with salt water for both water and earth elements. Say any words of blessing that you choose. Decorate the stick with ribbons, feathers, beads, and so on by tying them around the top. Hold the stick in your hand as you pray or meditate. You can also stick it in the ground outside and sit before it. On a breezy day the wind will move the ribbons and feathers and you can meditate on this movement.

Ember

Notes:

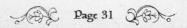

February 4
Friday

 4th ♐

    Color of the day: Pink

Incense of the day: Thyme

Setsubun Spell

The noisy, joyous Japanese holiday than ends winter and opens spring, Setsubun is the day that falls between one season and the other. While many traditions are associated with Setsubun, one of the most loved traditions is the *mame maki* ritual performed to cast out evil demons from the home and to promote good fortune for the household. During the ritual, the head of the household walks from room to room, scattering handfuls of roasted soybeans as all shout: *"Oni wa soto. Fuki wa uchi!"* (Out with the ogre. In with happiness!) Everyone in the household then eats one bean for each year of their age in order to bring personal good luck. Try the mame maki ritual at home to bring in your own good luck and to kick out any lingering ogres and demons.

Laurel Reufner

Notes:

February 5
Saturday

 4th ♐

    ☽ → ♑ 9:32 am

Color of the day: Gray

Incense of the day: Lilac

Transfer Anger to Energy Spell

The moss agate stone is known for its ability to hold energy and healing powers. With the aid of this stone and this simple spell you can store your anger and transform it into a more useful form of energy. When you are angry, take the stone in your right hand. Allow the anger to stream through your palm into the stone. When you are done, store the stone away. When you need to make use of this energy, take the stone into your right hand and visualize white light filling it, saying:

> What once was destruc-
> tive, now is pure. Where
> once was uncertainty,
> now is sure.

Place the stone on your altar, or boil it to infuse your home with its energy.

Tammy Sullivan

Notes:

February 6
Sunday

 4th ♑

Color of the day: Orange
Incense of the day: Clove

Shopping Spree Spell

Place a ten-dollar bill on the desk or table where you keep your bills. Fold the bill in half, and place a magnifying glass on top of the bill. See how large the bill becomes under the glass. Now think how valuable the large bill could be in a perfect world. Leave the bill under the magnifying glass for three days, and each morning and evening say:

> Goddesses of fertility,
> Come with me on my
>   shopping spree.
> Guide my steps to plenty;
> Make my ten dollars
>   spend like twenty.
> Let my wishes prevail,
> So I find everything on
>   sale.

Take the bill with you when you go shopping, and watch for signs that the Goddess has heard your petition.

Paniteowl

Notes:

February 7
Monday

 4th ♑
☽ → ♒ 9:26 am

Color of the day: Lavender
Incense of the day: Daffodil

Peace and harmony Spell

This is a good day to work toward emotional peace and harmony within yourself and among your friends and family. Soak three olives in a half cup of olive oil. Placing both hands around the container, visualize peace and love spreading through your circle of loved ones. Chant silently or aloud:

> Three olives I do see,
> Granting peace and
>   harmony.
>
> Olive oil, do your part,
> heal us all—body, mind,
>   and heart.

Cook dinner with the olive oil, knowing that this spell is permeating your food. The olives may be eaten to help manifest the spell: one by you, one by a family member, and one by a friend. Alternatively, the olives may be buried in the earth. Ask the earth to ground this energy into you and your loved ones that this peace and harmony might spread through you and into the rest of the wider world.

Kristin Madden

Notes:

February 8
Tuesday
Mardi Gras

 4th ♒
New Moon 5:28 pm

Color of the day: Maroon
Incense of the day: Evergreen

Start a Creative Project Spell

We are in the season of Brigid, the goddess of poets and smiths. With the New Moon in innovative, creative Aquarius, the light of Brigid shines upon those who work in creative fields. Place orange candles for mental energy on your altar and light a Celtic blend incense. Sit in a room with an electric light and remove its shade. At dusk, call Brigid:

> Brigid of the forge,
> Forge for me
> New creativity.
> Light and growth
> Aids us both.

Now close your eyes and mentally picture a light bulb lit above your head, such as when a cartoon character has a new idea. Laugh if this seems at all funny! Play and laughter are important aspects of creativity. Meditate on the creative project you would like to begin. When you have the idea firmly in mind, light the candles and turn on the light. The bulb symbolizes the initiation of the creative project. Say:

> Brigid the bard
> I will work hard
> To see this new creation
> To successful completion.

From now until the Full Moon, spend as much time as possible working on your new creative project.

Denise Dumars

Notes:

Holiday lore: Today is the Buddhist Needle Memorial. On this day, as part of the principle of endless compassion espoused by the Buddhist faith for all sentient and nonsentient beings, all the sewing needles that have been retired during the year are honored. That is, needles are brought to

the shrine and pushed into a slab of tofu that rests on the second tier of a three-tiered altar. Priests sing sutras to comfort the needles and heal their injured spirits.

February 9
Wednesday
Ash Wednesday – Chinese New Year

 4th ≈
)→ ♓ 8:59 am

Color of the day: Yellow
Incense of the day: Coriander

Time to Crow Spell

Each year of the Chinese calendar is represented by an animal. This is the year of the rooster, the cocky king of the barnyard who exudes confidence. He doesn't just walk, he struts, head held high and challenging anyone who seeks to usurp his authority. At this transition time, wrap yourself in a spell of confidence that no one will be able to ignore. Appearing confident impresses your boss, and makes your family feel secure in your presence. Strangers will also believe you're a potent force they do not wish to battle. If you look like you know what you're doing and where you're going, would-be attackers will leave you alone to seek an easier mark. Connect with this cocky confidence in a place where you will not be seen or heard for at least thirty

minutes. Add a Chinese atmosphere to your working area with various decorations. You will also need four sturdy candles. If using candles is not practical, substitute pen lights, flashlights, light sticks, or anything else nonflammable. Place one at each directional point of your working area. Stand tall and visualize a rooster—how he moves, how he sounds, how he knows he's at the top of the pecking order. When you feel your inner rooster, begin to move like him. Strut, flap, cock your head, and crow! The rooster's caw is a cry of leadership and success. Walk the circle as a rooster might if he was if presenting himself to the elements. Light the candles as walk around. Keep in mind south is transformation and courage; west is intuition and the home of the deities; north is the stable earth and all her creatures, and east is home of the rising Sun to which the rooster crows to announce start of each day.

Edain McCoy

Notes:

 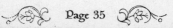

February 10
Thursday
Islamic New Year

 1st ♓
☽ → ♈ 10:21 am

Color of the day: White
Incense of the day: Geranium

Your Wishes Come True Spell

Every culture acknowledges a new year, and a celestial event is most often used to mark the transition. One old lunar calendar still in active use is the Islamic calendar. Unlike other cultures who make adjustments every few years to keep their lunar calendars falling within specific seasons, the Islamic calendar does not. Therefore their new year begins at sundown on February 10. But in 2006, it falls about 29 days earlier. Any new phase of the Moon is an excellent time to think about what your religion means to you and, if you feel so moved, to rededicate yourself to the deities you worship. Others use this time in between to make magic. As the last ray of the Sun settles behind the western horizon today, take note that the sky appears empty except for a few bright stars. There is no visible Moon, and the Sun has passed from view. You now have a universal canvas on which to paint a mental picture of your most precious desire. Lie down on the ground or an outdoor chair, just be comfortable. As more stars appear in the darkening sky, welcome them into your painting. Try to incorporate as many as possible into this huge image of your future. Remember that all those stars are suns, some much larger and hotter than our own, and the more of them you add to your canvas, the more energy you have to feed your goal. Chant:

Twinkle, twinkle, little
   star,
I watch you flicker from
   afar:
Yet millions of miles
   cannot impede,
This picture of my will
   and need.

A universe awash in tiny
   lights,
Many others hide from
   sight:
The power to change is
   in your fire,
As I will, so comes my
   desire.

                    Edain McCoy

Notes:

February 11
Friday

 1st ♈

Color of the day: Rose
Incense of the day: Sandalwood

A Dream Spell

You've cast your spell incorporating the "as above" energy with the "so below" physical action. And despite all of the work, nothing happens. The universe may have other plans for you, or perhaps the conscious mind misinterpreted the universal insight that was spoken to the unconscious mind. During sleep, the connection between the conscious mind and the unconscious mind is strongest. Dream memories, impressions, and feelings often yield the information that directs you to your goal. Write your latest dream on a small piece of paper. Place this paper in a pouch with an amethyst or some mugwort. Place the pouch on your pillow, and say:

> As I dream tonight, this
>   spell burns bright.
> Paths of manifestation
>   are revealed in morning
>   light.

Before rising from bed, record any impressions on paper. Be alert for any directions that you may receive over the coming days.

Karen Follett

Notes:

February 12
Saturday
Lincoln's Birthday

 1st ♈

Color of the day: Brown
Incense of the day: Juniper

Win Diana's Favor Spell

In the Hellenic tradition, today is the Festival of Artemis. This independent and sharp-tempered goddess champions the forest and its wildlife. Honor her by doing her work today. Fill a bird feeder, and leave some corn on the ground for squirrels and other critters. Sit down with your favorite nursery catalog and order some plants that provide food or shelter for wildlife. Donate to a conservation organization. To win Diana's favor, light a silver candle in a moon-motif candleholder on your altar and recite this invocation:

> Maiden of the silver bow,
> Mistress where no men
>   may go,

heed your servant here
below.

See the work that I
have done
By the light of Moon and
Sun:
Simple things, but well
begun.

Grant your blessings in
exchange
On the places where I
range.
Make them magical and
strange.

Elizabeth Barrette

Notes:

Holiday lore: Lincoln is called the
Great Emancipator and is thought
of as one of our great presidents.
Know this, however: Lincoln was a
rather unknown figure until the age
of forty, when he first entered the
Illinois state legislature. His later
assassination threw the country into
widespread mourning, inspiring Walt
Whitman to write:

Coffin that passes
through lanes and street,

through day and night
with the great cloud
darkening the land . . .
I mourned, and yet shall
mourn with ever—
returning spring.

February 13
Sunday

 1st ♈
☽ → ♉ 3:18 pm

Color of the day: Gold
Incense of the day: Poplar

Roman Purification Spell
This date marks the Roman festivals of Parentalia and Feralia,
a time for purification that will bring
peace and love to the household. The
goddesses to be honored now include
Hestia, Brigid, and Freya. Sprinkle
the floors with salt and rosemary,
visualizing all discord and negativity
being swept away. Burn scented white
candles to purify the air and lend
an aura of peace and contentment. It
is also traditional not to wear any
"badges of office" today, so try a day
without your pentacle, magical jewelry,
or other pagan finery, understanding
that outward displays are much less
important than what you carry inside.
Wear white for simplicity. Place
some rose quartz on the windowsill,
to invite love in. Spend the day in
calm reflection and be aware of the

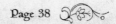

love, contentment, and peace that fills your life.

Ruby Lavender

Notes:

February 14
Monday
Valentine's Day

1st ♉

Color of the day: Silver
Incense of the day: Rose

Singing with Wolves Spell

An unusual park can be found in north-central Indiana. It exists not for the people of the state, but as a preserve for wolves and other wild canines that still roam this industrialized state. On Friday evenings, just before sundown, a guide takes parties out to small hill. There is no light except the Moon's. Everyone stands in silence waiting for the ancient song of the wolves to begin. You may feel you've been holding your breath when finally the first howl of the night is heard echoing from another hilltop. Soon the chorus is picked up by the other wolves, a discordant yet beautiful song. As you raise your head to join the chorus, you may feel a primal stirring inside you. You know without being told that this is an ancient magic. Wolves mate for life, and often will remain in their birth packs unless dominance issues force part of the pack out of the area. In honor of this love and loyalty, the Romans instituted the festival of Lupercalia, or the Festival of the Wolf. Later on the church would rename this festival in honor of St. Valentine. If you want to call out for a mate, or you wish to strengthen your bonds with your present partner or coven, go outside on Lupercalia Eve and raise your voice high in the ancient wolf song. This will help bond you with your partner, and bond all who participate to beautiful Mother Earth.

Edain McCoy

Notes:

February 15
Tuesday

 1st ♉

Second Quarter 7:16 pm

Color of the day: Gray
Incense of the day: Sage

Warrior Goddess Spell

One of America's greatest social reformers, and a key feminist icon, Susan B. Anthony, was born on this day. Her passion for social equality parallels many of the characteristics attributed to the warrior goddess Diana of ancient Roman mythology. Diana protected those who were less fortunate. To connect with your own inner warrior goddess, go to a grove of pine trees or place some pine branches on your altar, and say: "Lady of the fields and trees, I thank you for all the bounty you have brought to me." Continue with a specific request, then, to finish the spell, give thanks to the warrior goddess by leaving a small gift. To do so, decorate a pine branch with a silver star, a crescent moon, or an ornament shaped like an arrow.

James Kambos

Notes:

February 16
Wednesday

 1st ♉

☽ → ♊ 12:18 am

Color of the day: White
Incense of the day: Eucalyptus

Begin with a Thought Spell

Everything begins with a thought. As soon as you think of an outcome you would like to experience or witness, you have created the energy for it to happen. With further thoughts, you can continue to feed that energy with positive visualizations and affirmations that program your desire in your conscious and subconscious brain. Meanwhile, in the material realm, you can take further steps to achieve your goal. To do so, first light a green candle. Green is the color of abundance and success. In your Book of Shadows, or in a note pad if you do not have such a book, write this spell with green ink, if possible. This will further empower the magic. If you have a tiger's-eye stone, hold it firmly as you speak the following words:

Only for the good of all
This change will come.

Only if it is meant to be
Will this manifestation
be done.

Emely Flak

 Page 40

Notes:

rubbed on your wallet, purse, checkbook, on contracts, and on cash registers.

S. Y. Zenith

Notes:

February 17
Thursday

2nd ♊

Color of the day: Turquoise
Incense of the day: Musk

Prosperity Oil Spell

Making a prosperity oil on the sacred day of the planet Jupiter enhances the effectiveness of the oil. Add to a glass jar one part spearmint, one part basil, two drops cinnamon essential oil, and six parts of a base oil such as sunflower, almond, or virgin olive. Mix all the ingredients fully, and seal the jar. Let the concoction stand for three weeks in a dry, cool, and dark place. After three weeks, shake the jar and strain the oil through cheesecloth or muslin, and decant the oil into a dark glass bottle with a mouth wide enough for a few small coins to be inserted. Next, add a sprig of basil and a lodestone to the bottle. Store it away from sunlight. Prosperity oil may be

February 18
Friday

2nd ♊

☉ → ♓ 8:32 am

☽ → ♋ 12:13 pm

Color of the day: Coral
Incense of the day: Ylang-ylang

The Rite of Februa

February honors the ancient festival of purification called Februa. Use this day to cleanse your altar, ceremonial tools, sacred space, and self. Charge your stones and crystals in a solution containing the essence of the sea mothers: one-half cup of sea salt dissolved in a bucket of water. Burn old culinary herbs and botanicals, such as corn or gourds, from your altar in an outdoor *chimena* or barbeque grill. Cleanse your home with a bucket of spring water to which you've added one-half cup orange flower water, a tablespoon of lemongrass, and the juice of a lemon. Run a bath. Add one cup of full-fat cow's, goat's, or almond milk. Stand up in the tub, and pour the milk bath over your body as you recite:

> White as snow,
> Fresh as dew
> Cleanse, strengthen, and
> banish evil,
> My soul, please renew
> Tis the time of Februa
> We know what we must
> do.

Stephanie Rose Bird

Notes:

called her the "goddess of a thousand works." Writing a poem, making music, or beading a necklace are ways to give form to ideas. Make your altar beautiful today with symbols of your own handiwork. If you are new to the joy and deep satisfaction that comes from crafting, just do what feels natural. There are no expectations before the goddess. Decorate your altar with materials for a project of your choosing or with sheet music from a musical instrument you've decided to take up. Light an olive candle and wish the goddess happy birthday. For at least an hour, work your craft in a sacred space.

Lily Gardner-Butts

Notes:

February 19
Saturday

 2nd ♋

Color of the day: Blue
Incense of the day: Pine

Crafting by hand Spell
Today is the birthday of the goddess Minerva. Although Minerva was a warrior goddess, she also governed poetry, music, and crafts. Ovid

February 20
Sunday

 2nd ♋

Color of the day: Yellow
Incense of the day: Cinnamon

Essential Oil Calming Ritual
Fresh patchouli reminds me of moist, rich, hummus-filled earth. It grounds and energizes at the

same time. It's a good oil to grab when life is full of chaos and I start to get a little frazzled around the edges. Check out an aromatherapy book for other essential oils that calm and ground, then go to the nearest New Age or health food store to see which of the oils you are drawn to. This is important: Do not just go by what the book says. You want to choose a scent that appeals to your own senses. Also, pick up a bottle of grapeseed oil and an empty glass bottle. Fill the empty bottle with an ounce of grapeseed oil and twenty to forty drops of your chosen essential oil. As you mix the two, inhale the scent and envision it calming your stressed emotions. Set your bottle on the windowsill in the moonlight for a night to absorb the Moon's calm energies.

Laurel Reufner

Notes:

February 21
Monday
Presidents' Day (observed)

 2nd ♋

☽ → ♌ 12:54 am

Color of the day: Ivory
Incense of the day: Frankincense

A Kitchen Spell for harmony

A kitchen is a very special place in the home. Food sustains a family, and when prepared with love food satisfies more than mere hunger. A kitchen should be filled with caring thoughts and with harmony—what begins here spreads throughout the rest of the home. Use this charm to bless your kitchen. At twilight, create a personal sacred space by mixing a pinch of allspice, one sprig of dried and crumbled basil, nine coriander seeds, five juniper berries, half a teaspoon of dried lavender, and one teaspoon salt. Pour the mixture into a small dish or jar. Place a stone (a geode, moonstone, or quartz) in the center of the mixture, and set the dish in the kitchen someplace where it won't be disturbed.

Ember

Notes:

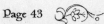

February 22
Tuesday
Washington's Birthday

 2nd ♌

Color of the day: Scarlet
Incense of the day: Musk

New Year New Wand Spell

The Full Moon this month is called the Chaste Moon. What would you do if you could have a clean slate? Artemis/Diana, the Moon goddess of chastity, independence, and feminine strength, is the solitary huntress who teaches us to fend for ourselves. The trees sacred to her are hazel, hawthorn, myrtle, and willow. Call to the east, as this direction signifies dawn and new beginnings. Search for a tree sacred to Artemis and cut a wand for yourself. Ask permission of the tree, and do not cut any more than the small branch you need. Leave an offering behind worthy of the sacrifice: a coin, a crystal, nuts, incense resin. Craft your wand with magical intention, imbuing it with the qualities of the goddess by meditating on her. If you keep the bark on your wand, attach a crystal, ribbon, leather, or other decoration; if you strip the bark off, polish it with oil. Each time you use your new wand, imagine Artemis imparting her blessings of courage and capability to you.

Ruby Lavender

Holiday lore: We all know the lore about our first president—cherry tree, silver dollar, wooden teeth—but the truth behind this most legendary of American figures is sometimes more entertaining than the folklore. For instance, did you know that once, when young George went for a dip in the Rappahannock River, two Fredericksburg women stole his clothes? This story was recorded in the Spotsylvania County records. Picture then the young man scampering home flustered and naked, and the icon of the dollar bill becomes just a bit more real.

February 23
Wednesday

 2nd ♌

☽ → ♍ 12:44 pm

Full Moon 11:54 pm

Color of the day: Topaz
Incense of the day: Cedar

Pre-Spring Cleaning Ritual

What is cluttering up your home, both literally and metaphorically? Now is a good time to clear your home of clutter and to clear whatever blocks your progress. Begin with your altar. Is it cluttered? Clear it, put down a fresh altar cloth, and place a new white candle on it. Take a cleansing bath or shower with sage, lavender, or hyssop, chanting "Pure, pure, I am pure" as you bathe. (Purity was very important to the priests and priestesses in ancient times.) At dusk, light the candle. Look into the candle flame and meditate on its solitude and purity. Feel burdens slip off your shoulder, and open the shades so you can see the Moon. Promise the Moon and Virgo the Virgin that you will focus on what is important in life and remove whatever is blocking you. Set aside the time between the Full and New Moon to clear clutter from your life.

Denise Dumars

Notes:

February 24
Thursday

 3rd ♏

Color of the day: Purple

Incense of the day: Jasmine

Southern Charm Spell

Southern charm usually brings one thing to mind: polite and genteel behavior. But let us think of Southern charm as a tool for magic. The South is renowned for its many variations of folk magic. This charm is from my own background that includes a bit of Hoodoo and various Celtic beliefs. To win financial luck, take a green gris-gris bag and place inside it three quarters, a magnet, a pair of dice, a cabbage leaf, and a sprinkle of cinnamon. Assemble all of the ingredients before a lit green candle, kiss the bag three times, and then whisper: "What you will now do for me is multiply good luck times three." Do this for thirty days until all of your bills are paid. Carry the bag with you, and kiss it once a day.

Tammy Sullivan

Notes:

 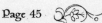

February 25
Friday

 3rd ♏

☽→ ♎ 4:22 am

Color of the day: White
Incense of the day: Nutmeg

Love and Confidence Spell

Recreate yourself as a god or goddess of love and confidence today. After your shower or bath, spritz yourself with rose water, or moisturize using glycerin and rose water. While the steam clears, stand before your mirror and draw a heart around your image, visualizing a deep rose-colored light filling the heart and reflecting back to merge with your energy. Say to yourself:

> I am confident and filled with love.

> I attract confident and loving people.

> My day will bring me abundant love.

Periodically throughout the day, take a brief moment to remember this image and this feeling. Visualize a rose light surrounding you and filling you with a sense of contentment all day. Treat the people you meet as if they were loved ones, and see how they respond.

Kristin Madden

February 26
Saturday

 3rd ♎

Color of the day: Black
Incense of the day: Lavender

Finding Lost Keys Spell

To find lost keys, draw a floor plan of your home. Make a pendulum by tying a small key to a string. Hold the string in your left hand, and run the fingers of your right hand down the string, starting at the top and ending at the key. Do this three times while saying: "Tell me yes." Watch the movement of the key. Do the same thing again, three times, while saying: "Tell me no." Hold the pendulum over the floor plan and ask: "Are the keys in my house?" If the answer is yes, start moving the pendulum over the floor plan, stopping in each room, and asking: "Are the keys in this room?" Once you get a firm "yes" answer from the pendulum, go to that room and search for your keys.

Remember to thank the pendulum for its help.

Paniteowl

Notes:

February 27
Sunday

 3rd ♎

Color of the day: Amber
Incense of the day: Peony

Rune Meditation for Clearing Energy Flow

We have all felt the frustration of spells that flop. While it's possible that a failed spell is just an indication that the universe has another agenda for you, it's also very possible that there is a hidden obstacle in the energy flow. Issues with confidence and empowerment are among the greatest saboteurs that block energy. The runes of Ken (ᚲ), Haegl (ᚺ), and Gyfu (ᚷ) will be used in a guided imagery to open and uncover disruptions and to balance

the chakra energy flow. Visualize Ken over the root chakra. Focus on opening the energies flowing from your root to your crown. Reveal any blockages by positioning Haegl over your root chakra. Visualize this rune uncovering disruptions as its energy flows to your crown. Return Haegl's flow from the crown to the root, uncovering any "manifestation" blockages. Visualize Gyfu flowing from your root to your crown to balance your chakra energy. Focus on and journal any feelings or perceptions that you encountered. Reprogram any obstacles that were uncovered.

Karen Follett

Notes:

February 28
Monday

3rd ♎
☽ → ♏ 7:21 am

Color of the day: Gray
Incense of the day: Gardenia

Sure-Footing Spell

Toward the end of winter, there is ice everywhere, as snow falls and melts and refreezes. This spell helps you get a grip on things. Goats are famous for their sure footing; they jump around on mountains and never seem to fall. So begin by finding a goat symbol—a picture, small statuette, piece of goat horn or hair, whatever works for you. Place the symbol on your altar, and light a brown candle. Then invoke Pan:

> Goat-footed god,
> Lend me your balance
> And your certainty.
>
> Let me dance through
>   my days
> As gracefully as you
>   dance
> Down the mountain
>   paths.
>
> Keep my feet light
> And my step sure.
> So mote it be!

Let the candle burn itself out. Keep the goat symbol and any remaining candle wax on your altar until the last ice of winter is gone for good.

Elizabeth Barrette

Notes:

 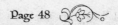

March

March is the third month of the year according to the Gregorian calendar, and the first month of the Roman calendar. Its astrological sign is Pisces, the fish (Feb 18-March 20), a mutable water sign ruled by Neptune. The name of the month itself comes from the Roman god of war, Mars. March heralds the end of winter and coming of spring. It is a transitional time, when warm spring rains and green budding plants return. The robin is a herald of spring, and a symbol of March—along with other migrating birds. Pruning season begins now in the garden, and branches are gathered and bundled together to dry for the coming Beltane Fire on May 1. As trees are still dormant, it is a good time to collect wood for wands now. It is also time to make use of a besom, or a Witches' broom, traditionally made of an ash handle and a bundle of birch twigs. Ritual sweeping is practiced at this time to purify. The main holiday of March is Ostara, or the Vernal Equinox, a time when day and night are equal once again after the dark winter. Seeds saved from the autumn harvest are celebrated and blessed now to ensure a good planting, and the March Full Moon is called the Seed Moon. Eggs are a symbol of the season. They are dyed or painted and used to make talismans, or else they are ritually eaten.

March 1
Tuesday

 3rd ♏

Color of the day: Red
Incense of the day: Maple

Protection Ritual for healers

This ritual is particularly useful for health workers, alternative health professionals, and fortunetellers. Consecrate a mirror and keep it in a drawer along with some charcoal disks, a heat-proof dish containing sand, some foil, a blue towel, a lighter, and the gum resins of frankincense, myrrh, and benzoin. Perform this ritual at least once a week. Position a small table in the middle of the consultation room and cover it with the blue towel. Put a length of foil over the towel. On top of the foil, prop the mirror against a sturdy object with the mirror facing the door. Put the sand-filled heat-proof dish in front of the mirror, light a charcoal disk, and place the disk on top of the sand. Burn grains of gum resin on the charcoal to fumigate the room. Upon completion, douse the charcoal disk with water. Pour the sand, charcoal, and resin remnants into the foil. Wrap the foil up, and dispose of the remnants outside on your premises. Be sure there is a fresh supply of sand for each new ritual.

S. Y. Zenith

Notes:

Holiday lore: On March 1, Roman matrons held a festival known as Matronalia in honor of Juno Lucina, an aspect of the goddess Juno associated with light and childbirth. Some records indicated that her name was derived from a grove on the Esquiline Hill where a temple was dedicated to her in 375 BC. Whenever a baby entered the world in Roman times, it was believed that the infant was "brought to light." Women who worshipped Juno Lucina untied knots and unbraided their hair to release any entanglements that might block safe delivery.

March 2
Wednesday

 3rd ♏
☽ → ♐ 1:29 pm

Color of the day: Yellow
Incense of the day: Cedar

Clean Your Well Spell

Today, in many parts of Europe, Holy Wells Day is celebrated. This festival is dedicated to Ceadda,

the Nordic goddess of holy wells and healing springs. Traditionally, on this day wells were cleaned. It would be unrealistic to expect you to find a well and stand neck-deep in muck and water, as was done in pre-Christian times, just for this quick meditation ritual. Instead, why not celebrate this festival with a contemporary approach? Dedicate this day to honoring your creative life force. Make an offering of flowers on your altar. Undertake a symbolic cleansing. If you live near mineral springs, wash your face and hands in the water. Take a drink of invigorating mineral water, and continue to drink it throughout the day. In the morning, state this affirmation:

> Beginning today, I will nurture my life force by drinking clean water to maintain a healthy body.

Emely Flak

Notes:

March 3
Thursday

 3rd ♐

Fourth Quarter 12:36 pm

Color of the day: Green
Incense of the day: Jasmine

Wind Spell for Making a Decision

Today is the feast day of old Saint Winnold, the third member of the "windy" saints. The ancient saying went:

> First comes David
> Next comes Chad
> Then comes Winnold,
> Roaring like mad.

Often stormy weather occurs these first three days of March. If you can't make a decision, write each of your options on a piece of paper. Tie each paper to a separate feather, using red thread. Place your feathers on an outdoor table. It is important that the table not be sheltered from the wind. The wind will move your feathers about. The last feather that remains on the table represents the option you should choose.

Lily Gardner-Butts

Notes:

March 4
Friday

 4th ♐

☽→ ♑ 5:12 pm

Color of the day: Pink
Incense of the day: Ginger

Inner Sun Spell

In honor of today's Feast of the Egyptian Sun god, Ra, try this inner Sun spell. Count down from ten to one, breathing deeply as you do. Visualize a golden star, or a small Sun, glowing in the center of your body. See and feel this golden star expand and grow brighter. Its radiance extends out beyond your body in a protective egg of light. Say to yourself that this inner Sun will keep you safe and healthy, and that you may use it in any way you choose. Whenever you need help in making a decision, all you need to do is look to your inner Sun. It will give you all the answers you need by glowing brighter or dimmer. Fully experience this inner Sun before you count back up from one to ten.

Kristin Madden

Notes:

March 5
Saturday

 4th ♑

Color of the day: Brown
Incense of the day: Patchouli

Garden Blessing

Use this chant to bless your garden this spring:

Tender seeds,
Take root and grow,
Take strength from earth,
And water's flow.
Reach for the sky,
Taste warmth of Sun,
Bear flower and fruit
Before you're done.

At harvest time,
The seeds remain
to share again
The life they contain.

Ember

Notes:

March 6
Sunday

 4th ♑
𝄰 → ♒ 6:49 pm

Color of the day: Gold
Incense of the day: Parsley

A healing Wind Spell

The wind of March brings with it hope and the fresh smell of the soft brown earth. Let the March wind purify your body and mind by performing this healing wind spell. Go outdoors to a secluded spot on a windy day. Hear the wind rushing through the trees, and see last year's dead leaves being tossed about. Facing east, breathe deeply and spread your arms as if you can fly. Feel all of the emotional baggage you've been carrying with you being blown by the wind. Now ask the four winds for their special help. Face east and say: "Bring me positive change." Then turn south and say: "Bring me warmth and comfort." To the west wind say: "Bring me emotional balance." Lastly, face north while saying: "Let me understand the mysteries." Thank each of the directions. Now you can face the coming spring with a fresh attitude.

James Kambos

Notes:

March 7
Monday

 4th ♒

Color of the day: Lavender
Incense of the day: Lilac

Yemaya Ritual

Yemaya is the Yoruban angelic spirit that resides in the ocean. She embodies, love, nurturing, and mothering. Monday is her day; seven is her number. Her stone is moonstone; sea kelp, peppermint, eucalyptus, and passionflowers are her ewe (herbs). To honor her, boil water in a teakettle. Put one teaspoon of peppermint and passionflower ewe in a strainer or a muslin bag. Run a bath. Add 1/8 cup of ground sea kelp and 1/2 teaspoon of eucalyptus essential oil. Add a moonstone. Fix a cup of tea, and place it near the bathtub. Light a blue and a white candle. Get in the tub. Go under the water, hold your breath as long as you can, and contemplate the divine generosity and caring spirit of Yemaya. As you hold your breathing, feel the very fragility of your life force. When you can no longer hold your breath, come up for air. Repeat this act seven times. Place the moonstone on your belly. Then recite: "Praise be to Yemaya, sustainer of life." Relax and enjoy your tea.

Stephanie Rose Bird

Notes:

Key Ring of Protection

For this protection charm you'll need a key chain that can fit comfortably in a pocket, a white candle, and a clove of garlic. Light the candle, and hold key chain and garlic above the flame, visualizing the light of the candle entering and surrounding both items. Gently rub the garlic clove over the key chain, picturing its protective qualities coating the key chain. You don't have to saturate the key chain with the garlic. The goal is to form a protective charm, not keep everyone at bay. Now hold the key chain in both hands and pour some protective guardian energy into it. Let it bathe in candlelight until the candle has burnt itself out. Carry your new charm whenever you're in an uncertain social situation or out traveling. If you need its protective powers, simply carry it in your hand.

Laurel Reufner

Notes:

Holiday lore: Although the month of June is named for Juno, principal goddess of the Roman pantheon, major festivals dedicated to her are scattered throughout the year. For instance, today marks Junoalia, a festival in honor of Juno celebrated in solemnity by matrons. Two images of Juno made of cypress were borne in a procession of twenty-seven girls dressed in long robes, singing a hymn to the goddess composed by the poet Livius. Along the way, the procession would dance in the great field of Rome before proceeding ahead to the temple of Juno.

March 8
Tuesday
International Women's Day

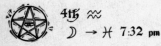

4th ♒
☽ → ♓ 7:32 pm

Color of the day: Black
Incense of the day: Poplar

Holiday lore: While most holidays across the world celebrate the lives and achievement of men, this is one day wholly dedicated to the

 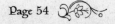

achievement and work of women. Originally inspired by a pair of mid-nineteenth-century ladies' garment workers strikes, today the holiday is little-known in its country of origin; though this day's legacy is clear in March's designation by the U.S. Congress as Women's History Month. Throughout the month, women's groups in American towns hold celebrations and events, concerts, exhibitions, and rituals that recall heroic and gifted women of every stripe.

wise direction. Move to the doors, bless them, and ask they stay strong. Go through each part of the car body in this manner. You may incorporate symbols if you like to add more protection to the blessing.

Tammy Sullivan

Notes:

March 9
Wednesday

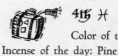 4th ♓

Color of the day: Brown
Incense of the day: Pine

Transportation Blessing

Today is the traditional feast day of Saint Frances of Rome, the patron saint of motorists. This is the day when Romans have their cars blessed. To take advantage of unique travel and transportation energies today, prepare a protective water to anoint and bless your transportation. To do this, take a shallow dish of water and crumble white sage and rosemary into it. Stir the mixture clockwise six times. Starting at the tires of your vehicle, sprinkle water on them, and say: "I bless these tires and ask that they stay safely on the road." Continue working in a clock-

March 10
Thursday

 4th ♓

New Moon 4:10 am

☽ → ♈ 9:03 pm

Color of the day: Purple
Incense of the day: Sandalwood

Neptunian Magic

The power of the sea is awesome, and anyone who has ever sailed upon it or swum in it has felt that power. Today we can begin to access the power of the sea in our own lives today with the New Moon in Pisces. If you live near the ocean, do this ritual on the shore. If not, create Neptune's Kingdom on your

 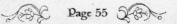

altar. For this, you will need a shell-anointing oil, a blue altar cloth or beach towel, a Mason jar, and a tape of ocean sounds. Anoint yourself with the oil. If at the beach, wet your feet (even if it's cold). Take the jar and fill it with seawater and a little sand. Add pebbles, small shells and a drop of the anointing oil, then place it on the altar. Say:

> King Neptune, mighty ruler,
> Look fondly on me.
> Grant me ocean strength,
> Ocean power.
>
> King Neptune,
> I bow to you.

If doing the ritual at home, fill the jar with salted water and purchased sand, shells, and pebbles. Whenever you need ocean strength, shake the jar and repeat the words above.

> Denise Dumars

Notes:

March 11
Friday

 1st ♈

Color of the day: Rose
Incense of the day: Rose

Egg-Coloring Spell

As Ostara approaches, a bit of egg magic gains potency. To do some egg-coloring magic, hard-boil some white eggs. Draw symbols on them using a white crayon or wax pencil. These symbols—runes, hearts, dollar signs, or words—should represent what you want to manifest in your life. Mix food colors to dye the eggs, and add a bit of salt and vinegar to some boiling water. Let the water cool slightly, and add the food coloring to the water. Dip the eggs in the dye with a spoon. If you wish, you may repeat the dipping in order to create more vivid colors. The symbols you drew on the eggs in white crayon will stand out against the vivid colors. Dry the eggs on paper towels, then refrigerate them. Each day thereafter, peel and eat an egg and reflect on the wishes that you hope to manifest. As you feed yourself this nutritious, high-protein food, an ancient symbol of sacred fertility, spend a few moments imagining its good and magical qualities giving you the power and will to achieve your desired goals.

> Ruby Lavender

 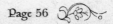

Notes:

Flames burn,
Paths unite,
Love so true
Is called with this rite.

Nourish the cooled ashes' energy in the earth of your yard or in a potted plant.

Karen Follett

Notes:

March 12
Saturday

 1st ♈

Color of the day: Gray
Incense of the day: Lilac

Flame of Love Spell

Light a red candle today. Draw two outlines of people on a piece of paper. One will represent you, the other represents your future love. Create a binding rune by overlapping Gyfu (✕), Wynn (ᚹ), and Is (ᛁ) on the front of an envelope. Arrange your hands, with thumbs and forefingers touching, to form a triangle over the outline of your. Focus on your whole being, including both the light and the shadow sides of you. Then, place your hands in a triangle over the other outline. Focus the universal energy of Gyfu's balance, Wynn's fulfillment, and Is's protection into this outline. Place both of the outlines into the envelope. Light the envelope with the candle's flames, and put it in a fireproof container, chanting:

March 13
Sunday

 1st ♈
☽ → ♉ 1:05 pm

Color of the day: Yellow
Incense of the day: Cinnamon

Seven-Flower Health Bath Ritual

This Southeast Asian multipurpose bath recipe ensures smooth transitions as a person recovers from an affliction. The ingredients are seven different flowers of seven different colors, a handful of lime leaves, and two tablespoons of sea salt. Epsom salt may be substituted for sea salt. While a bath is running, put the flowers, lime leaves, and salt into the

water. When ready, get into the bathtub for a good soak and scrub. Before getting out of the bath, use a bowl to pour water over the head seven times. Rinse off the flowers and leaves, towel dry, and dress in fresh clothing. This bath also purifies the seven psychic centers of the soul. For those severing old ties, this bath assists with integration into new directions.

S. Y. Zenith

Notes:

also make individual pages and send them to relatives as gifts. Craft stores carry lots of gorgeous paper, photo-safe adhesives, decorations, and other supplies for scrapbooking. Look closely and you'll find Pagan-friendly images like woodland scenes, magic wands, even five-pointed stars. Make copies of two or three favorite photographs. Fasten them to background paper that matches the theme, like tulip paper for spring outings. Then write your memories of the pictured event on a piece of contrasting paper and attach it to the photos. Embellish with stickers or drawings, and you're done.

Elizabeth Barrette

Notes:

March 14
Monday

 1st ♉

Color of the day: Gray
Incense of the day: Chrysanthemum

Fun Indoors Spell

Ruled by the Moon, Monday concerns the home and family. Forget about braving the chilly, wet, spring weather. Strengthen your family ties by doing something fun together indoors. One great project is scrapbooking. If you already have a scrapbook, work on new pages. If not, now is a perfect time to start one. You can

March 15
Tuesday

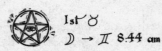 1st ♉
)) → ♊ 8:44 am

Color of the day: Maroon
Incense of the day: Juniper

Keep a Pet from Straying Spell

It can be heartbreaking when a dear pet runs away. To help prevent this from happening, we should try to form a psychic bond with our pets. One way is through the use of positive magic. Here is one spell that may help. In the early morning, face the east and obtain three hairs from your pet. Place these beneath your welcome mat at your front door, and say: "Here you are and here you'll stay, now and forever more!" Give your pet a treat and a hug, and spend some quality time with him or her. Let them know the best place they could be in the world is with you.

James Kambos

Notes:

Holiday lore: Why is March 15 considered so unlucky? On this date in 226 BC, an earthquake brought the Colossus of Rhodes—one of the seven wonders of the ancient world—to its knees. But a more famous incident probably accounts for the superstition regarding the "Ides of March." Julius Caesar's family may have belonged to the "Peoples' Party," but somewhere along the way he became a tyrant. In February of 44 B.C., Caesar had himself named Dictator Perpetuus—Dictator for Life. Brutus assassinated him on March 15, 44 BC. Caesar's murder was foretold by soothsayers and even by his wife, Calpurnia, who had a nightmare in which Caesar was being butchered like an animal. Caesar chose to ignore these portents and the rest, of course, is history.

March 16
Wednesday

 1st ♊

Color of the day: White
Incense of the day: Neroli

Healing by Moonlight Spell

The Moon has always fascinated us with its beauty and the magnetic pull it exerts on the tides buried within each of us. We can use the Moon's energy to help us heal. For a quicker recovery from an illness, place a clear glass bowl on a mirror. Put the mirror and bowl outside on an even surface. If you can't go outside, place them in a window that will catch the light of the Moon as it passes through its phases. Fill the bowl with clear spring water, and say this three times:

"The Moon will rise, and so will I." When you see the New Moon reflected in the water, take a drink of the Moon-kissed water. Add some extra water, and continue to take a sip each night, envisioning your body being healed and energized with Moon glow. During the next Full Moon, drink all of the water.

Paniteowl

Notes:

namon powder, and a shamrock in the center. Tie the corners together to make a small bundle. Kiss the bundle three times, and say:

> Brigid, watch o'er and
> bless me. Allow only good
> fortune to come. Open
> my eyes, so that I may
> see prosperity where I
> saw none.

Carry the bundle with you through the day and make sure to touch it at least every hour to maintain your connection with it.

Tammy Sullivan

Notes:

March 17
Thursday
St. Patrick's Day

 1st ♊

Second Quarter 2:19 pm

☽ → ♋ 7:44 pm

Color of the day: Turquoise
Incense of the day: Carnation

Magic of the Shamrock Spell

Why not combine Jupiter's monetary aspects with a wee bit o' Irish luck today? The magic of the shamrock is triple-fold and a perfect representation of the triple goddess Brigid. Take a bit of green cloth, and place a magnet, a pinch of cin-

Holiday lore: Much folklore surrounds St. Patrick's Day. Though originally a Catholic holy day, St. Patrick's Day has evolved into more of a secular holiday today. One traditional icon of the day is the shamrock. This stems from an Irish tale that tells how Patrick used the three-leafed shamrock to explain the Trinity of Christian dogma. His followers adopted the custom of wearing a shamrock on his feast day; though why we wear green on this day is

 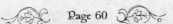

less clear. St. Patrick's Day came to America in 1737, the date of the first public celebration of the holiday in Boston.

March 18
Friday

 2nd ♋

Color of the day: Coral
Incense of the day: Dill

Alder Moon Spell

Alder is the tree of wholeness; it is tough, resilient, and healing. This Moon appears a few days before the Spring Equinox, a time when day and night are nearly equal. This is the day to treat your mind, body, and spirit. Lavender coordinates well with the Spring Equinox. Hoodoos believe lavender is a neutral, balanced plant, suitable for all relationships—heterosexual, gay, lesbian, and trans-gendered. It is also medicinally balancing, as it can stimulate or calm as needed. Sip lavender bud tea today to attract positive spirits and alleviate negativity. Dab pulse points with lavender essential oil. Lavender essential oil attracts good spirits, has a positive effect on your mood, and is antibacterial. At midnight, bring lavender, a charcoal block, some matches, and a flat large stone out-side. Sit down on the ground in a clear space. Set the stone in the moon-light. Light the charcoal, and set it on the stone. Add a few pinches lavender at a time. Lavender incense is calming and very fragrant.

Stephanie Rose Bird

Notes:

March 19
Saturday

 2nd ♓

Color of the day: Blue
Incense of the day: Pine

New Beginnings Spell

To start anew at this time of year, collect circular objects—rings, buttons, bracelets, key rings—and put them in a bowl, cup, or cauldron. These should be items you have used or worn and that you have a history with or that mean something to you. Choose items that have a hole all the way through them. Consider each object—what it is actually is, how it functions, and what is symbolizes in your life. Use these items to create a spell for endings and beginnings—that is, to end a current cycle and create a new beginning for whatever your need. This can be personal or professional, or just generally for healing or renewal. Thread a string through the items, recognizing what each means to you, and as you tie the ends together in a knot, visualize the cycle you wish to complete and the new beginning you hope for.

Ember

Notes:

March 20

Sunday

Ostara – Spring Equinox –
International Astrology Day

2nd ♋

☉ → ♈ 7:33 am
☽ → ♌ 8:17 am

Color of the day: Amber
Incense of the day: Sage

A Spell of Reawakening

The Spring Equinox, called Ostara by many, is a day of perfect balance between night and day, darkness and light, slumber and awakening. Many craft traditions, covens, and solitaries have devised their own rituals for awakening Mother Earth at this time. Many of these can be traced back to England. One common practice is to walk through a natural area, tap the earth three times with a staff or wand, and make a joyful noise to welcome the Goddess's return. This ritual is performed three times in keeping with the sacred number of many of the Pagan sects from western European countries. Now is not only a good time to awaken Mother Earth, but also to awaken ourselves. We should ask: Are we only going through the motions now? Or are we reawakening our spiritual selves, and seeing anew all the magical possibilities of spring? To awaken your own body, mind, and soul to spring's rebirth, give back to Mother Earth some of the things we've taken from her. Plant a tree, herb garden, or flowers. Feed her animals and birds. As you do any of these things, consecrate your offering by saying:

Mother Earth,
Goddess we walk upon,
May my gifts be of value
Even after I'm gone.

Today, while I'm here,
May my offering be,
An act of love for you
from me.

Edain McCoy

Notes:

and place it on your altar. For example, a person who is creative at sewing might use a needle or some embroidery cotton. For a painter, it could be a brush or paints. With pride in your art, speak this spell:

> With this tool
> I dedicate my art
> To nourish the creativity
> That flows from my
> heart.

Dedicate your next creative product to Minerva.

Emely Flak

Notes:

March 21
Monday

2nd ♌

Color of the day: Silver
Incense of the day: Myrrh

Artistic Empowerment from Minerva Ritual

The ancient Roman festival of Quinquatria is also known as the Festival of Minerva. Minerva is the Roman goddess of war and of wisdom, the arts, and the trades. She is the Roman counterpart to the Greek goddess Athena, who is honored by artisans and students. To enhance your artistic talents at this time, empower your spell with the energies of Minerva. Find a tool that represents your craft or trade

March 22
Tuesday

2nd ♌
☽ → ♍ 8:10 pm

Color of the day: White
Incense of the day: Honeysuckle

Amethyst Protection Spell

Amethyst is known to balance energies and bring strength, stability, and peace to its bearer. While it is a powerful stone, it backs up its protective energies by bestowing a sense of warmth and comfort. Find an amethyst that feels strong yet welcoming to you. Run it under clear water for three minutes while visualizing all unwanted energies flowing out of the stone. Allow the water to carry these bad energies away for purification. Now sit with your stone and ask it to partner with you for protection. Imagine yourself living your life with a strength based on the knowledge that you are being protected on all levels of being. Fill the stone with these energies. Carry this amethyst with you for at least seven days to attune your energies to this effective partnership.

Kristin Madden

Notes:

Holiday lore: Cybele was the Great Mother of the gods in Ida, and she was taken to Rome from Phrygia in 204 BC. She was also considered the Great Mother of all Asia Minor. Her festivals were known as *ludi,* or "games," and were solemnized with various mysterious rites. Along with Hecate and Demeter of Eleusis, Cybele was one of the leading deities of Rome when mystery cults were at their prime. Hila'aria, or "Hilaria," originally seemed to have been a name given to any day or season of rejoicing that was either private or public. Such days were devoted to general rejoicing and people were not allowed to show signs of grief or sorrow. The Hilaria actually falls on March 25 and is the last day of a festival of Cybele that commences today. However, the Hilaria was not mentioned in the Roman calendar or in Ovid's *Fasti.*

March 23
Wednesday

 2nd ♍

Color of the day: Topaz
Incense of the day: Coriander

Psychic Housecleaning Spell

In March the forces of nature begin to stir. The brook beyond my garden is free of winter's grip and the water is rushing again. It's time not just for springcleaning,

but for psychic housecleaning as well. Over the winter our homes may collect unwanted energy. By using some of nature's elements we can ritually cleanse our living space. Begin by opening all windows and doors to let the spring air in. Go through your house and pour bottled spring water down each drain. Visualize trapped negativity being rinsed away. Light a pale blue candle that you have blessed, and moving clockwise about your house, pause at each door, window, and fireplace. Use your power hand to trace the shape of a cross or pentagram before each opening. End the ritual by placing some potted hyacinths in a special place. They have a protective quality and will bring the scent of spring indoors.

James Kambos

Notes:

March 24
Thursday

2nd ♏

Color of the day: Crimson
Incense of the day: Evergreen

Visions of Abundance Spell

All physical action begins with mental thought and with visualization. Whether this is a sudden and instantaneous action brought on by a particular stimulus, or a well-planned attempt to achieve success and abundance, action begins with thought. To start this spell, light a gold candle. Burn a mixture of cinnamon and nutmeg on a charcoal block. Write your goal on a piece of paper. Be concise about the goal while incorporating the universal "or something better" provision. Focus on the goal using vivid sensory detail. Chant the following words over and over as you make your visualizations:

> My prosperity grows in
> visions that I see.

> Visions manifest,
> Abundance flows to me.

Allow yourself to open to any visions and universal guidance that may come to you. Write down your plan of action to achieve your goals of abundance.

Karen Follett

Notes:

you someone who shares your interests and will appreciate you for who you are. Fold the parchment, and place it under the pink candle if you are seeking a woman, the green if seeking a man. Go outside and stand under the Full Moon, letting its rays fill you with silvery, magical, love energy. Go out to a dance or other social event, but do not overtly try to meet someone new; now is the time to reflect on what you want in a partner. If you prefer, go to a film, concert, or other event you would like to share with a new love interest. Feel confident that by the next Full Moon that person will come into your life.

Denise Dumars

Notes:

March 25
Friday
Purim – Good Friday

 2nd ♏

☽ → ♎ 6:00 am

Full Moon 5:38 pm

Color of the day: White
Incense of the day: Almond

Meet That Special Someone Spell

oday, call upon Libra's ruler, the planet Venus, and the goddess it was named for to maximize your chances of meeting a new love interest within the month. Wear something green or pink with silver jewelry. Place a green and a pink candle on your altar. Write your finer qualities, interests, hobbies, and desires on a piece of parchment. Light the candles, and ask Venus to bring

March 26
Saturday

 3rd ♎

Color of the day: Indigo
Incense of the day: Lavender

Plowing Day Spell

In agrarian calendars, this marks Plowing Day, the day after the Full Moon when the soil is ready for tilling in spring. Farming and planting are powerful metaphors for those who work magic for self-transformation. At this time, our desires and goals are like seeds that need to be carefully tended so they may grow and bear fruit. To encourage this, fill a small bowl with potting soil. Choose a seed symbolic of your goal—such as an acorn for protection and health, a poppy seed for fertility, a walnut for healing, an almond for wisdom, brazil nuts for love, and so on. Or else use any seed or nut to represent what you wish it to through you intention. As you plant the seed, chant your intention:

> By seed and root, by bud
> and stem, by leaf and
> flower and fruit, I invoke
> the power to achieve my
> goal.

When your goal is achieved, add the soil to your garden or a nearby park, releasing its power to the earth.

Ruby Lavender

Notes:

March 27
Sunday
Easter

 3rd ♎

☽ → ♏ 1:29 pm

Color of the day: Orange
Incense of the day: Basil

Easter Resurrection Spell

Many of us have hypnotically regressed into a past life at one time or another. Some of us had file folders stuffed with these tidbits of a forgotten past. While there are many ideas about where these memories come from, we can't deny that they happen and help us change our lives, explain behaviors, or explain why a strange place is familiar. In the end, we can't deny that time is omnipresent and surrounds all of us. This means the past, present, and future are all being lived simultaneously. The question is, though, why do some people refuse to consider that it is possible to send our consciousness to another place and time? If we accept the subtle truth of omnipresent time, we can do hypnotic progression to see what our future lives will bring. These are the currents a psychic taps into when she or he has an image come to her or him. Start your progressing experience by inducing dreams of the future. To do this you will need to make a small, round pillow (about

two inches around), and fill it with a mixture of some or all of the following: mugwort, sage, chicory, jasmine, or rosemary. Before you go to bed at night, place this pillow under your own and say:

> If far—back memories
>   can come to me,
> It means the future I
>   can also see.
> Wheel of time, where
>   there is no time,
> Open my eyes to a future
>   of mine.

Edain McCoy

Notes:

undertaken frivolously. Bathe and dress in fresh, white pajamas. At midnight, walk the perimeter of a churchyard or garden. Throw hemp seed over your left shoulder and say:

> hemp seed I sow.
> hemp seed, grow.
> That is to marry me,
> Come after me and mow.

You should see the spirit of your future mate form behind you, mowing with a scythe. If nothing is visible, that means you will not marry this year.

Lily Gardner-Butts

Notes:

March 28
Monday

  3rd ♏

Color of the day: Ivory
Incense of the day: Daffodil

St. Mark's Eve Spell

This potent divination has been performed on St. Mark's Eve for centuries and is for anyone who seeks to discover their future mate. It is important that this spell is not

March 29
Tuesday

  3rd ♏
☽ → ♐ 6:56 pm

Color of the day: Scarlet
Incense of the day: Musk

Divination Party Ritual

Hold a divination party with your magic-minded friends today. Each person should bring at least one divinatory tool: a tarot deck, a set of runes, a pendulum, or whatever you tend to use. Make sure these are items you don't mind sharing for a little while. The greater variety of tools people bring, the more magic will be generated. If you like, dress up as carnival fortunetellers. Seat everyone around a well-lit table, and lay out the different tools. Each person should describe the tool they brought—its history, how it works, the pros and cons of using it. Then, exchange the tools with each other, and try your hand at someone else's kind of divination. Take turns reading each other's fortunes. This is a great way to decide what you want to acquire for your own collection.

Elizabeth Barrette

Notes:

March 30
Wednesday

 3rd ♐

Color of the day: Brown
Incense of the day: Sandalwood

Hermes Invocation for Travel

Hermes was the Greek guardian of travelers. Invoke his aid while traveling with this very simple incantation. Repeat it at least three times as you envision your vehicle surrounded by protective white light.

Hermes, hear my plea.
See us safely there,
And safely back again.
This is my will,
So mote it be.

Laurel Reufner

Notes:

March 31
Thursday
The Borrowed Days

 3rd ♐
☽ → ♑ 10:48 pm

Color of the day: White
Incense of the day: Carnation

Druidic Stone–Blessing Ritual

This spell may be used for blessing large stones, such as those placed in your garden or on your altar. Touch or hold the stone in your hand, saying:

> I call upon thee, stone of
> earth. Formed by fire,
> sculpted by water, and
> weathered by wind.
> Impart the deepest
> secrets of the earth to
> me. Teach me how to be
> silent, how to listen, how
> to be strong without
> force, and how to be firm
> without anger. Lend me
> your strength.

Stones, even though they tend to be less dramatic than fire, swords, or glittering goblets, can be very powerful magical tools. Crystals are one type of stone used for magic and meditation, but see what lessons the humble pebbles, rocks, and boulders hold for you.

Ruby Lavender

Notes:

April

April is the fourth month of the year of the Gregorian calendar, and the first month of the astrological calendar. Its astrological sign is Aries, the ram (Mar 20-Apr 19), a cardinal fire sign ruled by Mars. The name of the month comes from the Latin *aprilis*, which derives from *aper*, or "boar," as April was thought to be the month of the boar. April is the month of burgeoning life force, sunshine, and life returned to the forests. Birds are building nests now; lambs are romping on greening hillsides. Apricot trees are blossoming, and herb gardens are filling out. Now is the time to plant your garden. Potatoes, onions, lettuce, and tomatoes are sacred to various divinities now. It is a good time to create a circle for meditation outside, either of stones or shrubberies. The four cardinal directions should be marked in the circle, and connected by a crossquarter cross. Cut mazes and labyrinths now in turf or in fields. Plant tree saplings too—maples, hawthorn, and holly are sacred in April. Bunnies and hares are symbols of fertility at this time of year, associated with rites of spring. The Full Moon in April is called the Hare Moon. Holidays in April include April Fools' Day, which comes from Roman celebrations of the New Year rebirth. Earth Day on April 22 celebrates the bounty of the planet. April 30 is called May Eve and is celebrated with revels and bonfires.

April 1
Friday
April Fools' Day

 3rd ♑

Fourth Quarter 7:50 pm

Color of the day: Purple
Incense of the day: Thyme

Merry Meet the Lord of Misrule Spell

April Fools' Day seems like a celebration created by a practical joker just to legitimize his games for one day a year. April Fool's Day has its origins in changes made to the old Roman calendar when the new year began around March 25. To add more confusion, we changed calendars again from the Julian to the Georgian, thus cutting eleven days out of our year. In sparsely populated areas many people became unsure where April was on the calendar, thus they were April fools. The Lord of Misrule, the trickster and jester, appears at many Pagan celebrations. Like his consort, Discordia, he seeks to bring novelty and, perhaps, something fresh and new to our festivals. Remembering that we have vowed to harm none, the Lord of Misrule can be called upon to inspire you with fresh ideas for tricks and revelries. Speak these words for April Fools' inspiration:

> Lord of Misrule,
> Your time has come,
> help me make an April
> Fool of someone;
> I ask for inspiration so a
> Trickster I shall be,
> help me to harm none,
> In fun, so mote it be.

> Edain McCoy

Notes:

April 2
Saturday

 4th ♑

Color of the day: Gray
Incense of the day: Jasmine

Change Yourself Spell

The first thing a spell changes is you. Stand before a mirror and decide what changes you feel you need to improve your life. It may be losing a little weight, or breaking a bad habit. It may even be that you'd like to change your hair color! The choice is yours. Gaze into your mirrored eyes and make a promise to yourself to follow up on doing those things that will help you to achieve your goal. Enchant your image by saying:

> Mirror, mirror on the wall,
> Listen to my heartfelt
>   call.
> To be the person I should be,
> I trust that you will help
>   me see
> All the things I need to do
> To help my fondest
>   dream come true.

Tie a blue ribbon to a corner of the mirror, and look into it every day. Remember the promise to yourself. When you've achieved your goal, tie a yellow ribbon on the mirror to remind yourself that you can do anything you truly want to do.

Paniteowl

Notes:

April 3
Sunday
Daylight Saving Time Begins 2 am

 4th ♑

☽ → ♒ 1:31 am

Color of the day: Amber
Incense of the day: Coriander

An Empath's Emergency Kit

Empathy is a gift. Well, I should state that developing skills in empathy can be a gift. While it is good that we can sense the emotions and issues of other people, we can also inadvertently absorb the emotions and issues of others. We may walk away from a conversation feeling angry and not know why. We may pass a stranger and then feel suddenly exhausted without apparent reason. One of the skills that you build as an empath is the ability to discern what issues belong to you and what issues you have absorbed from others. Once discerned, you will want to cleanse this other "issue" from your energy. Carry a black tourmaline. When you notice a sudden emotion or feeling that appears without reason, visualize it draining into the tourmaline. "Neutralize" this energy by storing your tourmaline in a container filled with rock or sea salt.

Karen Follett

Notes:

April 4
Monday

 4th ≈

Color of the day: Silver
Incense of the day: Rose

honoring the Great Mother Anew Spell

This date, according to the ancient Roman calendar, began an important week-long celebration honoring Cybele, the Great Mother Goddess, the deity who was credited for creating everything. All creatures, humans, animals, plants, trees, even the gods were created by her and under Cybele's control. Her role is so complex and her strength so great, to honor her it is best to keep your ritual simple. Here is one idea. Decorate your altar with pine and a small bouquet of wild violets, both of which are associated with her. In the center of your altar, place one plain, white, hard-boiled egg as a symbol of the eternal life cycle—birth, death, and rebirth. Thank Cybele by saying:

> Great Mother,
> Guardian of all,
> hear me and favor me
> with your bounty.

Eat the egg and crush the shell, scattering it on the earth. Or, keep the shell for a future spell.

James Kambos

Notes:

April 5
Tuesday

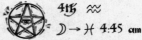 4th ≈
☽ → ♓ 4:45 am

Color of the day: Red
Incense of the day: Gardenia

Kwan Yin Compassion Spell

In China today, the festival of Kwan Yin is celebrated. Kwan Yin, also spelled Quan Yin, is the goddess of compassion and mercy. Her name translates to "the one who heals the cries of the world." As one of Asia's most revered and popular goddesses, Kwan Yin's qualities are altruism, service to others, and unconditional love. She is often invoked for protection from danger and to heal illness. A ritual to honor Kwan Yin reminds us of the importance of showing compassion, a quality that is often overlooked in our fast-paced lifestyle. To invoke Kwan Yin qualities, sit in a quiet place and ask yourself: How can I serve others without neglecting my own needs? How can I improve a relationship with a partner, friend, or family member by showing more compassion and less judgment?

Emely Flak

Notes:

your thoughts and feelings to the picture, and visualize his or her essence in the same room. Tell him or her what you want or ask questions. The response will enter your mind. When this communication session is completed, blow out the candle and wave the photograph through the smoke from north to south, then west to east. Return the snapshot to where you usually keep it.

S. Y. Zenith

Notes:

April 6
Wednesday

 4th ♓

Color of the day: Yellow
Incense of the day: Eucalyptus

Communicate with an Absent Partner Spell

For telepathic communication with a partner who is away from home and not been able to make contact by telephone, letter, or other modern means, light a white candle and sit comfortably in your favorite chair. Hold a clear quartz crystal in your left hand. With your right hand, pick up a photograph of a loved one and gaze deeply into the eyes. Speak

April 7
Thursday
World health Day

 4th ♓
☽ → ♈ 4:45 am

Color of the day: Green
Incense of the day: Geranium

Osain's healing Energy Spell

World Health Day is the perfect time to reflect on Osain, angelic spirit of herbs and healing of the

Yoruba practitioners of Ifa. Osain kept his healing medicines high up in a tree in a calabash. The other spirits got jealous and angrily brought the calabash of herbs down to earth. Osain's story teaches us to share healing energy, be it through some herbal tea, a heartfelt hug, a generous smile, a thank-you card, or just a phone call. Today is simply the day to contribute to the well-being of others. Peppermint is well suited to World Health Day. It eases nervousness, insomnia, headache, stomachache and vomiting, and symptoms of colds. Peppermint is a good additive to baths, herbal sachets, salves, and it is considered an aphrodisiac. Put one-half pound dried peppermint in a bag. Tie the bag with a turquoise ribbon, and place it inside a dried calabash, gourd, or simple wooden salad bowl. Share the story, and share good health.

Stephanie Rose Bird

Notes:

April 8
Friday
Buddha's Birthday

 4th ♈
New Moon 4:32 pm

Color of the day: Coral
Incense of the day: Ylang-ylang

Luck of the Draw Spell

Eclipse magic has always been dicey at best. Many practitioners warn us away from doing magic on a day when there is an eclipse, but hey, some of us like to gamble with fate . . . so why not try a gambler's spell tonight? On your altar place a picture of Thoth, the Egyptian god of writing, academia, and gambling; a symbol of Mars, Aries' ruler; and either some dice or playing cards. Tell the universe that you will be open to surprises (such as the elusive perfect lottery number combo, perhaps?) and will accept what is given. Mars is, after all, unpredictable, and Thoth in his aspect as Hermes is a bit of a trickster. To acknowledge this you may want to sing the lyrics to a classic gamblers' song such as "Luck Be a Lady Tonight" or "The Gambler." Roll the dice if you've chosen them as your symbol. Did you roll a seven? If so, book a flight to Vegas right now! If, on the other hand, you pick at random the Queen of Hearts, then Lady Luck smiles on you. Remember, however, never to bet more than you can afford to lose.

Denise Dumars

Notes:

nado it is far too dangerous to attempt a capture. Decide on the goal of the spell. Write it on paper and rip the paper to little bits. Place the bits in your left palm. Now conjure the tornado. Visualize it getting stronger and blowing fiercely. Hold your left palm up to your mouth and blow, hard. See the tornado burst from your mouth in a pulsating white cloud.

Tammy Sullivan

Notes:

April 9
Saturday

 1st ♈
☽ → ♉ 11:50 am

Color of the day: Blue
Incense of the day: Violet

Tornado Spell

On this day in 1947, tornadoes killed 169 people in three states. Tornadoes are a prime example of nature at its most powerful. To harness the power of a tornado and put it to use in magical work, we must work in the astral realm. There is old lore that says you can capture the wind in a bag and magically seal the bags with cords and knots, thus harnessing the wind. But when dealing with a tor-

April 10
Sunday

 1st ♉

Color of the day: Orange
Incense of the day: Clove

Spell for Courage

We all need courage sometimes, whether for standing up to someone, for leaving an unhealthy situation, or for starting something new. Living through fear is hard on your body, mind, and spirit. With three major planets in Aries today, this is an ideal time to develop the courage that already lies within you. Brew yourself a cup of black tea. Sprinkle a small amount of thyme into your tea. Holding the cup in your hands, call upon your spirit guides and ask for their help. Gaze into the cup of tea and see yourself as a courageous being, able to handle any situation with ease and confidence. Take three deep breaths, and with each exhalation blow a feeling of courage onto the surface of the tea. As you drink, imagine these energies filling every cell in your body and resonating throughout your complete being.

Kristin Madden

Notes:

Suit of Wands Spell

This spell helps improve your tarot skills by attuning you to the suit of wands. Cast it in the morning, as you will continue working with the imagery all day. Begin by taking out the Ace of Wands from your favorite tarot deck. Place the card on your altar. Burn some incense with a woodsy fragrance—such as cedar, sandalwood, or pine—then say:

> Wand of power,
> Wand of might
> Touch my mind with
>   magic's light.
>
> Give direction,
> Point the way
> Show yourself to me
>   today.

Open your deck's guidebook and read the section on wands. Meditate for a while on the imagery and interpretations. Let the incense burn out on its own. For the rest of the day, watch for wand motifs wherever you go. Keep a record of what you see, and store it with your tarot-reading notes.

Elizabeth Barrette

Notes:

April 11
Monday

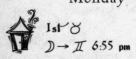

1st ♉
☽ → ♊ 6:55 pm

Color of the day: Lavender
Incense of the day: Frankincense

 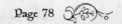

April 12
Tuesday

 1st ♊

Color of the day: White

Incense of the day: Ginger

Spell of Mars

This spell is used to gain personal strength and courage, to enhance our passion for a vocation, to deal with a difficult situation, to increase vitality, or to face coming changes. Mars can also help us to deal effectively with anger—either expressing it or absorbing it. The operative words are "fire" and "energy." Light six red or orange candles. Burn dragon's blood resin for incense. Wear a red robe or other similar article of clothing. Play music with drums and a primal rhythmic element. Stand before the brightly lit altar, swaying to the music, feeling the light and heat of the candles and the passionate rhythm of the drums fill you. Chant an invocation to Mars:

God of fire,
God of passion,
God of strength and
bravery;
Fill me now with all your
power;
Lend your might and
will to me.

Build the energy, and be sure to ground and center when finished.

Ruby Lavender

Notes:

Historical note: On 12 April, 1961, Yuri Gagarin piloted the first manned spaceship to leave the pull of our planet's gravity. This achievement is given much less attention than it deserves; part of it is politics, since Gagarin was a cosmonaut for the Soviet Union. Part of it, too, is time; today, space pilots live and work for months aboard space stations, so a simple space flight seems routine. Still, Yuri Gagarin's 108-minute flight in space represented not only a triumph of science and engineering, but also it broke a psychological barrier. It was literally a flight into unknown. "Am I happy to be setting off on a cosmic flight?" said Yuri Gagarin in an interview before the start. "Of course. In all ages and epochs people have experienced the greatest happiness in embarking upon new voyages of discovery . . . I say 'until we meet again' to you, dear friends, as we always say to each other when setting off on a long journey."

April 13
Wednesday

1st ♊

Color of the day: Brown
Incense of the day: Cedar

Water Blessing Spell

Today is traditionally a Buddhist water festival. Statues of the Buddha are cleansed and the water is thrown on the faithful to wash away the evil spirits that attach to a person. You can perform this ritual with a statue of the Buddha, or you can bathe any god or goddess statues you hold sacred. At twilight, add the water you used to cleanse your statues to your bath water. Bathe by the light of a new blue candle, and ask the divine for blessings. Like Wiccans, Buddhists believe in the sacredness of all life. By leaving food for the birds or wild animals in your neighborhood, you ensure that you receive blessings in turn.

Lily Gardner-Butts

Notes:

April 14
Thursday

1st ♊

☽ → ♋ 5:03 am

Color of the day: Crimson
Incense of the day: Musk

Looking for a New Job Spell

Take a little extra something with you when looking for a new job. Dress a green candle with essential oil of rosemary, and place it in a holder on your altar. Light the candle. Now, place your hands down on the altar on either side of the candle and gaze into the flame. Picture yourself getting an interview, being made a job offer, and even getting a first paycheck. Tell yourself that you are worthy of employment, and that you are getting a job you will enjoy and that will meet your financial needs. Get it all firmly planted in your mind, and believe it to be true. Let the candle burn for a half hour, then blow it out. Burn it on consecutive nights until it is no more.

Laurel Reufner

Notes:

April 15
Friday

 1st ♋

Color of the day: Pink
Incense of the day: Nutmeg

Spiritual Connection Spell

Spirituality isn't something that we practice. Spirituality is a lifestyle. Every action in the mundane can connect to and reflect our connection with the Goddess—our unity of mind, body, and spirit. Today, cut three equal lengths of cord. The cords, which represent mind, body, and spirit, can be of colored cotton or of natural hemp. Unify the three lengths of cord together by tying a knot at one end. Burn some sandalwood on a charcoal block, and focus on the union of mind, body, and spirit. Focus on specific actions that nourish this union. Be it personal meditations or public activism, decide on a daily action and tie a knot in your trio of cords. Repeat this daily until the Full Moon. On the night of the Full Moon, light a white candle. Burn your knotted cord in honor of your spiritual life.

Karen Follett

Notes:

April 16
Saturday

 1st ♋

Second Quarter 10:37 am

☽ → ♌ 5:17 pm

Color of the day: Indigo
Incense of the day: Patchouli

Language of Flowers Spell

There is a language of flowers. Lovers would send secret messages by using certain herbs and flowers in small bouquets known as tussies. You can make a magical wish for health, prosperity, and love by planting a small garden to "spell" your home. Use rosemary, for example, for remembrance; miniature red roses for love; oregano or echinacea for health; myrrh or money plant for prosperity; tansy or yarrow for protection. Plant the seeds and think about the things you will need to be happy and successful. As you tend the plants, chant: "Earth and water, fire and air, listen to my simple prayer. This garden tended lovingly, will bring my wishes home to me."

Paniteowl

Notes:

April 17
Sunday

2nd ♌

Color of the day: Yellow
Incense of the day: Poplar

Health Improvement Charm

This spell assists in improving the health of elderly persons, the frail, infirm, or those who are housebound. Obtain a horseshoe or find an iron nail. Bring some water to a boil in a saucepan, and add sea salt to the liquid. When the salt has dissolved, let the water cool down to a lukewarm temperature. Immerse the horseshoe or iron nail in the salt water to bless it. Take the horseshoe or iron nail to the garden of a sick person, and bury it with the tip pointing out of the soil. Or else, it can be buried in a potted plant and placed in a sunny part of the living room. Water the plant regularly, and feed it with fertilizer once in a while. Have the sick person sit near the plant whenever possible to absorb strong, fresh, and rejuvenating energies.

S. Y. Zenith

Notes:

April 18
Monday

2nd ♌

Color of the day: Gray
Incense of the day: Peony

Bedroom Spell for Restful Sleep

To bring restful energies to your bedroom, begin with a good practical cleaning. Vacuum or sweep, dust all surfaces, make the bed up with clean linens. Open any windows, and allow all negative energy to be dispelled. Burn sage in the room, and ring a bell nine times. Light candles, and assemble a talisman using a quartz, moonstone, amethyst, and a small seashell wrapped up in a piece of white fabric. Sprinkle with dried rosemary, chamomile, anise, lavender, and elderberries. Add a drop of real aloe gel and three drops of pure water, chanting:

Power of the silver
Moon, bless this room.
Bring restful sleep,
Safe and sound.
This promise keep.

Place the bundle under the mattress. Burn sandalwood incense visualizing peace and harmony in the room.

Ember

Notes:

April 19
Tuesday

2nd ♌

☽ → ♍ 5:27 am

☉ → ♉ 7:37 pm

Color of the day: Scarlet
Incense of the day: Pine

Bread of Opportunity Spell

Today is the last day of Cerealia, honoring Ceres, goddess of grains. On this day, her temple in Rome was first dedicated, bringing a horrible famine to an end. In honor of Ceres, bake a loaf of bread today. The recipe below is easy as it uses no yeast, eliminating rising times.

Soda Bread

1 cup all-purpose flour
1 cup wheat flour
2 tablespoons brown sugar
1 teaspoon baking powder
1/2 teaspoon baking soda
3 tablespoons butter
1/2 cup buttermilk
2 eggs, beaten separately
1/2 cup raisins or currants

In a large bowl combine the flours, sugar, baking powder, and baking soda. Cut in the butter in bits, and mix the mass with your hands until the mixture is crumbly. In a small bowl combine the buttermilk, one beaten egg, and the raisins. Pour the liquid into the flour mixture and stir until everything is moistened. On a floured surface, knead the dough gently about fifteen times, working in a little more flour as needed. Place the dough on a greased baking sheet, shaping it into a rounded loaf. With a sharp knife, cut a cross into the top of the bread. Brush the surface with the remaining beaten egg. Bake at 375°F for about thirty-five minutes or until golden brown.

Laurel Reufner

Notes:

April 20
Wednesday

2nd ♍

Color of the day: White
Incense of the day: Maple

The Legend of Dogwood Winter

The rural people of Appalachia are keen observers of nature and weather. Over the years they've accumulated a wealth of knowledge concerning seasonal weather lore. One of these legends concerns a natural phenomenon that occurs each spring known as "dogwood winter." In April, the Appalachian landscape is starred white by the blossoms of the dogwood tree. But during this blooming, there is always a cold spell, which brings a dramatic drop in temperature and an occasional snow flurry. This became known to the old-timers as dogwood winter, and I've observed it too, occurring almost every year without fail. Farmers and gardeners expect it and curtail planting until warmer weather returns. See if you can learn more about the weather lore in your area. It's not only fun, but it will help you understand the cycles of nature, and this can enhance your magic.

James Kambos

Notes:

April 21
Thursday

 2nd ♏

☽ → ♎ 3:27 pm

Color of the day: Purple
Incense of the day: Sage

Car Protection Spell

Whether we live in a large city or in a rural area, our lifestyles are largely urban. Most of us drive or ride in a car frequently. Driving relies on applying common sense:

> Stay alert.

> Drive at safe speeds.

> Never drive under the influence of alcohol or drugs.

> Turn off your cell phone.

Enhance your protection when on the road with some urban magic. Each time you are in a car, either as the driver or passenger, visualize a protective bubble around your vehicle. Write this spell on a card and keep it with you or in your car:

> My journey is safe,
> Vigilant in every way.
> In this vehicle and any
>   other,
> Grant me protection.

Emely Flak

Notes:

April 22
Friday
Earth Day

 2nd ♎

Color of the day: Rose
Incense of the day: Ginger

Eco-Magic for Earth Day

The Earth, its seasons, the lengthening and shortening of days, the swift phases of the Moon, the dense forests—we take all these things for granted, but it wasn't always this way. The Earth and its magic were once regarded with wonder, and treated as our mother. When the Earth is happy, you can almost feel her gentle chuckle below your feet. When we deface or scar her, we diminish all life. So help protect the Earth today by starting with one tree. Seek out a quiet spot with a huge old tree—one that seems to embody the wisdom of many centuries. Since it's Earth Day, no will think it strange that you, or your coven or friends, are cavorting around a tree. Take with you some small animal food, a sharp knife, and a bucket half full of water. Stand before the large tree, or, if you're with a group, stand in a circle. Chant: "Blessed be, old friend tree." At some point in the dance, leave the food for the tree's creatures. Scatter it liberally around the entire base of the tree, then place your palms on the tree, close your eyes, and try to communicate with her. Some trees have had traumatic experiences with people, so be gentle. Ask for permission to cut a small limb so you can plant another tree, an offspring. You may even offer her a gift of coins, food, or a colorful ribbon. If she says no, find another tree. If she says yes, sever only one limb with a careful and clean cut. Thank her, leave her a gift, then place the base of the branch into the bucket of water so it won't dry out.

Edain McCoy

Notes:

 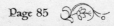

April 23
Saturday

 2nd ♎︎

☽ → ♏︎ 10:25 pm

Color of the day: Brown
Incense of the day: Lilac

Kokopelli Rain Ritual

Kokopelli is a hump-backed, flute-playing spirit intimately tied to the sacred rites of spring, gardening, birth, renewal, sexuality, and rain. To invoke Kokopelli, play a CD of Lakota flute music. Burn a mixture of tobacco, cedar, and mugwort in a censor over charcoal. Spread some blue or red cornmeal (substitute yellow if necessary) on the floor. Dip your finger into a glass of rain-water. Draw the simple shape of Kokopelli in the cornmeal. Wet your fingers well with the rain-water once more. Sprinkle a few raindrops over your head. Lie down next to the drawing and allow the sensual music and sacred incense inspire the flow of creativity.

Stephanie Rose Bird

Notes:

April 24
Sunday
Passover Begins

 2nd ♏︎

Full Moon 6:06 am

Color of the day: Gold
Incense of the day: Cinnamon

Protect and Serve Spell

The Jewish observance of Passover commemorates the exemption of the Jewish people from the killing hand of the angel of death (who took the lives of the first-born of their enemies). This year the day falls on the night of a Full Moon eclipse. The theme today is one of keeping hidden and safe. Place a spell of protection around you, your home and family today. You will need a bowl of lightly salted water, some rosemary, and a protective incense such as frankincense, pine, or cinnamon. All these items should be handled so they absorb your will. If possible, allow all others in the household to add their energies by handling the catalysts also. Begin your spell outside. Using your fingertips, scatter small drops of water against the base of the house. If your house has an unfinished basement, toss a little of the salt water there too. As you move clockwise around the house chant softly: "We are protected well, all who in here dwell." Back inside, take the incense

from room to room, still chanting. When you feel the incense has purged every part of your home, take the empowered herb and walk it through your house. Then go outside and walk three times clockwise around the building. On the third time around, sprinkle bits of the herbs to create a circle of protection. As soon as you're back inside, go to each window and door (even doors that don't lead outside), and mentally impress a symbol of protection on it.

> Herbs from Mother Earth
>   do spring,
> This gift we borrow so
>   we can sing,
> Feeling secure and safe in
>   her arms,
> Keeping her children free
>   from harm.

Edain McCoy

Notes:

picture. Record your feelings about each phase of the Moon and what it symbolizes in your life. Consider the pull of the Moon on the tides and on the tides within us. As you record your feelings and memories about each phase, consider using this notebook as a lunar journal to record any of your thoughts, feelings, spells, and rituals you have performed during specific phases of the Moon. See if a pattern emerges that reveals how your energy grows and wanes during certain Moon phases. This knowledge can inform you about patterns in both your mundane and magical life.

Denise Dumars

Notes:

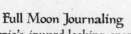 **Full Moon Journaling**

Scorpio's inward-looking energy lends itself well to tonight's lunar eclipse. This evening, place a picture of the Moon phases on your altar, or better yet, sit outdoors in a quiet place with a notebook and the

April 25
Monday

3rd ♏

Color of the day: Ivory
Incense of the day: Lavender

Burning Question Spell

Choose a place where you will be undisturbed for at least one hour. Make sure that this is a place you feel safe in. If you can go to a park or wilderness area, do so. If not, simply turn the ringer off your phone and lock yourself in a room in your home for a while. Burn some myrrh incense and gaze into the smoke, holding your question in your mind. Chant your name along with the names of your spirit guides and power animals. Feel these energies fill the space around you as you chant. Ask for their blessings and protection, and imagine them looking deep into the dark shadows within you. See a light illuminate the areas that relate to your specific question, and explore as much as you feel comfortable. Thank your guides when you are done.

Kristin Madden

Notes:

Fey Folk honoring Ritual

This is the month of oak, and a time of year when the devas and fairies seem to be awakening in the earth. Honoring the fey folk is a great way to bring blessings upon your home. The oak-tree nymphs who dwelt within oak trees were called *hamadryads* in ancient times. To honor one, go to an old oak in your neighborhood. Fairies and other nature spirits love gifts of all kinds. Something naturally beautiful and biodegradable is especially welcome— for instance fruit, flowers or herbs, a bit of fresh bread or cake, some nuts or seeds, or some milk, mead, or wine offered as a libation. After you make your offering, sit against the tree, close your eyes, and offer thanks for the tree's shade, strength, and beauty. Don't be surprised if you see a hamadryad out of the corner of your eye, shyly thanking you.

Ruby Lavender

Notes:

April 26
Tuesday

 3rd ♏

☽ → ♐ 2:46 am

Color of the day: Black
Incense of the day: Juniper

April 27
Wednesday

3rd ♐

     Color of the day: Topaz
Incense of the day: Pine

Flow of Life Meditation

While we are the masters of our own destinies, we are a part of the natural world and the order of that world. Nature has a pattern of flow. Each creation is given attributes and gifts that, when utilized, encourage our flow to the universal abundance of mind, body, and spirit. When we make choices that deviate from the life flow, we tend to find ourselves in need. Reattune yourself to the natural pattern by picturing a waterway that leads to a glorious Moon or starlit horizon. Burn sandalwood on a charcoal block and say:

> Lead me back to the flow
> of the universe, attune me
> to the pattern of my life.

Meditate, using the guided imagery. Write any perceptions that enter your awareness. Be alert for opportunities to improve your flow.

                      Karen Follett

Notes:

April 28
Thursday

3rd ♐
☽ → ♑ 5:33 am

Color of the day: Turquoise
Incense of the day: Jasmine

Bird Banishing Spell

Do you have a problem with birds in your garden? This spell shoos them away. Collect an assortment of sparkly bird-banishers. Garden stores sell tinsel streamers, pinwheels, mirrored mobiles, and so forth, or you can use aluminum pie plates. Hang them all around your garden, and say:

> Fairies wild, fairies free,
> Lend your ears to me.
> Come and see what I
>   have done,
> See the sparkle of the sun!
> Come to visit and to stay.
> Come to play.

Fairies love flashy things. Plus, their mischievous nature inclines them to tease anything that moves. Pesky birds will desert your garden in search of quieter feeding grounds.

          Elizabeth Barrette

Notes:

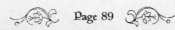

April 29
Friday
Orthodox Good Friday

 3rd ♑

Color of the day: White
Incense of the day: Rose

honoring Flora Spell

Flora was the Roman goddess of flowers, springtime, and gardens. Today is the second day of the ancient festival Floralia held in her glory. In honor of this weave a circlet of flowers to wear in your hair. Take a packet of flower seeds, and plant them in a special spot in your garden. Pour milk and honey over the seed bed, and say: "Goddess Flora, bringer of new life, I offer this garden to you. I open my eyes to see and my heart to feel the beauty and love on this Earth." Make sure to take the time to stop and smell the roses today.

Tammy Sullivan

Notes:

April 30
Saturday
May Eve

 3rd ♑
☽ → ♒ 7:54 am

Color of the day: Blue
Incense of the day: Juniper

Beltane Fertility Spell

As Beltane approaches, spells and enchantments to improve fertility are very appropriate. A good and subtle talisman is to make a grapevine wreath and decorate it with fertility symbols and colors—a small cinnamon broom, a bird's nest with three polished stones in it, some turkey feathers, a small stuffed rabbit, or any other items that represent fertility to you. Use florist wire to attach the items to your wreath. Add silk flowers, or fresh greens for their beauty. Hang the wreath on your front door, and each time you enter or leave touch the wreath and say: "Goddess of fertility, bring the spark of life to me." Remember, fertility is not just pregnancy, but also concerns new ideas; a new business, or simple good fortune.

Paniteowl

Notes:

May

May is the fifth month of the year. Its astrological sign is Taurus, the bull (April 19-May 20), a fixed earth sign ruled by Venus. The month is named for Maia, a Roman goddess and mother of the god Hermes (the word is from the Greek for "mother"). May is a month of full-blown growth and colors of every sort. The main holiday of the month—May Day, or Beltane (May 1)—is a celebration of color and flowers. A traditional part of the May Day celebration is the maypole, which traditionally was cut from a fir tree on May Eve (April 30) by the unmarried men of the village. All its branches, except for the topmost, were removed and then adorned with ribbons and placed in the village square. On May Day, dancers hold the ends of the ribbons attached to the top of the maypole—girls going one way, boys another. As the ribbons wind and shorten, the dance becomes a spiral, symbolizing death and resurrection. Making and exchanging wreaths of flowers is an old tradition in May. In some traditions, the Sacred Marriage— between the May Queen and the May King, also known as Jack-of-the-Green—is important on May Day to ensure a vigorous growth in the crops. The Full Moon of May is called the Dyad Moon, the time when the two become one and all things meet in perfect balance and harmony.

May 1
Sunday
May Day – Beltane

3rd ≈
Fourth Quarter 2:24 am

Color of the day: Orange

Incense of the day: Sage

A Beltane Binding Spell

In the Wiccan wheel of the year Beltane celebrates the marriage of the God and the Goddess. Many modern Wiccans enjoy a Beltane wedding because of the sexual imagery contained in this sabbat's rituals. One feature of the celebration is the tying together of the couples' hands. We call this handfasting, a name given to the Celtic customs of trial marriages. With a length of silk you can weave a spell to bind something to you. Wrap one end of the silk snugly around your left hand. Wrap the other end of the silk to something or someone else, provided you have consent. You may want to confirm your relationship to your best friend, a work partner, or with a small child. You may wish to keep objects, such as books, jewelry, or money, from being lost. You will need to personalize the words of power so that they are more specific to your purpose. What follows is a blueprint. The finished spell is yours to build.

high and hot the
   Beltane fire,
I bind you now by my
   desire.
No one shall harm, lose,
   or take,
Because a binding upon
   it I make.

When the silk is removed, the spell remains. Keep the silk and visualize the spell to recharge the binding as necessary.

Edain McCoy

Notes:

May 2
Monday

4th ≈
☽ → ♓ 10:43 am

Color of the day: Gray

Incense of the day: Coriander

Clear the Air Spell

Strong-willed children and adults under the same roof can sometimes together create a rather tense environment. This fun little ritual will not only clear out the edgy, argumentative energy, but will also improve everyone's mood. You need a stick of incense of your choice, and a musical instrument or noise-maker for everyone else participating. Go from room to room using first the incense, then the noise-makers at every door and window. Laugh and have fun as you move about.

Laurel Reufner

Notes:

can do it with harm to none. Write down the actions that are hurting you. As you are writing, visualize all the pain you have felt from these actions streaming through the pen onto the paper. With each thing you write, say it aloud and then say: "The hurt from this leaves me now." When you have finished speaking, burn the paper so no trace is left, only ashes. Take the ashes outside and bury them, preferably off your property. Now say, "I lay this hurt to rest now and forever. May the great Mother Goddess recycle the energy and put it to good use."

Tammy Sullivan

Notes:

May 3
Tuesday

 4th ♓
Color of the day: Red
Incense of the day: Honeysuckle

Releasing the Psychic Vampire Spell

If you should find yourself needing to rid yourself of another's harmful energy, there is a way you

May 4
Wednesday

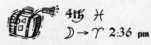 4th ♓
☽ → ♈ 2:36 pm

Color of the day: Yellow
Incense of the day: Neroli

New Employment Endeavor Spell

To prepare for a job search or new business enterprise, create the following charm. Burn frankincense incense as you make a sacred space or circle. Pass a dollar bill several times through the incense smoke, then fold the bill nine times—starting at one end and ending with a small strip. Repeat with each fold: "This venture will be blessed with prosperity and success." Tie a string around the folded bill, and carry it with you.

Ember

Notes:

Boy's Day Spell

On this day, the Japanese celebrate their boy children. They have two rituals that bring the family good health and good luck to the boys. The first is to prepare a bath with iris leaves to make the boys both healthy and courageous. The second ritual is to hang a wind sock in the shape of a strong, determined carp outside their door. Hang one sock for each boy, the largest going to the eldest. Burn a red candle for Kwan Yin, and say:

> Kwan Yin,
> Goddess of compassion.
> Thank you for the blessings
>   you have bestowed
>   upon my family.
>
> Thank you for the good
>   health and happiness
>   we have enjoyed.
>
> Please continue to watch
>   over us.
> Blessed be.

Lily Gardner-Butts

Notes:

May 5
Thursday
Cinco de Mayo

 4℞ ♈

Color of the day: Purple
Incense of the day: Vanilla

oliday lore: Don't confuse Cinco de Mayo with Mexican Independence Day on September 16. Cinco de Mayo marks the victory of the brave Mexican Army over the French at the Battle of Puebla. Although the Mexican army was eventually defeated, the *Batalla de Puebla* became a symbol of Mexican unity and patriotism. With this victory, Mexico demonstrated to the world that Mexico and all of Latin America were willing to defend themselves against any foreign or imperialist intervention.

May 6
Friday

 4♄ ♈

☽ → ♉ 8:01 pm

Color of the day: Pink
Incense of the day: Dill

Shango Invocation

Shango is the magnetic warrior spirit of the Yoruba people whose number is six. He is noble, elegant, protective, and tricky. To engage the positive aspects of his spirit go outside where there are plenty of trees. Face northeast, as it is his direction. Burn his favorite incense, frankincense tears, in a censer, being careful to use fireproof protective surfaces. Spread some cayenne peppers, hibiscus flowers, and bay leaves around the circumfer-

ence of a tree that has some of Shango's characteristics. Keep your head low; defer to this spirit. Walk away backwards, as quickly as you can without falling, until you are well away from the tree.

Stephanie Rose Bird

Notes:

May 7
Saturday

 4♄ ♉

Color of the day: Indigo
Incense of the day: Pine

Hidden Power of the Dark Spell

It's the dark period of the Moon now, just before the New Moon—a period that is sometimes called "the black Moon." Ironically, this is also the day of the Greek Crone goddess, Hecate. Like the Crone, the Moon maintains a low profile, but her power cannot be underestimated. In this phase, the Moon represents the crone, a symbol of hidden power waiting to be released. Many Wiccans don't perform manifestation spells in the dark Moon period. This is a time for reflection, planning, and wisdom-seeking instead of action. It's an ideal time to plant a seed for a project without taking any action. Keep the action for the waxing phase of the moon. While contemplating your plan, say these words:

> Goddess of darkness,
> In your sky without light,
> Withhold the very
>   manifestation
> Of plans made tonight.

Emely Flak

Notes:

May 8
Sunday
Mother's Day

4ħ ♉

New Moon 4:45 am

Color of the day: Yellow
Incense of the day: Basil

Mother's Day Beauty in the New Moon

Taurus, in the body, rules the neck and Taurus' ruler, Venus, rules beauty, so today is perfect for beginning new beauty rituals for the hair, face, and neck. Think in terms of healthy skin and hair today, and the beauty will follow. Use an herbal hair rinse, steeping dry or fresh herbs, and then using the "tea" as a rinse after shampooing. Rosemary is good if you have brown hair; chamomile if blonde; juniper if you have gray hair, and hibiscus if you have red. Rose is Venus' scent. Have someone give you a neck massage with rose-scented oil; wear rose perfume today and buy some rose water and glycerin hand lotion. Ask a beauty expert at a department store for the best skin care for your particular complexion. Get a free make-up demonstration while you're there. Keep using rose-scented products whenever possible and Venus will smile on you, increasing your beauty and positive outlook. Over the next lunar month, expect compliments!

Denise Dumars

Notes:

May 9
Monday

 1st ♉
☽ → ♊ 3:29 am

Color of the day: Lavender
Incense of the day: Chrysanthemum

Rebuilding Your Energies Spell

As the New Moon grows now, it is a good time to strengthen the body and build up our reserves. The waxing Moon signals the time when the body starts to absorb nutrients more efficiently. Winter has perhaps found us neglecting our healthy eating and exercise habits. As the weather turns fair, exercise your body outdoors. Eat spring vegetables that are particularly health-giving: asparagus, fiddle-heads, greens, and lettuces. Culpeper and other herbalists believed spring greens such as dandelion, dock, nettles, chicory, and so on, were nature's best tonic—replenishing everything the body needs. Eat lightly and make sure your food is full of nutrients. Stick to salads and vegetables, fish and lean meats, whole grains, and fresh fruit. As you feed yourself these foods, think about how our bodies mirror the seasonal changes around us. As the flowers bloom and fill the world with color, picture your own vitality increasing. In a few weeks, your winter sluggishness will be gone,

you'll shed a few pounds, and you will feel vibrant and alive for the upcoming summer.

Ruby Lavender

Notes:

May 10
Tuesday

 1st ♊

Color of the day: White
Incense of the day: Evergreen

Protect Your Garden Spell

During the month of May in colonial America, farmers would bless their land and pray for a good harvest. Revive this tradition by performing this spell to protect your garden.

On a May eve,
As the Sun forgets the
    light of day,
Fill an earthen vessel
    made of clay
With soil from your

sacred ground,
Then add a pinch of
cinnamon,
Spicy and brown,
And a bit of clove to
purify.

Let this be witnessed by
Mother Earth and
Father Sky,
Stir it all with a nail
aged with rust,
Blend these elements
until they're reduced
to dust.

Sprinkle this about each
bed and border,
As you announce your
magical order:
No beast nor fowl from
sky or land
Shall bring harm to this
garden,
Which I protect by my
own hand.

To secure your garden's
protection and fate,
Bury the rusty nail near
your garden gate.

James Kambos

Notes:

May 11
Wednesday

 1st ♊
☽ → ♋ 1:20 pm

Color of the day: Brown
Incense of the day: Eucalyptus

Lost Luggage Spell

Ruled by Mercury, Wednesday concerns matters of business and travel. Here is a spell to keep your luggage from getting lost in transit. You need two silver candles and a length of black ribbon. You also need one of those "Best Friends" or "Be Mine" pendants that breaks apart into two halves, though make sure it starts as one piece. Name one candle for yourself, the other for your luggage, lighting each as you do so. Carefully loop the ribbon around both and knot it, saying:

> Mine to me,
> Me to mine,
> Like this ribbon so
> entwine.
> Me to mine,
> Mine to me,
> As I will, so mote it be!

Touch the pendant to the candles. Snap it in half and attach one half to your luggage, carrying the other half with you. Leave the bound candles on your altar until you return home from your next trip.

Elizabeth Barrette

 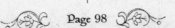

Notes:

paper under the glass money jar until your wish is fulfilled. Donate a portion of the money received to charity.

S. Y. Zenith

Notes:

May 12
Thursday

 1st ♋

Color of the day: Green
Incense of the day: Sandalwood

Spiral Coin Spell

To ensure prosperity, gather as many coins as possible. Anoint a green candle with virgin olive oil and place it on the left side of the altar. Light the candle and surround the base of the candleholder with a mixture of mint and honeysuckle. Form the stash of coins into a spiral shape on the right side of the table. Using a pen with green ink, write on a piece of white paper the sum of money you need for a useful purpose. Anoint the four corners of the paper with mint oil. Place the paper next to the spiral pile of coins and leave it there. Allow the candle to burn down before removing the coins for storing in a clear glass jar. Put the piece of white

May 13
Friday

 1st ♋

Color of the day: Rose
Incense of the day: Thyme

Awen Spell

Use the energy of Venus in Gemini today to inspire your love life. *Awen* is a Welsh word that relates to the flow of divine inspiration. Consider how inspiration might flow through you. Allow your creativity to flow freely. Fully experience the process of creating without judgment or any thought for the aesthetics of your creation. Smudge yourself with sagebrush, and create a sacred space in your preferred manner. Sit in

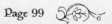

silent meditation for a few moments, and call upon the energy of your lover or the lover you hope to attract. Feel this energy fill your space, and let it excite you. Imagine the ideal relationship—one that is full of sensuality, trust, and fun. Feel that energy fill your space. Paint a picture with color, music, or words that manifests these feelings into the physical. Allow the awen to assist you in honoring and creating the ideal relationship.

Kristin Madden

Notes:

Perpetual Sunlight Spell

Today the Scandanavians celebrate the first day of the Midnight Sun, ten weeks of perpetual sunlight that lasts through the summer. It is the festival of Sunna, the Sun goddess. It is said of Sunna that she is chased by the celestial wolf, Skoll, who at the end of the world will at last catch her and devour her. For the next ten weeks Sunna is at her strongest. She has run far from the sky wolf, and for now, the world is safe. Take a Sun bath today and soak up Sunna's strength. Sun magic uses change to achieve its purpose. Light a yellow candle, and visualize what you wish to manifest this summer. Write down what you need to change to accomplish your goals.

Lily Gardner-Butts

Notes:

May 14
Saturday

 1st ♋
☽ → ♌ 1:17 am

Color of the day: Gray
Incense of the day: Lavender

May 15
Sunday

 1st ♌

Color of the day: Gold
Incense of the day: Coriander

Ides of May Spell

During an illness, we may have to take medicines that take time to work. To enhance the properties of the medication, follow the directions printed on the label, but also do this simple meditation both before and after you take your prescription. First, take a deep cleansing breath for a slow count of four. Then, hold your breath for another slow count of four. Now breathe out, for a slow count of four, and hold for another slow count of four. Repeat this breathing exercise three times, while envisioning your body getting ready to receive the help it needs. Pause for a few moments and a few stray breaths, then take the medication very deliberately and with conscious thought. Next, perform the breathing technique described above three more times—each time envisioning your body accepting the medication and readily sending it along the pathways of your blood stream, delivering its message of relief and improved health.

Paniteowl

Notes:

May 16
Monday

 1st ♌

Second Quarter 4:57 am

☽ → ♏ 1:46 pm pm

Color of the day: White
Incense of the day: Myrrh

Personal Power Spell

Personal power means many things to many people. The common denominator in personal power is confidence—confidence with who you are and what you can accomplish, and that allows you to take the path of your choosing while honoring others in the paths they choose. Power is a divine spark that burns in each of us. This power chant can be used to ignite a power spark for any desired goal. Visualize yourself as a powerful person obtaining a specific goal. Begin

the chant by saying: "Power divine, your spark is mine." Feel the energy's warm flow. Allow the warmth to build through your chakras. As you feel the warmth intensify, change the chant to: "Power divine, your flame is mine." Release the energy as it crests. Draw your power back through your chakras from crown to root, and ground any excess energy.

Karen Follett

Notes:

ably, and calm your breathing. Feel your body coming to rest. Now, take an extra-deep breath and begin building a mental shield around yourself. Feel layer upon layer building up, wrapping itself around you in a warm protective coating. Feel the shield becoming translucent, even porous. Let it become a part of you, and then visualize yourself reaching out a hand to touch the shield, seeing a static pulse appear under your fingers. Know that when any strong emotions come toward you they will be "vaporized" in a similar pulse. Let the shield damp itself down, remaining dormant until needed. To activate at any time, visualize the shield "powering up" around you like a forcefield brought back to life.

Laurel Reufner

Notes:

May 17
Tuesday

2nd ♍

Color of the day: Black
Incense of the day: Sage

Shielding Meditation for the Strongly Empathic

The psychic shield this meditation creates will allow you, when it is activated, to filter out strong emotions that can be disorienting or even draining. To start, sit or lie comfort-

May 18
Wednesday

2nd ♍

Color of the day: Topaz
Incense of the day: Cedar

Anubis Travel Spell

Anubis the Egyptian jackal or hunting dog is a protector, guardian, and opener of ways. Its nature is movable and when invoked for guidance prior to a journey away from home, Anubis navigates the traveler through unforeseen obstacles during the trip. Obtain a picture of Anubis and tuck it into your luggage. This will ensure that it will arrive at the same destination upon your disembarking, instead of turning up in the town of Usa in Japan. Being the patron of navigators, Anubis is the St. Christopher of the Western world and guards and protects your welfare and belongings. After you return home from a successful and happy trip, place the picture of Anubis on the altar and give thanks.

S. Y. Zenith

Notes:

May 19
Thursday

2nd ♍
☽ → ♎ 12:30 am

Color of the day: Turquoise
Incense of the day: Dill

Civil Rights Keep Marching On Spell

On this day in 1925, Malcolm X was born. Also on this day in 2001, a young Chinese woman was put to death for refusing to be sterilized by authorities. To honor the bravery of these two very different civil rights activists, and to keep the movement for civil rights moving forward throughout the world, take a newspaper and fold it into an airplane. It doesn't have to be fancy or fly very well; the idea is what counts. Charge the little toy with your intent, speaking how important are the rights of individuals in the face of injustices of the world. Sail it into the air and say:

> Wind,
> Take this plane high,
> As a reminder that we
> Should always take the
>   high road.
>
> Give this plane
>   movement,
> As a reminder for us
>   to grow.

Finally, lay the plane down. As a reminder that we are all one with the Earth, say: "So it is done."

Tammy Sullivan

Notes:

of lilac, rose, or apple blossom. Her colors are rose pink, pale green, and pale blue. Her perfumes are sandalwood, rose, and orange. After decorating a suitable altar to the goddess of love, put on some romantic, sensual music. Sit and breath deeply, or dance slowly, letting Venus' love and beauty radiate within you and in the room, which is perfumed and adorned in her honor. Venus loves all gestures of beauty, so honor her each day with a small offering. She will surely send love your way.

Ruby Lavender

Notes:

May 20
Friday

2nd ♎︎
☉ → ♊︎ 6:47 pm

Color of the day: Coral
Incense of the day: Ylang-ylang

Lusty Month of May Spell

Ah, the lusty month of May! Beltane rites fill us with the sensuality and passion of the season. Some Witches like to do some love magic to increase the romance in their lives at this time. Of course, never focus your intention on specific individuals, as this might compromise their free will, but instead focus on preparing yourself for love. The gifts of Venus are all around us at this time. On Friday, her day, decorate your ritual space with branches

May 21
Saturday

2nd ♎︎
☽ → ♏︎ 7:49 am

Color of the day: Blue
Incense of the day: Jasmine

Bear Waking Time in Norway

The hibernating mother bear has inspired many myths through time. For instance, one intriguing myth is that mama bear gives birth to her cub as she dreams in her den. In Norway, this day, May 21, is recognized as the time when the bear awakens and begins tending to her cubs. To inspire your ability to have potent, creative, and prophetic dreams at this time, make the following dream pillow. Mix a handful mullein, mugwort, jasmine flowers, chamomile, and lavender in a bowl. Then, mix one-quarter teaspoon each of the essential oils of chamomile and lavender, and add six to eight drops of attar of roses. Stir this mixture, and then add it to the herbs. Place the herb blend into a muslin bag, and tie the bag up with a new purple ribbon. Place the pillow near your bed at night, and before you go to sleep recite in a soft, but clear voice:

> Dream by day,
> Dream by night.
>
> Dream herbs do your best
> To stimulate insight.

Repeat this three times, pausing to consider your dream pillow after each time. Then add:

> So it is written,
> So mote it be.

Stephanie Rose Bird

Notes:

May 22
Sunday

 2nd ♏

Color of the day: Amber
Incense of the day: Parsley

Anam Cara Spell

The *anam cara* is the Celtic soul friend. This is someone that loves you unconditionally, either physically or spiritually. Cover a mirror with a scarf or translucent cloth. Light one yellow, one white, and one pink or green candle, and place them on a table beside the mirror. Turn off the remaining lights in the room, and light some cedar incense. Turn the mirror slightly to the left side and greet your anam cara. Imagine that your soul friend is joining you through the mirror and is listening lovingly to you. Speak from the heart, and share all that you need to share. Tell everything to this

 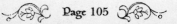

friend that you are afraid to tell others. Be completely honest. Stop every now and then and be silent, allowing messages to come through. When you are finished, thank your friend and blow out your candles.

Kristin Madden

Notes:

May 23
Monday

 2nd ♏
)→ ♐ 11:38 am

Full Moon 4:18 pm

Color of the day: Silver
Incense of the day: Daffodil

healing the Earth Ritual

Jupiter's influence on the Moon in bull's-eye Sagittarius can help you strengthen and hone your psychic abilities. Try scrying with a black mirror or crystal ball. The intense focus required should raise your energy and your ability to concentrate. Start with a darkened

room lit only with white or silver candles. Burn copal or frankincense to accentuate your mood. A tape of chanting or other evocative sounds can help you concentrate. Begin by closing your eyes and taking three deep breaths in and out. Open your eyes and concentrate on the scrying device. Empty your mind of its chatter; use the music and incense to think about whether you must let your mind wander. Sit comfortably and do not strain your eyes. Blink naturally and let your vision go slightly off-focus. Repeat this at several brief intervals throughout the evening. Record any interesting visions you receive.

Denise Dumars

Notes:

May 24
Tuesday

 3rd ♐

Color of the day: Gray
Incense of the day: Musk

Protective Shield Spell

Imagine a silver shield, wall, or bubble around yourself or those you wish to protect. Think of it as an impenetrable, invisible, but flexible substance that surrounds you and that keeps out anything that is unwanted. Speak these words as you visualize the protective barrier growing: "Shield hold true, no harm pass through." You can invoke this shield any time, any place, whenever you feel the need. Know that your words will bring it into existence.

Ember

Notes:

Protection from a Negative Coworker Spell

To protect yourself from a negative coworker, get a small picture of the person. Take an egg, and punch a hole in it. Remove the insides of the egg, and put them in a cup, being careful not to break the shell. Take the empty shell put one-half teaspoon of salt into the hole, and shake the egg. Roll up the picture of the person aggravating you, and put it into the shell. Place the shell in a clay pot, and put small pieces of mirror in the pot around the eggshell. Cover the pot, and put it in a safe place where no one will disturb it. Eat the egg you extracted from the shell. Use no oil or butter to cook it, but you can add a pinch of salt. As you eat the egg, say: "This spell I cast responsibly. Your harmful thoughts will mirrored be, and fall on you, not on me."

Paniteowl

Notes:

May 25
Wednesday

 3rd ♐

$\math…{D} \rightarrow \text{♑}$ 1:11 pm

Color of the day: White
Incense of the day: Maple

May 26
Thursday

3rd ♑

Color of the day: Crimson
Incense of the day: Carnation

Strength and Justice Day Spell

The Moon wanes today, on Thursday, the day of strength and justice. You are feeling empowered today to take on challenges and work on diminishing anguish, for instance, those people at work or school who cause you stress. Now is the time to deal with this, and to address any unnecessary imbalances in your life. Start with some simple Thursday visualizations. If you see "difficult" people in your life today, look at them and visualize their physical body being spiralled away from you. Picture their image fading from your mind. If you will not see the troublesome person today, do this visualization anyway. Just remember you do not to wish them any harm. You simply want them out of your personal space. If you find they are verbally intimidating you, imagine yourself holding a mirror to them. In this visualization, you see their negative energy bouncing back to them and away from your own impenetrable, invisible shield.

Emely Flak

Notes:

May 27
Friday

3rd ♑
☽ → ♒ 2:10 pm

Color of the day: Purple
Incense of the day: Almond

Mother of Arles handfasting Spell

In France, people hold a festival called the "Mothers of Arles." It is celebrated mostly by Gypsies who gather from all over Europe to honor the ancient ways. Three women dress up to represent the Goddess in her aspects of life, death, and beauty. Traditional activities include boating, processions, fortunetelling, street fairs, and weddings. Today is an auspicious day for handfasting. It also a good time for festive gatherings. Get your witchy friends together

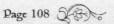

and throw a Gypsy bash. Decorate the space with bright colors, glittery scarves, gold coins, and lanterns or candles. Crown three ladies as the aspects of the Goddess. Play Gypsy music and teach people traditional dance styles. Break out the tarot decks, tea leaves, and crystal balls. See who can tell the most outrageous fortunes!

Elizabeth Barrette

Notes:

May 28
Saturday

 3rd ≈≈

Color of the day: Brown
Incense of the day: Violet

Memorial Day Weekend Remembrance Spell

You can perform this spell at a family gravesite or at your altar. Place photos of your beloved dead on the grave or altar. Make bouquets of their favorite flowers and set objects that once belonged to them on your shrine. Play the music they used to enjoy. Imagine your dead relative or friend as a reincarnated person. The Buddhists believe that we reincarnate forty-nine days after we die. How old would your dead be in their new life? Visualize each of your beloved dead as they were and how they may be in their reincarnated life. Say:

> Grandma is safe and protected. Grandma is content and pleased. her body supports her with strength. her mind supports her with strength. her life unfolds smoothly with ease. She realizes her higher self.

Begin again with the name of your next beloved dead.

Lily Gardner-Butts

Notes:

May 29
Sunday

 3rd ♒

☽ → ♓ 4:09 pm

Color of the day: Orange
Incense of the day: Clove

Kite Spell for health and happiness

Derived from the Orient where kites are used in rituals to carry wishes and petitions to the gods in heaven, this is both spell work and good physical exercise for the body. Wishes can either be written on kites or on several pieces of cloth and paper for tying to the kites' tails. Use creativity and intuition to adorn your personal kite with health and happiness symbols after writing your wishes and aspirations. Go to a location where you can fly the kite freely, and let the wind carry your kite upwards. Control the flight of the kite to build up a ritual momentum. Concentrate on the kite's movements, the push and pull of the wind, the rise and fall of the object in space. Watch the sky around the kite and observe its colors, the clouds, any other details. Let loose more string so the kite can soar higher. The kite will eventually break free and rise further up in the sky. If not, cut the string to release the kite so it can carry your wishes to the cosmos.

S. Y. Zenith

Notes:

May 30
Monday
Memorial Day (observed)

 3rd ♓

Fourth Quarter 7:47 am

Color of the day: Ivory
Incense of the day: Rose

Remembering Saint Joan Spell

She was a French peasant girl who became known to the world as Joan of Arc. On this day in France in 1431 she was burnt at the stake by the English. Known for the visions that told her to help liberate her country from the English, St. Joan was eventually brought to trial on charges of witchcraft and religious heresy. The witchcraft charges were dropped, but the charges of religious heresy eventually led to

her execution. The Vatican, however, pronounced her innocent in 1456, and she was declared a saint in 1920. Today, St. Joan would have been called a psychic or visionary. Her life serves as an example of how psychic abilities have been misunderstood over the centuries. Understandably, she is friend and patron of soldiers. And on a deeper level magical people identify with her as the embodiment of the warrior goddess aspect.

James Kambos

Notes:

side). At the end of the war, this soldier was allegedly overheard commenting that in the Old World people scattered flowers on the graves of dead soldiers. In May of 1868, a Union army general suggested to Commander John A. Logan that a day be set aside each year to decorate Union graves. Logan was game, and he set aside May 30 for this ritual. His proclamation acknowledged those "who died in defense of their country" and "whose bodies now lie in almost every city, village, or hamlet churchyard in the land." This patriotic holiday was later amended to include all the dead from all the wars, and its date was shifted to a convenient Monday late in May.

May 31
Tuesday

 4th ♓
)) → ♈ 8:07 pm

Color of the day: Maroon
Incense of the day: Gardenia

Elemental Chant
This chant can be used during circle-casting to invoke the elements, or simply as a way to meditate on their properties. Although this begins with east, it can be changed since some traditions prefer to begin with north. To start, simply say:

Holiday lore: Opinions are divided concerning the origins of the holiday of Memorial Day in the United States. This is a day set aside for honoring the graves of American war dead. While most historians credit the origins of the custom to Southern women, there is also a rumor, historically speaking, of an anonymous German who fought in the American Civil War (no one is sure on which

I greet the east,
The Sun will rise,
The power of air,
The breath of skies.

I greet the south,
Warm and bright,
The power of fire,
To pierce the night.

I greet the west,
Rain and sea,
The power of water,
To comfort me.

I greet the north,
Tree and stone,
The power of earth,
I'm not alone.

Ember

Notes:

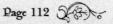

June is the sixth month of the year. Its astrological sign is Gemini, the twins (May 20–June 21), a mutable air sign ruled by Mercury. It is named for Juno, the principal goddess of the Roman pantheon, wife of Jupiter, the king of the gods; she is the patroness primarily of marriage and the well-being of women. The warm breezes dry the fields now, and the hay is mown. The air is perfumed with the fragrance of honeysuckle and wild rose and filled with birdsong. Fireflies dance in tall meadow grass. Toads are common in wet areas. Fuchsia, foxglove, and lavender blossom, attracting bees and birds. Culinary herbs are ready for harvesting. Squirrels and chipmunks bicker in the garden over prized plants. Birds are busy feeding hatchlings now. Broken birdshells are to be found cast away from nests under the trees; finding a hatched eggshell is a sign of great fortune and favor. Birds are also molting their old feathers now, which can be used in magic. By mid-June, the weather moves into the full heat of summer. The June Full Moon is the Mead Moon, named for the fermented drink made from honey. June is considered the best month for marriage. The main holiday in June is the Summer Solstice, which marks the time of year when the waxing Sun reaches its zenith and days will begin to shorten again.

June 1
Wednesday

 4♄ ♈

Color of the day: Yellow
Incense of the day: Pine

Nine Fishes Spell

To ensure the flow of smooth business and trade today, install an aquarium containing eight gold fish of different sorts and one golden-black fish in the reception area of your business establishment or office. Ideally this should be positioned at the left corner that is farthest from the entrance to the space. This is, according to feng shui principles, the "prosperity corner." Since ancient times, gold-colored fish have been considered by the Chinese to be auspicious. The eight gold-colored fish, then, symbolize good luck, while the golden-black fish represents protection. Decorate the bottom of the aquarium with smooth, colorful pebbles. Consecrate and place three tumbled stones each of jade, green tourmaline, and moss agate among the pebbles to enhance good business turnover and general harmony. Feed the fish daily, and change the water regularly to prevent it from turning murky. If the area is too small to comfortably fit an aquarium, a large fishbowl works just as well.

S. Y. Zenith

Notes:

June 2
Thursday

 4♄ ♈

Color of the day: Turquoise
Incense of the day: Geranium

Farewell Ritual

Ten years ago on this day, a nation wept for the innocent lives lost in the bombings at the Federal Building in Oklahoma City. Our purpose is twofold today. We will send strength to those who remain behind from that day, and we will bid farewell to those we have lost. Charge a white candle with strength, and say:

> With the lighting of this flame, I send energy of love and goodwill to the survivors. May they know no strife today. May they feel the comfort of a mother's arms. So mote it be.

 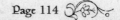

Light a blue candle in honor of the departed, and say:

> Gone, but not forgotten. Your memory lives on. Rest and rejoice in this, your time of replenishment. Be in peace. Farewell.

Tammy Sullivan

Notes:

what we want and what we truly need. Allow the darkening Moon to speak its wisdom through your dreams now. Dreams communicate the messages of your unconscious mind to your conscious mind. Fill a pouch with eyebright or sandalwood, and place it on your pillow. State these or similar words:

> Send visions through my dreams in illuminating light, lifting the veils of illusion while the Moon dims in the night.

Repeat this until the New Moon. Upon awakening, write in your journal and reflect on any perceptions or dream memories.

Karen Follett

Notes:

June 3
Friday

 4♄ ♈
☽ → ♉ 2:20 am

Color of the day: White
Incense of the day: Nutmeg

Dream Vision Spell

We view situations, actions, and outcomes based on our unique perceptions. Having roots that are based in our own personal history and our wants and needs can guide us to better our lives. These perceptions can also be misinterpreted in a veil of illusion that comes because we misinterpret the difference between

June 4
Saturday

 4♄ ♉

Color of the day: Indigo
Incense of the day: Cedar

Down the Drain Spell

On a clean square of white toilet paper, write down everything that you want to let go of. Include all your negative patterns, unfinished business, basic fears, limitations, and anything you feel is preventing you from creating the life you want. Bring up all the memories and frustrations that these things have created for you. Allow the paper to soak up all these feelings as you write. Throw the paper into the toilet, and visualize the water beginning to break up the energies bound to it. Flush the toilet, saying:

> Flowing water purge my
>   pain,
> Release my troubles
>   down the drain.
> Cleanse me now so that
>   I am free,
> Unblock my boundless
>   creativity.

Close the lid as you leave the bathroom, and feel that you are free to create what you want.

Kristin Madden

Notes:

June 5
Sunday

 4th ♉

☽ → ♊ 10:36 am

Color of the day: Orange
Incense of the day: Cinnamon

Brighten Your Space Spell

We are often forced to spend a great deal of our day in an environment other than our home. To keep that space filled with positive energy, create an amulet. To start, sprinkle a cotton ball with orange and lemon oils, and place it in the center of a small square of bright fabric—whatever appeals to you. Sprinkle dried basil, cloves, and crushed frankincense resin over the cotton. Add some small stones, such as tiger's eye, carnelian, pyrite, or citrine. Surround the fabric with a circle of candles, making sure they're not too close to each other, and allow the candles to burn out. When finished, pull up the sides of the fabric and tie it up with gold string. Use more string to hang the bundle and brighten your surroundings.

Ember

Notes:

June 6
Monday

 4th ♊
New Moon 5:55 pm

Color of the day: Gray
Incense of the day: Clove

Spell for More Effective Communication Between Family Members

For this spell, you will need a candle, some Cleopatra or other spicy oil, some dried rosemary, basil, and lavender, and a cherry pie. The candle and oil represent closeness, love, and friendship. The herbs facilitate communication. (The pie is for dessert!) Anoint the candle with the oil. Place it on a plate, and sprinkle a bit of each dried herbs around it. Anoint yourself as well, if you wish, and place the pie on the altar in front of the candle. Light the candle, and say:

> Family of mine,
> Loved ones divine,
> Speak and be heard,
> Truthful of word,
> Respectful of each other.
> Bring us together
> friends and loved ones
> forever!

Get the kids involved with the spell, they may enjoy chanting the rhyme. Have the pie after dinner. Let people play with their food just this once.

Expect happy chatter and honesty in communication tonight. Repeat this spell whenever awkward silences threaten to come between family members or when misunderstandings occur.

Denise Dumars

Notes:

June 7
Tuesday

 1st ♊
☽ → ♋ 8:46 pm

Color of the day: Lavender
Incense of the day: Ginger

Playful Meditation Wave Tube

To make a meditation wave tube, you will need a clear, thin bottle with a secure lid, some baby or vegetable oil, some food coloring, and some water. Make this simple tool for whenever you need a little distracting, calming energy drawn to you. Fill your bottle two-thirds full with the oil, then top it off with water. A test tube is ideal for this, but a twenty-ounce water or soda bottle will also work. Add twelve to twenty drops of food coloring, close the lid, and shake well to mix. To use, simply tilt the bottle gently back and forth, sending the waves of color rolling. Or, shake it like crazy and watch the light reflect off the smaller beads of water suspended in the oil. For a special touch, add a pinch or two of fine glitter before you seal the bottle.

Laurel Reufner

Notes:

from which we get the term "honeymoon." (Traditionally, a honey liquor called mead was consumed the night after a wedding). The idea of a sacred marriage comes from medieval alchemy, in the search for the ideal union of opposites. That is, in this system, fire and air (male elements) and earth and water (female) were united to form matter. A ritualized marriage ceremony often means offering a vision of the sacred marriage. In general, you should open your mind and heart to unification and harmony in all aspects of your life. If there are opposing forces or active conflicts manifesting in your life, ask yourself if reconciliation or compromise is possible. By seeing opposing forces for what they are, and giving appropriate consideration to all sides, we gain perspective and learn how to achieve balance and so enjoy the fullness of existence.

Ruby Lavender

Notes:

June 8
Wednesday

 1st ♋

Color of the day: Brown
Incense of the day: Neroli

Marriage Month Spell

June is the marriage month, and the month of the Mead Moon,

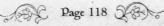

June 9
Thursday

 1st ♋

Color of the day: Crimson
Incense of the day: Musk

Blessing the Family Ritual

The eight-day Roman festival, Vestalia, commenced on this day. In honor of Vesta, goddess of fire and the hearth, the Romans made offerings of food baked on their own hearths. Vesta'a temple was opened to all married women for just this brief time. Once the festival ended, the temple was open only to the goddess' attendants, the Vestal Virgins. The festival was a nature celebration that remained popular with indigenous communities. As keeper of the sacred hearth, Vesta is regarded as a homebound goddess. Today, devote some time to making your home a sacred place. Commit thirty minutes to creating order and harmony for your sanctuary. This can be a simple task like organizing one drawer or tidying a cupboard.

Emely Flak

Notes:

June 10
Friday

 1st ♋
☽ → ♌ 8:39 am

Color of the day: Pink
Incense of the day: Rose

First Day of the Oak Moon Spell

Oak Moon begins today. Oak is a hardy tree revered for its strength, longevity, and perennial knowledge. Oak represents the great mother in Native American belief. Oak is special to the Druids, whose very name is derived from the tree. *Dru* translates as "oak," while *wid* means "knowledge." Thus the Druids were keepers of the knowledge of the oak. To absorb some of the precious gift of oak tree knowledge, go outside and gather ten pliable oak leaves. Draw a bath at dusk or midnight. Place seven oak leaves in tub. Use the other three to wash your body. Wet, then lather up one leaf at a time, rubbing it over your body as you recite:

> Strength and courage,
> I summon thee.
> Wisdom of the mighty
> oak tree.
> Cleanse me, treat me,
> touch my soul.
> Thereby others I can
> make whole.

Stephanie Rose Bird

Notes:

or white clover. Sprinkle this on the paper and fold. Keep your grass and paper until Midsummer's Eve, then burn them in a ritual fire to release the spell.

James Kambos

Notes:

June 11
Saturday

 1st ♌

Color of the day: Blue
Incense of the day: Sandalwood

A healing Love Charm

The cutting of grasses to make hay is one of the most important and ancient of agricultural activities. According to tradition, today is one of the days for the beginning of haymaking season. Most of us have forgotten how potent grasses can be when used in spell casting. Use them to attract protection, prosperity, and good fortune. The following spell, if begun now, can be completed on the Summer Solstice. On a sheet of yellow paper write these words: "I was, I am, and I will be." Visualize a specific goal as you write. Using a ceremonial knife, harvest three blades of grass. These could be lawn grass

June 12
Sunday

1st ♌
☽ → ♏ 9:22 pm

Color of the day: Gold
Incense of the day: Basil

Protect Your Teenager Spell

Take three fresh leaves from a new corn plant. Lay a strand of your teenager's hair on each leaf. Fold each leaf in thirds, making an envelope for the hair. Braid the leaves together. Place three votive candles—a red one, green one, and white one—on a round plate in a triangular formation. Place

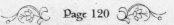

the braid in the middle of the triangle. Light the white candle, and say: "Demeter, I call to you, as one who loves her child too." Light the green candle, saying: "A mother's love is strong and true. I seek your help to see me through." Light the red candle, saying: "Protect this child from harm and strife, that he (or she) may lead an honorable life." Allow the candles to burn down, and the melted wax pool around the braid. Put the wax-coated braid in a jar or box, and keep it in a secret place.

Paniteowl

Notes:

June 13
Monday
Shavuot

 1st ♏

Color of the day: Ivory

Incense of the day: Peony

Pilgrimage to the Source Spell

Shavuot is a minor Jewish holiday, one of the three pilgrimage observances. It comes seven weeks after Passover. One of its themes is thankfulness for finding oneself in a safe and sacred place. This is just one more step in our soul's goal of reuniting with the supreme creator. This ritual spell will take you into the deepest part of yourself so higher spirits can give you hints about where you should be going spiritually or about how to get back on your path when your energies have scattered. (Note to covens: This spell is perfect for group use too, especially if you have a labyrinth or maze to work with.) To start, find a safe, quiet place. Sit comfortably on the floor or in a chair. Lie down only if you're sure you can stay awake. In your mind imagine yourself entering a labyrinth or maze. You are alone but unafraid. Approach the center with confidence. At the center is a huge cauldron. It's literally twice as tall as you, and you notice there is a door on the side facing you. Open the door and enter. You are now in the realm of spirit. Feeling like Alice in her rabbit hole, begin to explore. Listen to the deities and spirits you trust for guidance. You may hear someone speaking to you, or you may see flashes of scenes, or the run of an entire movie. You may awaken at will. Immediately record any special impressions you remember from your journey.

Edain McCoy

Notes:

an object or picture representing each, such as a dance slipper for Terpsichore, and so on. Then say:

> Muses of old,
> Now hear my plea.
> Reach deep inside
> and set me free.
>
> As I come to you, come
> to me:
> Bless me with creativity.

Meditate on the Muses for a while, then blow out the candles. Go attend a poetry reading, a play, or a dance performance. Honor the arts, and the Muses will send inspiration in return.

Elizabeth Barrette

Notes:

June 14
Tuesday
Flag Day

 1st ♏
Second Quarter 9:22 pm

Color of the day: Black
Incense of the day: Poplar

Flag Day Protection Spell

Today is the birthday of the Muses, the Greek goddesses who gave us creativity. Born of the Greek goddess Mnemosyne (memory), they are Calliope (epic song), Clio (history), Euterpe (lyric song), Thalia (comedy), Melpomene (tragedy), Terpsichore (dance), Erato (erotic poetry), Urania (astronomy), and Polyhymnia (sacred hymn). For more creativity in your life, invoke them with this spell. On your altar, light a white candle for Mnemosyne, and nine candles of different colors for the Muses. Include

June 15
Wednesday

 2nd ♏
☽ → ♎ 8:59 am

Color of the day: White
Incense of the day: Coriander

St. Vitus Spell for Early Risers

Do you have difficulty waking up in the morning? St. Vitus, whose feast day is celebrated today, is the patron saint of the early riser. His emblem is the rooster. For this spell you will need the likeness of a rooster, an orange candle, and an alarm clock. Arrange the rooster, the candle, and the clock on your night stand. Light the candle, and close your eyes, as you say:

> St. Vitus,
> For whom the angels
>   danced,
> Grant me a rested body
> And an alert mind in the
>   morning.

Visualize the alarm going off at the time you have set. You rise feeling refreshed and ready to begin the day.

Lily Gardner-Butts

Notes:

June 16
Thursday

 2nd ♎

Color of the day: Green
Incense of the day: Sage

Prosperity Potpourri Spell

Boost prosperity and financial luck with this synergistic potpourri combination. Gather two cups dried rose petals, two teaspoons mint leaves, one cup cloves, two cups dried chamomile flowers, and two cups dried honey-suckle flowers. Combine these in a big glass bowl. In a smaller bowl, mix one cup orrisroot powder with one drop cinquefoil oil, one drop basil oil, and three drops mint oil. Add this mixture to the bowl of flowers and herbs. Blend gently but thoroughly with clean hands. Store the potpourri in a large jar with a tight lid for three weeks in a dry, dark, cool place. Every few days, open the jars and stir the contents. After three weeks, transfer the potpourri to a decorative bowl for the living room. Add a sachet of silica gel to keep contents dry.

S. Y. Zenith

Notes:

June 17
Friday

 2nd ♎

☽ → ♏ 5:23 pm

Color of the day: Rose
Incense of the day: Dill

Love Yourself Spell

June is sacred to the Roman goddess Juno. Orris root is sacred to her as well and can be used to draw love. Juno is also known as our higher self. Today we will honor Juno, and in doing so, honor ourselves. Take a bit of orris root, and say, "You represent Juno and the love I have for myself." Place the root between two hand-held mirrors, and say:

> As the reflection is now
>   never-ending,
> So too is my confidence
>   and self-esteem.
> I shall grow and help
>   others to grow.
> Mighty Juno, I take
>   strength from your aid.

Leave the orris root between the mirrors until you feel it is no longer needed.

Tammy Sullivan

Notes:

June 18
Saturday

 2nd ♏

Color of the day: Gray
Incense of the day: Maple

Self-Transcendence Spell

Cleanse a clear quartz crystal by soaking it in salt water for three days. Create a sacred space in your usual way. Light some patchouli incense, and smudge the crystal with the smoke. Sit in meditation with the crystal, and invoke the great spirit. Ask to be blessed with the ability to see life beyond the confines of a single human mind. Imagine you are looking at your life with the perspective of someone who has lived forever. You are a wise observer of the human experience, and your reactions to events have a new sense of balance. Send this new perspective into the crystal. Ask the stone to help you recall this feeling when you need to. Thank the great spirit and the stone, and carry the stone with you.

Kristin Madden

Notes:

June 19
Sunday
Father's Day – Pentecost

2nd ♏︎

☽ → ♐︎ 9:45 pm

Color of the day: Amber

Incense of the day: Parsley

Father, hunter, Magician, Warrior, Sage Spell

Thanks to the greeting card industry, we have a day for just about everyone except plumbers and brain surgeons. In June, we set aside a Sunday to be Dad's special day, during which he can eat junk foods and watch whatever junk he wants on TV. He would probably rather do this on Super Bowl Sunday, but, hey, you take what you can get. Anything is better than another tie. Unlike the virgin, mother, and crone archetypes we assign to female deities and heroines, it's not quite as easy to differentiate between the male archetypes. Yet they are all embodied in one's father. After he eats the meal he has requested for himself, keep him seated at the table. Allow all others who are present to bless the father figure in your house. Allow someone to set a crown on his head to honor the king in him. Someone else may hand him a knife, the symbol of the hunter, to honor him for the food he helps provide for his family. A certificate of honor can be made to pay homage to his wisdom, and a pair of running shoes can symbolize the warrior who goes to battle each day out in the big, bad world. Before you close this circle at your table it's nice to offer a simple blessing in unison:

> Father, hunter,
> Warrior, king,
> You are all that,
> And many other things.
>
> Today is yours,
> And we depart,
> But every day,
> You're king in our hearts.

Edain McCoy

Notes:

June 20
Monday

2nd ♐︎

Color of the day: Silver

Incense of the day: Lavender

Vestalia Day Spell

Vestalia honors the Roman goddess of hearth and home, Vesta. This is a day for beautifying, purifying, and purging what is old and dead from the home. Sweep your floors with a besom whose bristles have been dipped into spring water laced with lavender. Gather debris, remove large articles, and clean up any dirt and dust. Deposit this dirt in the nearest body of running water. If none is available, flush it down the toilet. Place fresh violets on your altar. Put whole-grain muffins or mini-loaves of bread on the altar along with a shot glass of the lavender water. Light a white candle and recite:

> Vesta, sweet keeper of
> hearth and home,
> I honor your spirit on
> Vestalia Day.
> May your warmth forever
> stay.
> Bless this home,
> Dear Vesta, I pray.
> Keep it safe
> by night and by day.

Stephanie Rose Bird

Notes:

June 21
Tuesday
Summer Solstice – Litha

2nd ♐

☉ → ♋ 2:46 am

☽ → ♑ 10:52 pm

Color of the day: Gray

Incense of the day: Frankincense

Looking for a Promotion Spell

With the Sun riding high in the sky, you can absorb that energy and put it into your job hunt or into your efforts to get that promotion you know you deserve. Allow the Sun's energy to infuse an amulet or talisman of your choosing. You may choose a tiger's-eye stone, a piece of gold jewelry, or any other item you feel is represented by the Sun. Hold it out so both you and the Sun can see it glow. Visualize yourself in your ideal job situation, and imagine your bank balance growing. While you do this, say:

> Golden and high is this
> midsummer Sun,
> The task has now begun.
>
> Rewards and riches for
> me I seek,
> With harm to none, so
> mote it be.

Carry this with you as often as you can, and always have it with you during a job interview. Feel confident in the power the Sun has given you. When you feel confident others feel it too, and this will make an impression on any potential employer.

Edain McCoy

Notes:

June 22
Wednesday

 2nd ♑
Full Moon 12:14 am

Color of the day: Topaz
Incense of the day: Sandalwood

Good Traveling Luck Spell

Today's magical associations of Woden and Mercury mix with the Full Moon to make for a good day to consecrate a traveling charm. The purpose of this charm is to protect you during vacations and travels far from home. Begin with a green or blue flannel bag. Add a "lucky" penny, as copper is a metal associated with today's gods. Add a small symbol of the way you prefer to travel, such as a small toy airplane, a car, ship, and so on. Write these words on parchment:

> Fleet-footed Mercury,
> Keep my travel swift
>   and steady,
> Efficient and without
>   delays.
> Bless this charm
> With your traveling
>   magic.
>
> Father Woden,
> Patron of travelers,
> Watch over me.
> Keep me safe
> When I am far from
>   home,
> And bless me to return
>   home again,
> happy and carefree.

Anoint the parchment with geranium or lemon oil and place it in a pouch. Carry this when you travel and reconsecrate the charm each time you take a trip.

Denise Dumars

Notes:

June 23
Thursday

 3rd ♑

☽ → ♒ 10:36 pm

Color of the day: Crimson
Incense of the day: Carnation

heart's Desire Spell

Always remember it is you who makes the magic. The power is within. When you have a need or sincere desire, use your altar to help manifest it. If you don't have a personal altar, use another space such as the top of a dresser or fireplace mantle. Find a picture, symbol, or simply write your need on paper, and place this on the altar. Speak these words:

> With heartfelt need, and
> sincere desire, I ask for
> this, which I require. For
> highest good, and harm
> to none, grant me this
> wish, may it be done.

Think of these words each time you walk past the altar. Keep the picture or symbol in full view always. Look at the representation of your desire often and reaffirm your need. As always, be open to whatever form the answer to your desire manifests. That is, your answer may not be exactly what you think you want, but it may be exactly what you need.

Ember

Notes:

June 24
Friday

 3rd ♒

Color of the day: Purple
Incense of the day: Thyme

Celebrating Uniqueness Spell

We are all unique. It's easy to lose our appreciation for our own "uniqueness" in the day-to-day, "follow the flock" mentality of societal expectations. Being unique takes courage. It is also wonderful and deserves to be celebrated. Light any color candle that reflects your mood of the moment. Select a gemstone that reflects your unique self. Using colored pencils, draw a self-portrait. Allow your imagination free rein. If you want pink hair, color pink hair. Set your gemstone on top of your portrait. Focus on the wonderful attributes that make you unique into your gemstone. State these or similar words: "I am what I am and that's all I need be. Unique and perfect, that's me!" Place your picture in a special place. Carry the gemstone to remind you that you are a divine treasure.

Karen Follett

Notes:

How many of us don't feel stressed out or emotionally depleted from time to time? If you're feeling out of sorts from time to time, try adding this herb to your daily dose of vitamins and supplements. As the Moon wanes, drink a cup of St. John's wort tea each day. Sit in quiet reflection, and tell yourself that as the Moon grows smaller, your stress and depression will lessen. What else can you do to alleviate stress in your life? Try eliminating some of your activities and see what you can do without. Simplify your lifestyle. Remember: The best things in life are free.

Ruby Lavender

Notes:

June 25
Saturday

 3rd ♒︎

☽ → ♓ 11:03 pm

Color of the day: Brown
Incense of the day: Lilac

St. John's Wort Reflection

St. John's wort blooms in profusion in the days surrounding the Summer Solstice. This plant has been prized by herbalists for centuries, but in recent years it has been discovered that St. John's wort helps alleviate mild depression without the side effects of prescription drugs.

June 26
Sunday

 3rd ♓

Color of the day: Yellow
Incense of the day: Cinnamon

Mint Spell for Sleep

The mints in my herb garden reach their peak in June. Their leaves glisten in the Sun, and their scent fills that corner of the garden. Herbalists have long regarded mint as a healing herb that calms us physically and mentally. If you're tense and can't rest, the scent of mint can help ease you into a peaceful sleep. To work this spell, cut at least three stems of mint—spearmint or peppermint are best—and place the stems in a small vase by your bed. Finely chop another three stems of mint, and place these on a white cloth. Tie the cloth up with blue ribbon. Inhale the scent deeply. Place the bag of mint beneath your pillow, and repeat these words three times: "Mint so green, bring me peaceful rest."

James Kambos

Notes:

June 27
Monday

3rd ♓

Color of the day: Lavender
Incense of the day: Chrysanthemum

Beautiful Bouncing Wishes Spell

A friend once said that you should never pass a row of gumball machines without stopping. There is a small thrill in not knowing what exactly will come tumbling out. Will it be a nifty new treasure or a true piece of junk for which you have just wasted your money? Four small rubber bouncy balls—as can be found in a gumball machine—are required for this spell. The spell must be cast where children play: a school playground, the park, your own front yard. It is best done when there are very few children around to observe. Holding one of the balls, face east and infuse the ball with a good wish appropriate for the direction—perhaps that the finder do well on an upcoming test or that he or she find the necessary inspiration of a school project. Having charged it with your wish, toss the ball eastward, sending your wishes with it. Do the same with the remaining three balls, making directionally appropriate wishes.

Laurel Reufner

Notes:

June 28
Tuesday

 3rd ♓
☽ → ♈ 1:51 am

Fourth Quarter 2:23 pm

Color of the day: Scarlet
Incense of the day: Honeysuckle

Journey Protection Spell

Today's spell is designed to protect you on a journey, whether it is by road, air, or sea. This could be travel related to your work or simply for your personal enjoyment. Find an item that represents your mode of transportation. For example, if you are flying, your symbol could be an airline ticket or a small model airplane. On your altar, light a white candle to represent safety and protection. Close your eyes and focus on the image representing your trip. Hold this image as you visualize a circle of white light around you and the transport vehicle. In your mind's eye, imagine yourself reaching your destination safely. Continue to hold the image in your mind, and then imagine returning home again safely.

Emely Flak

Notes:

June 29
Wednesday

4th ♈

Color of the day: Brown
Incense of the day: Eucalyptus

Magical Pudding

For a magical pudding, peel, core, and cut three apples into bite-sized pieces. Peel and segment three oranges. Peel and slice two bananas, and drain one large can of fruit cocktail and one large can of pineapple and reserve the juice. Put the fruit in a large bowl, and mix together stirring deosil. Heat the reserved juice to a simmer in a pan. Add two tablespoons of tapioca, and one-half cup of sugar, stirring deosil until it begins to thicken. If it begins to boil, reduce the heat and stir widdershins until it returns to a simmer. Pour the juice over the fruit. Add two cups of cream, whipped, and fold in gently. Put the bowl in the refrigerator to chill for an hour. Before serving, say: "North, south, east, west—nurtured at our Lady's breast. Above, below, within, without—our Lord provides, we have no doubt."

Paniteowl

Notes:

June 30
Thursday

 4th ♈
☽ → ♉ 7:45 am

Color of the day: Purple
Incense of the day: Geranium

Everything from the Sun Ritual

Everything we have comes from the Sun. Without its light and heat, there would be no life on Earth. Use this time of long, hot days to give thanks for all that you receive. Don't ask for anything, just express your gratitude. Dress in solar colors of orange, red, and gold. Fill a bowl with things that remind you of the Sun: chocolate coins covered in gold foil, packets of sunflower seeds, stickers with happy faces, postcards of astrological art, and so on. Place the bowl on your altar, and light the biggest gold candle you can find. Name the things for which you feel grateful. Then say:

> Helios and Lugh,
> Amaterasu and
>   Sekhmet,
> I thank you for your
>   many gifts.
> Let me learn to be as
>   generous as you.

Blow out the candle. Keep the bowl by your door and give away its contents to people who visit your home.

Elizabeth Barrette

July

July is the seventh month of the year. Its astrological sign is Cancer, the crab (June 21–July 22), a cardinal water sign ruled by the Moon. The month is named for Julius Caesar. The heat of July is oppressive, only occasionally interrupted by sudden summer storms. Leaves wilt on trees and plants suffer in the parched fields. July is the traditional month for visiting the seashore or other body of water as an escape. Sand and seawater are useful in magical rituals at this time; as are shells, particularly cowries, which resemble and symbolize the sexual organs of the Goddess. Snails and shellfish, such as mussels and clams, have magical resonance. A visit to the beach is a perfect time to perform magic; an incoming tide (and waxing Moon) is a time to cast spells of increase, prosperity, and fertility. An outgoing tide (and waning Moon) is a time for spells of banishment. One of the most magical objects you can find on the beach is a stone or pebble with a natural hole in it. July harvest time begins with cabbage, from which one makes sauerkraut for the winter months, followed by all the herbs of the garden. The Full Moon of July is called the Wort Moon; *wort* is old Anglo-Saxon for "herb." Use a white-handled ritual knife to harvest herbs for magical purposes. Give thanks to the spirits that dwell in the herb garden.

July 1
Friday

 4th ♉

Color of the day: Coral
Incense of the day: Sandalwood

Iroquois Green Bean Ceremony

Various groups hold thanksgiving and sharing ceremonies for each of the important American harvests, and one such day is today. The Iroquois green bean ceremony is the time of the year to thank the creator for fertility. It is designed to inspire in particular a productive harvest. Start by acknowledging your ancestors by burning tobacco in a censer. Beans are symbolic of life and are considered lucky. Try this main course. Wash, sort, and break green beans into two or three sections. Mince a small onion and four rashers of bacon. Put the bacon in skillet over medium heat. As the bacon begins to brown, add onion. Turn until both brown. Add the green beans and two cups of water to the pan, taking care to avoid spattering grease. Season all with a splash of apple cider vinegar, a pinch of salt, some black pepper, and some cayenne pepper. Cover and continue cooking about twenty-five minutes or until the beans are tender. Enjoy this green bean dish, preferably outdoors with family and friends.

Stephanie Rose Bird

Notes:

Holiday lore: Today is the first day of the season for climbing Mt. Fuji in Yamabiraki, Japan. Mt. Fuji is the highest peak in Japan and is revered in Japanese culture. Considered the foremother or grandmother of Japan, Fuji is an ancient fire goddess of the indigenous Ainu people. In modern times, the Ainu mostly resided on the northern island of Hokkaido. The name *Fuji* was derived from an Ainu word that means "fire," or "deity of fire." Each year since the Meiji era, a summer festival has been held to proclaim the beginning of the climbing season and to pray for the safety of local inhabitants and visitors or pilgrims to the sacred mountain. The two-month climbing season begins today, and ends on August 30.

July 2
Saturday

 4th ♉
☽ → ♊ 4:26 pm

Color of the day: Gray
Incense of the day: Juniper

Pleasure of Ishtar Spell

July is the month of Ishtar, the goddess of resurrection. Ishtar was worshiped in Babylonia for over 2,500 years. As the patron goddess of temple prostitutes, she had no shame in pleasuring her body and pleasing numerous lovers. This makes today an ideal day for women to honor their sexuality and minimize any guilt or hangups they have about their body. Decorate your altar with the symbols of Ishtar. Use a piece of paper to cut out her symbol, an eight-pointed star and a statue or photograph of a lion. The lion is her sacred animal. In candlelight, say these words:

> Ishtar, I invoke thee.
> With your acceptance
> and love bathe me.
>
> My body is a gift,
> A shrine of pleasure.
> I am woman,
> I am a goddess treasure.

Emely Flak

Notes:

July 3
Sunday

 4th ♊

Color of the day: Orange
Incense of the day: Sage

Sunburn Bath

A few years ago my husband got badly sunburned while working outside. This bath not only worked wonders on the pain, but also on the burn itself. Use equal amounts of chamomile, crushed juniper berries, lavender, rose petals, and witch hazel to make an infusion. Pour the liquid into a cool bath and add one-half cup of finely ground oatmeal. The contents of a packet of commercial oatmeal bath would also work. Have the injured party soak for about a half hour and then finish using a moisturizing lotion containing aloe vera.

Laurel Reufner

Notes:

July 4
Monday
Independence Day

4th ♄ ♊

Color of the day: White
Incense of the day: Myrrh

Freedom from Fear Spell

The twenty-first century is turning out to be much more than a just a number. While our European allies have been dealing with terrorism for decades, we Americans thought the anger and hatred of reactionaries and fundamentalists would never touch our lives. English folklore includes two war legends, probably based on true events, that we can draw on a magical people to help affect a dangerous world for the better. The legends claim that England's Witches and Druids stirred up the massive storm that wrecked the dreaded Spanish Armada in 1588, and then turned back a planned invasion by the Nazis in 1940. We can gather, raise power, and send out magic to let the world know that the United States and our allies will not live in fear. To do this, gather as many other Pagans as you can find. If you're a solitary you can still do this alone. Go outside if you can, and sit on the ground of your own homeland. Raise an impenetrable curtain of safety surrounding the coastlines and borders of your nation.

Feel the strength of the cone of power rising around you. When it has reached its peak, release it into the imagery your mind created.

Edain McCoy

Notes:

Holiday notes: On July 4, 1776, the Second Continental Congress adopted the Declaration of Independence. Philadelphians were first to mark the anniversary of American independence with a celebration, but Independence Day became commonplace only after the War of 1812. By the 1870s, the Fourth of July was the most important secular holiday in the country, celebrated even in far-flung communities on the western frontier of the country.

July 5
Tuesday

 4th ♊
☽ → ♋ 3:07 am

Color of the day: Maroon
Incense of the day: Evergreen

Seashell Amulet Spell

Seashells connect us with the element water, our home before we were born. Therefore, seashells serve as a direct link to the life-force. They can be an awesome object of power and protection. Like most natural magical objects, we come upon them by chance. This summer if you are at the shore, take a walk along the beach and see if you're attracted to a particular seashell. If so, bring it home and magically charge it by holding the shell and speak these words softly:

> The divine has brought
> you to me
> Safe and sound from the
> sea.
>
> You have been bathed by
> the water
> And drenched by the
> light
> Of Moon and Sun.
>
> Now, our magic has
> begun.

Protect your shell and use it as a focal point for certain spells, especially those related to travel.

James Kambos

Notes:

July 6
Wednesday

 4th ♋
New Moon 8:02 am

Color of the day: Yellow
Incense of the day: Cedar

Consecrating a Magical Moonstone Ritual

The moonstone is a semiprecious stone that can aid in any magic you wish to do involving the Moon, water, or the astrological signs Cancer, Scorpio, and Pisces. A cabochon-shaped piece of moonstone should be easy to find in rock shops or in New Age stores, and the stone is relatively inexpensive. Once you find it, bathe the stone in salt water. Go outside to face the night sky. Hold it and visualize it becoming the Moon while you say:

Moon in my hand
Lovely to see,
You are mine to hold,
Mine to find
When no Moon I see.

When I wish the Moon's power
Indoors with me,
Moon in my hand
You will abide with me.

Take the stone inside and place it on your altar. Burn a silver candle and place the stone before an image of a Moon god or goddess, such as Thoth or Diana. Meditate on the stone, imbuing it with the powers of the Moon and the sea. Scry with it. Write down what you observe. Repeat the washing of the stone and presentation of it to the Moon each night until the Full Moon for maximum moonstone power.

Denise Dumars

Notes:

July 7
Thursday

 1st ♋
☽ → ♌ 3:11 pm

Color of the day: Green
Incense of the day: Musk

Summer Love Spell

On the seventh day of the seventh month, Vega joins Altair over the Milky Way. The king of the sky had one daughter who worked long hours as the court weaver. Her name was Vega, and she thought of nothing but the clothes she designed and wove—that is until she met Altair. The two fell in love and spent so much time together that in time the king's robes grew threadbare. The couple ignored the king's warnings about their irresponsibility. Enraged, the king separated them on either side of the Milky Way. As a result, the lovers became ill with grief. Eventually, the king relented and allowed the lovers this one day in the year to be together. To find your true love today, you must decorate your altar with spools of colored thread and flowers. Light two candles, one pink, one red, and pray to the heavenly couple that you find your soul mate.

Lily Gardner-Butts

Notes:

July 8
Friday

 1st ♌

Color of the day: White
Incense of the day: Ylang-ylang

Increase Love Spell

Problems are inevitable in all relationships, so it's important to keep loving thoughts in mind—especially during times of conflict. If not, hurtful words can be spoken that you may later regret. To remind yourself to keep feelings of love, wear rose quartz or any heart-shaped pendant next to your skin every day for as long as you need. Chant:

help me see,
past wrong and right.

For each shadow,
there must be light.

Ember

Notes:

July 9
Saturday

 1st ♌

Color of the day: Indigo
Incense of the day: Pine

Spell to heal a Broken Connection

Ancient Greece celebrated the festival of Panathenaea on this day to honor the goddess Athena. Create an incense on this, the goddess of wisdom's day, that is designed to enhance your powers of foresight and concentration. Start by combining one tablespoon of powdered benzoin resin, two teaspoons sandalwood powder, one teaspoon of powdered frankincense resin, one teaspoon of crushed lavender flowers, and one-half teaspoon of powdered rosemary. Blend together the ingredients in your mortar and pestle, then add three drops white wine. Burn the resulting incense on hot charcoal disks in a heat-proof bowl or cauldron. When invoking Athena, slightly sweet vanilla fragrances are called for. Therefore, light some vanilla or sandalwood candles, and spray some labdanum/amber (also known as Peru balsam) perfume around the room. To make some Athena perfume oil, to an almond oil base add four parts sandalwood essential oil, two parts Peru balsam, two parts tonka bean essential oil, and one part patchouli essential oil.

Ruby Lavender

Notes:

July 10
Sunday
Lady Godiva's Ride

 1st ♌

☽ → ♍ 3:57 am

Color of the day: Amber
Incense of the day: Clove

Cashew and Tea healing Energy Spell

Brew a cup of strong chamomile tea today to start raising some good healthy energy. Sit with the tea in both hands, and visualize a protective energy egg surrounding you. See this energy protecting you on all sides. This healing energy permeates every cell of your being and flows out through your skin into your home. Visualize healing energy filling your home and the space around your home. It creates a healing buffer that helps maintain your health and keeps your energy balanced. Charge the tea with this energy. Steep a cashew in the tea for three minutes, allowing it to fully soak up the energies you charged the tea with. Plant the cashew in a household plant in the center of your home. As you plant it, imagine the healing energy radiating out from this central spot to fill your home. It will revitalize everyone that enters this place and bless all who live here.

Kristin Madden

Notes:

Historical notes: Lady Godiva's original name was Godgifu, meaning "God-given." She was a Saxon noblewoman who was outraged at a tax levied on the people of Coventry by her mischievous husband Leofric. He offered a deal, though: He would cancel the tax if she rode through the town naked. Godgifu's ride has been commemorated by the grateful townspeople of Coventry for many years on this date with whimsical parades and a festival.

July 11
Monday

 1st ♍

Color of the day: Gray
Incense of the day: Rose

Slumber healing Spell

Before sleep tonight, call to the ancient healers, spirit guides, and angels. Asked to be enveloped in a ray of healing energy. Visualize this ray surrounding you in the color of its choice. Focus on your body, beginning with your feet and ending with your head. Allow each part of your body to relax and yield to this healing ray. Request that the ray remain with you during the night while you drift off to sleep. In the morning, prepare a glass of healing water by placing in your hands in a triangle, with thumbs and forefingers touching, over the glass. Visualize healing rays entering the glass, and afterward drink the entire glass of water. Create and consume a glass of healing water at least eight times per day.

Karen Follett

Notes:

reasons unknown, prepare and use this charm sachet immediately. It may be carried on the person, put into a handbag, or placed in your living room or bedroom to ward off malevolent energies. It is also helpful to those susceptible to attacks of nervous energy or prone to fragile emotional states. Cut a square of red cotton cloth, and in the middle of it place a pinch of white pepper, a portion of sage, a little garlic powder, a tiny dash of cayenne pepper, a wee bit of tobacco, a thorn plucked from a cactus, and a red jasper tumbled stone. Fold the square into a rectangle, and sew up the sides with a needle and red thread. Dab the four corners and the middle of the charm bag with basil oil before you use it as a charm. If troubled by nightmares, sleep with it under the pillow at night.

S. Y. Zenith

Notes:

July 12
Tuesday

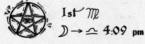 1st ♏
☽ → ♎ 4:09 pm

Color of the day: Red
Incense of the day: Sage

Protection Charm Sachet
When feeling threatened or intimidated by others or for

July 13
Wednesday

 1st ♎

Color of the day: Brown
Incense of the day: Maple

Child healing Spell

In Portugal, people celebrate Our Lady of Fatima today. Mary, the Mother of God, is an aspect of the Queen of Heaven. This goddess usually appears when her children need healing. In this case, she instructed people to build a shrine in Fatima for curing the sick. Set your altar with a blue cloth, white flowers, blue and white candles, and other items that remind you of the Queen of Heaven. Light the candles and say:

> We who light candles
> upon your shrine,
> Ask for your healing,
> Goddess divine.
> Flowers we bring to honor
> your name,
> Loved by all people,
> One and the same.
> Merciful mother,
> Queen above all,
> Open your hands and let
> blessings fall.

Pray for sick people you know, or for strangers. If you have get-well cards to send, place them on the altar to gather energy while the candles burn down.

Elizabeth Barrette

Notes:

July 14
Thursday
Bastille Day

 1st ♎
Second Quarter 11:20 am

Color of the day: Turquoise
Incense of the day: Jasmine

Carnelian Passion Stone Spell

July is one of the hottest months of the year. Fittingly, the spiritual stone of the month is the gorgeous red carnelian. Carnelian has many significant qualities, but since today is Friday let's engage the sensual, sexual aspects. Carnelian gives confidence, and obliterates self-doubt and negative thoughts that deter romance. Carnelian is a stimulating, energizing stone that attracts love. Go to a bead shop or gem store, and pick out a piece of carnelian. Take it home and charge it. Soak the stone in salt water for three days outdoors so that it can be purified by the Sun, and absorb the power of the Moon at night. Hold it in your hands to see if it is charged. If it is not, repeat the process until the stone feels right. Keep carnelian in a mojo bag, and carry it on your person when you need it.

Stephanie Rose Bird

Notes:

night of the Full Moon, sprinkle a pinch of rosemary, echinacea, and mugwort over the papers, and set them afire. Speak this petition as the papers burn:

> To mother Moon I send
> this plea,
> May those in need be
> trouble-free.
> Through the power of
> these herbs,
> And my will,
> So mote it be.

Paniteowl

Notes:

July 15
Friday

 2nd ♎

$\mathbb{D} \rightarrow \mathbb{M}$ 1:51 am

Color of the day: Pink
Incense of the day: Nutmeg

Cauldron of Care Spell

When you hear of friends or loved ones in need, write their name on a slip of paper along with a brief note about their troubles, or what you wish for them. This may be "better health, ease of mind, prosperity," and so on. Put the slips of paper in a small cauldron. Each day, take time to look through the slips of paper to remind you of the people in need. On the

July 16
Saturday

 2nd ♏

Color of the day: Blue
Incense of the day: Lavender

Goddess of Justice Spell

Can you think of a time when either you or someone close to you was mistreated and felt that justice never was served? Saturday is a day of reckoning and karma. Align your magical work on this day to invoke the energies of Nemesis to restore or correct this injustice. In Greek mythology, Nemesis is the goddess of justice and vengeance. Her vengeance is thought to be purely positive, as it is only directed at those who disrupt harmony or pervert justice. Burn frankincense incense, and focus on the issue that is imbalanced. Frankincense is known for its protective and spiritual qualities. Visualize a set of scales readjusting themselves to balance, and say:

> Goddess of justice,
> hear my plight,
>
> Balance the evidence
> To make the situation
> right.

Emely Flak

Notes:

July 17
Sunday

 2nd ♏

☽ → ♐ 7:35 am

Color of the day: Yellow
Incense of the day: Basil

A Spell to Protect Sleeping Children

Saint Marina is a little-known saint honored today only in certain areas of the eastern Mediterranean. She is said to be the protector of sleeping children. Some say she never existed, but her spirit is still prayed to. To weave a web of protection around your children, obtain three charms—one shaped like an anchor, one shaped like a heart, and one simple blue turquoise bead. As your children sleep, empower the charms by saying:

> With this anchor you'll be
> safe and secure.
> With this heart, our bond
> will endure.
>
> With this stone, blue as
> the sky,
> May you never be harmed
> by the evil eye.

The anchor, heart, and turquoise are symbols of protection in the Near East. You should hide the charms. When your children are old enough, give them the charms as a gift with a gold chain. They don't have to know you have enchanted these charms, so be sure not to tell them.

James Kambos

Notes:

around me. Love and light surround me. Laughter and happiness fills my soul. As I said it, let it be so.

Continue chanting until you feel happy. Keep the candles in case you want to repeat this spell. Carry the hardened wax drippings with you as a joy and laughter charm.

Tammy Sullivan

Notes:

July 18
Monday

 2nd ♐

Color of the day: Silver
Incense of the day: Poplar

Laughter Spell

To bring yourself the energy of a little laughter, draw a warm bath, and add orange, lemon, and lime essential oils and a handful of sea or Epsom salts. Charge a yellow candle with laughter, and light it. Charge an orange candle with joy, and light it. Turn off the electric lights, and settle into the warm water. Affirm to yourself by saying:

> I will the water and flame to put my energies in harmony with joy and laughter. Happiness flows freely through my life and the lives of all

July 19
Tuesday

 2nd ♐
D → ♑ 9:26 am

Color of the day: Black
Incense of the day: Musk

Tree Spirit Honoring Ritual

Today is the Lucaria, an ancient Roman festival honoring the spirits who lived in trees. This is a time when land was cleared to make way for new fields. Land-owners wanted to propitiate the spirits and prevent them from interfering with crop production. Normally a pig would be slaughtered and a ritual prayer given. To honor the tree spirits in your area make an offering of red wine, grape juice, or even water to a grove or single tree while uttering: "In honor of the Lacuria."

Laurel Reufner

Notes:

music, redecorating or cooking, or just fantastic daydreams. Remind yourself that you are a creative being, and send that knowledge into the nut. Visualize the nut as a seed of this creativity that sprouts and grows in your being. Ask that the nut find its own healthy outlet through you. Carry the nut with you, trusting that this energy blossoms and grows stronger each day.

Kristin Madden

Notes:

July 20
Wednesday

 2nd ♑

Color of the day: White
Incense of the day: Pine

Nut of Creativity Spell

With Mercury in Leo, this is an ideal time to work toward creative self-expression, particularly in school or business. A subtle yet powerful way to do this involves gathering one common nut—preferably an almond, pecan, or pistachio. Take the nut into circle with you, creating sacred space as you do. Breathe deeply and relax. Call upon the memories of times in your life when you were creative. This may involve traditional artwork, dance or

July 21
Thursday

 2nd ♑
Full Moon 7:00 am

☽ → ♒ 8:55 am

Color of the day: Purple
Incense of the day: Chrysanthemum

honoring the Epagomenal Days

Today is an auspicious day to honor the birthdays of the Egyptian gods Isis, Osiris, Nephthys, Set, and Horus the Elder. Purify yourself with hyssop and sea or Epsom salts in a morning bath. Wear white or blue cotton or linen clothing and an ankh. Offer bread and beer on your altar before images of the gods. Burn kyphi incense, and anoint five white tea lights □with jasmine and nephthys. When the Moon rises, light the candles and incense and say the following:

> Gods of heliopolis
> I honor you.
> Born this season,
> You are the light of the
> Sun and the Moon,
> The fertility of the earth,
> The wisdom of the
> ancients,
> And the magic of the gods.
>
> Live em hotep, neteru.
> Live in peace, gods and
> goddesses.
> Live em Ma'at, neteru.
> Live in truth, gods and
> goddesses,
> Sacred of Egypt.
> Bless my life with peace
> and truth.

Follow with any Egyptian ritual or magic you wish to perform.

Denise Dumars

Notes:

July 22
Friday

3rd ≈

☉ → ♌ 1:41 pm

Color of the day: Rose
Incense of the day: Ginger

Sun Energy Meditation

This month's Full Moon is called the Wort Moon, because so many plants bloom in this season of Sun and rain. This day also marks the beginning of the sign of Leo, the lion ruled by the Sun. Leo's tarot cards are the Sun and Strength, and some solar gods include Apollo, Helios, Hyperion, Ra, Lugh, Chango, Christ, and Mithras. The Sun's force is both necessary and dangerous. Think of the difference between a golden suntan and a severe sunburn, or a pleasant sunny day and a heatwave followed by drought. Ancient peoples worshiped the Sun, its constancy, as well as its unpredictability, its life force and its capacity from great destruction.

Ruby Lavender

Notes:

July 23
Saturday

 3rd ≈
☽ → ♓ 8:12 am

Color of the day: Coral
Incense of the day: Violet

Spell for horse Racing

Today is the festival of Neptunalia, to honor Neptune, god of the sea. Neptune's mother saved him from his child-eating father, Cronus, by offering the father a horse in place of the child. Neptune was saved and grew up to be the god of horses. For this spell, etch a three-prong trident shape on a blue candle dressed with two parts frankincense, one part pine oil. Light the candle, and ask Neptune to bless your horse. Write the name of the horse you wish to win nine times. Write your name nine times. Watch how the candle burns. If the wax drips mostly on the left side, chances are your horse will lose. If the wax drips mostly on the right side, chances are your horse will win. It is never good magic to gamble more than you can afford to lose.

Lily Gardner-Butts

Notes:

July 24
Sunday

3rd ♓

Color of the day: Gold
Incense of the day: Coriander

Candle Consecration Spell

To cleanse a candle prior to spell work, collect the following: some cedar oil, a second candle, dried sage, salt, and water. The object is to consecrate the candle with each of the four elements. As you expose the candle to each item, say the words, "Power of earth, air, water, and fire—this candle is made pure for my desire." That is, roll the candle in salt, pass it through the smoke of burning sage, rinse it with water, and pass it quickly through the flame of another burning candle. Afterward, anoint the candle with the oil using the method of your choice. Don't charge the candle for its purpose at this time, but imagine clearing it of any prior associations. Later, you can charge the candle for a specific spell by visualizing your need and carving an appropriate symbol into its side.

Ember

Notes:

July 25
Monday

3rd ♓

☽ → ♈ 9:23 am

Color of the day: Ivory
Incense of the day: Peony

Decisions, Decisions Spell

Sometimes having a multitude of options is even more frustrating than having limited options. Use this spell to help you attune to your own inner voice of wisdom in making a difficult decision. Light a white candle, and burn eyebright on a charcoal block. State these or similar words: "I call to the night and the shadows to guide me in my decision." Write out your possible choices and the pros and cons of each choice. Pay attention to any sensory perceptions you may encounter. Allow yourself to meditate, listening to the voice of inner wisdom. The wisdom may not come immediately, but be alert for the next few days. Allow extra relaxation and meditation time, as the voice is more apt to speak when the mind is open and at rest.

Karen Follett

Notes:

July 26
Tuesday

3rd ♈

Color of the day: White
Incense of the day: Gardenia

Tarot Awareness Spell

To improve your grasp of the tarot, cast this spell in the morning. It will help you attune you to the suit of swords. First, sort out the Ace of Swords from a tarot deck, and put it on your altar. Light a stick of incense with a fiery scent, such as cinnamon, dragon's blood, or frankincense. Then say:

> Unsheathe the hidden sword,
> Fate's lady, magic's lord.
>
> Slice through what hinders me,
> Bring truth and clear words.

Read what your deck's guidebook has to say about the suit of swords, then spend some time meditating on their symbolism. Allow your incense to burn out on its own. All day, keep a sharp eye out for any sword imagery you may come across. It will have a special meaning and can help you understand the suit. Record what you see in your tarot notebook.

Elizabeth Barrette

 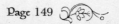

Notes:

spoon. Bring the vinegar to a boil, and then pour it into the jar and leave contents to cool before covering. Shake the jar once a day for two weeks before straining into glass bottles. Store the excess at home in the refrigerator.

S. Y. Zenith

Notes:

July 27
Wednesday

 3rd ♈

☽ → ♉ 1:54 pm

Fourth Quarter 11:19 pm

Color of the day: Topaz
Incense of the day: Neroli

Vinegar Travel Protection Potion

When planning travel to foreign lands, concoct this protective toiletry vinegar two weeks before you take off. Some drops may be added to your bath water while on the trip, or if stored in a spray bottle it can be used for spraying the body before stepping outdoors. It can also be layered with perfume during trips to places with cool climates. To make the perfume, gather one cup orange peel, one cup lemon thyme, three drops bergamot oil, five drops lavender oil, two drops geranium oil, and five cups of quality cider vinegar. Put the orange peel and lemon thyme in a large jar and crush them with a

July 28
Thursday

 4th ♉

Color of the day: Crimson
Incense of the day: Evergreen

Release Bad Spending Habits Spell

Azna, the mother goddess, is here to aid us no matter what our troubles may be. Azna carries a golden sword that she uses to draw negative energy from us. Petition Azna for relief from your bad spending habits, saying:

> Mother God, I cannot
> control my spending
> habits. Take them from
> me. Instill within me the
> knowledge of what to do.

I ask you to take the pressure from me with your sword.

Visualize Azna lowering her sword to draw all of the negative energy away from you. Go forth knowing you no longer need to fret.

Tammy Sullivan

Notes:

piece of paper, roll them into a tiny scroll, and tie them together with a piece of ribbon. Put the scroll into the jar of honey. With a pair of scissors, snip off the stems of both roses. Use a spoon to gently insert them into the jar. Infuse the roses with honey, and position the scroll between both blooms. Tighten the lid of the jar, and place it on your altar.

S. Y. Zenith

Notes:

July 29
Friday

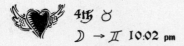 4th ♉

☽ → ♊ 10:02 pm

Color of the day: Purple
Incense of the day: Parsley

honey-Rose Love Spell

This love spell is very useful for refreshing long-lasting relationships that have gone stale, or for sweetening things after a serious quarrel. Fill a large jar with honey, and pluck two pink or red roses from the garden. If you don't have a garden, purchase the roses instead. Write your full name on one small piece of paper. On another, write your partner's full name. Kiss each

July 30
Saturday

 4th ♊

Color of the day: Black
Incense of the day: Cedar

Aid to Clarity Spell

Gather together a star sapphire, a moonstone, a garnet, an amethyst, and a citrine—and put them on a small mirror. Place the mirror outside, or inside on a windowsill that catches the moonlight. Leave in place for one Moon cycle. When the stones have been fully Moon charged, mount them in like settings that have an open back.

Attach the set gemstones to a band of ribbon or silver. The band can be sized for a bracelet or headpiece, depending on your choice. Meditate on the meaning of each stone. When you wear the band, concentrate on its magical powers before working any spell.

Paniteowl

Notes:

July 31
Sunday

 4th ♊

Color of the day: Amber
Incense of the day: Poplar

Summer Song Spell

Where has the summer gone? It seems like it was just the other day that I prepared my garden for planting. Let the following meditation fill you with summer's joy, even as you are aware of its inevitable ending. Take time to think where your life is going.

> I am life force at its peak,
> I am what you seek.
> My days of the seasoning
>   are here.

> I will sustain you through
>   the coming year.
> You trusted me with your
>   crops to raise,
> Now they stand tall in
>   the sunny haze.
> I color the corn yellow in
>   the field,
> I swell the orchard's yield.

> The ripening days have
>   come.
> Sing with me as I sing
>   summer's song.

James Kambos

Notes:

August

August is the eighth month of the year and named for Augustus Caesar. Its astrological sign is Leo, the lion (July 22-Aug 22), a fixed fire sign ruled by the Sun. August begins with Lammas, the celebration of the first harvest, especially the grain harvest of corn, rice, millet, rye, barley, oats, and wheat, brought in from the fields in sheaves. In the past, such grains were associated with gods and goddesses of death and resurrection—Tammuz in ancient Sumeria, Adonis in Babylon, Demeter in Greece, Ceres in Rome. Small figurines representing these goddesses were buried with the dead to ensure their resurrection into the afterlife. Baking bread is celebrated now, in all of its steps: grinding the grain, moistening the grain with water, shaping it into a loaf, and baking it. In some Mediterranean countries, women ritually sprout grain seed in dishes or pots to be given as offerings, either thrown in rivers or left at churches, to harvest gods. By midmonth, we begin to transition from the high heat of summer. The harvest is over and signs of the coming fall and winter begin to appear for the first time. Birds have begun to vanish from the trees, cooler air has moved in. The August Full Moon is called the Barley Moon, a time to contemplate the eternity of life evident in the grain of the fields.

August 1
Monday
Lammas

 4th ♊
☽ → ♋ 8:52 am

Color of the day: Gray
Incense of the day: Lavender

Lammas hospitality Spell

Lammas has been characterized since prehistory as a time for the sharing of bread. In the Celtic countries, clan chieftains were obliged to be hospitable to all guests, even their enemies. The sharing of food bonds people together. In humanity's deep past, breaking bread together was an offering and acceptance of friendship. In many ways, eating with others is a very intimate event. Recall all of your first dates that began by dining out. Wasn't that the most uncomfortable part of the evening? Create a grand feast this Lammas, and invite as many as many people as your home can hold. Be sure to include a few people who don't like you, a few you don't like, and any people who have been quarreling with each other. For your feast, bring the warm loaves of bread to the table after everything else has been placed. Announce that you will be passing the loaves so that everyone can break bread. While the bread is being passed you may tell the story of Celtic hospitality—how

the sharing of bread is a symbol of peace and unity. End your explanation with a simple prayer that will not offend anyone's religious beliefs, or, depending on the size of your feast, allow everyone a chance to also offer a prayer. The ending of yours might sound something like this:

From the womb of
   Mother Earth comes
   bread,
From this gift we all are
   fed.
Sharing the creator's
   bounty together,
May generosity and
   peace be with us forever.

                Edain McCoy

Notes:

Holiday lore: Lammas is a bittersweet holiday, mingling joy at the current high season's harvest with the knowledge that summer is soon at an end. Many cultures have "first fruit" rituals on this day—the Celt's version is called Lughnasadh; the Anglo-Saxon version called *hlaf-masse*. In the Middle Ages, the holiday settled on August 1, taking its current form for the most

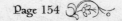

part, with sheaves of wheat and corn blessed on this day.

August 2
Tuesday

 4th ♋

Color of the day: Black
Incense of the day: Ginger

Purification Paste Spell

Lammastide is traditionally a time of honoring the gods of harvest—whose myths were associated with ritual sacrifice. One modern novel, *Harvest Home* by Thomas Tryon, describes a modern-day community that still performs human sacrifice for their crops. Many modern Witch covens select a harvest lord and corn maiden, as in the novel, to preside over their rituals for a full year. The young lord is honored with praise and gifts before he is ritually "sacrificed" (we're talking symbolically, of course!) to feed the fields and ensure a good and bountiful harvest. The altar is decorated with produce. Bread is baked, and the scythe is displayed. Such rites are powerful as they capture the essence of the cycle of life—nature's design that rules all living things.

Ruby Lavender

Notes:

August 3
Wednesday

 4th ♋
☽ → ♌ 9:10 pm

Color of the day: Yellow
Incense of the day: Coriander

Discover New Secrets and Explore Deep Thoughts Spell

This day before the New Moon is a time to uncover secrets and mysteries and to explore your own deep thoughts. Take special note of your feelings throughout the day today, and write them down. It's likely you will look back on today's notes at some later date and find that your innermost thoughts that surfaced will have some significance. Perhaps you will be able to identify synchronistic events or a gut feeling about something that proves to be right. Optimize this time of the lunar cycle to tap into your subconscious to attract insightful dreams. When you retire for the night, cast a circle around your bed. Visualize the circle protecting you and attracting the right dreams to you tonight, and as you drift off say this simple spell:

> As I relax into this circle
> of light,
> Bring me the dreams I
> need to see tonight.

Emely Flak

Notes:

Success is within my
reach,
And my confidence soars.

You may also anoint yourself and any objects you wish to be charged—such as your wallet, company badge, or your new key to the executive washroom. Feel successful and lion-proud each day until the Full Moon by wearing an article of royal purple or royal blue. Success is within your reach—make it happen.

Denise Dumars

Notes:

August 4
Thursday

 4th ♌
New Moon 11:05 pm

Color of the day: Green
Incense of the day: Dill

Preparing for Career Success Spell

Before this work week starts, use the power of Leo during the New Moon to help revitalize your career. Continue this ritual through the next Full Moon. Take a symbol of the career you have or want, and place it on your altar along with a purple candle in a glass jar. Purify the space with sage. Combine success, prosperity, and steady work oil (or similar blends) into your own custom blend. Anoint the candle. Burn the candle a little each day, and say:

My career comes to
fruition,
Prosperity blooms like a rose.

August 5
Friday

 1st ♌
Color of the day: White
Incense of the day: Rose

Freya Love Invocation

Take a smooth piece of yellow-gold citrine, and by the light of a red candle rub it all over with vervain as you say:

Freya, Freya,
help me be

Loved by someone
Who is drawn to me.

Either wrap the citrine with gold wire to make a pendant, or carry it on your person where you can touch it often.

Laurel Reufner

Notes:

August 6
Saturday

 1st ♌
☽ → ♍ 9:54 am

Color of the day: Indigo
Incense of the day: Patchouli

Fairy Wine Recipe

It is said that if a human drinks from fairy wine, he or she will see fairies. If a fairy happens to drink from the same goblet, then the person will see fairies forevermore. The following is a traditional Welsh recipe for elderberry wine—also known as fairy wine.

> 7 lbs. elderberries, stripped and stalked

3 gallons boiling water
6 cloves
3 lbs. loaf sugar
1 lb. seedless raisins
1/2 oz. ground ginger
1/2 oz. yeast

Place the berries in a large pot, and cover with the boiling water. Let the pot rest for twenty-four hours, then mash the fruit and strain it through a jelly bag. Place the strained fruit back in the pan, and add the cloves, sugar, raisins, and ginger. Boil this mixture for one hour, skimming constantly. Let it cool, and add the yeast. Bottle and cork the mixture, and let it rest for at least three months.

Tammy Sullivan

Notes:

Historical fact: Today commemorates the day that atomic bomb Little Boy fell, in 1945, on the city of Hiroshima in Japan. In Japan, on this day, the people of Hiroshima celebrate a peace ceremony in memory of the dead. You may also take today to offer a silent prayer vigil, chanting: "Never again, never again."

August 7
Sunday

 1st ♍

Color of the day: Orange
Incense of the day: Cinnamon

Chinese Peach Wine for health

Used both as an appetizer and a nightcap, Chinese peach wine also serves as a blood cleanser and relieves constipation. No more than two small shot glasses should be drunk per evening. It is also an excellent offering to Pagan gods and goddesses. To make your own, take five unripe peaches, one pint of rice or white wine, and one-and-a-half ounces of refined sugar. Quarter the peaches, and put all the ingredients into a large sterilized jar. Seal the jar and store it in a cool, dry, and dark area for nine months. Afterward, strain and pour the wine into a dry sterilized bottle. The bottle may be stored in the refrigerator. For extra zing during festivals, add a dash of the wine to ice cream, trifles, and other deserts. In place of peaches, Chinese red dates or persimmons may be used.

S. Y. Zenith

Notes:

August 8
Monday
Dog Days

 1st ♍
☽ → ♎ 10:08 pm

Color of the day: Lavender
Incense of the day: Maple

Water Elemental Meditation

For this spell, you will need drinking water, an open glass container such as a jar or bowl, and some sounds of water if possible—either a recording of rain or running water, or if possible sit near a fountain or stream. You should be able to hear, see, smell, touch, and taste water. To start, listen to its sound. Next, look at the water source or at the water in your container. Pause to consider how vital water is to our existence. Think of all the ways we use it and how life would be without it. Be grateful for water. Touch it, and then take a drink. Engage all your senses in experiencing water. The element of water represents emotions and feelings. Try to get in touch with this aspect of yourself, and consider all the aspects of water—rain, lakes, springs, streams, and oceans, and its association with the womb. Do this for at least ten or fifteen minutes, then say:

> Ripples on the pond,
> Sacred spring and well,

The current and the tide,
Watch it flow and swell.

Water of the earth,
Water from above,
Waters of the world,
Fill us with your love.

Ember

Notes:

clothing today. Build a fire, and into it toss dried mandrake root and yarrow as an offering to the salamanders. Ask your question. Gaze into the flames as the fire burns down. You will see images that speak to your future.

Lily Gardner-Butts

Notes:

August 9
Tuesday

1st ♎

Color of the day: Gray
Incense of the day: Juniper

Fire Divination

August 9 is the festival of the salamanders. The Greeks were the first people to regard salamanders as the elemental spirits of fire. They often appear as small balls of light within a flame. Without the salamanders, there would be no warmth or light. You must always approach elementals with a sincere heart. Be warned that they hate cowardice and greed. Wear red, yellow, and orange

August 10
Wednesday

1st ♎

Color of the day: Brown
Incense of the day: Sandalwood

Abundant Balance Spell

I used to dislike the phrase "It takes money to make money." Like many people, I thought that this phrase spoke to the idea that only the rich get richer. Then it dawned on me that this phrase mirrors the concept of a balanced universal flow of abundance. Even the bills that you pay and the groceries that you buy start a chain of events that ensure money will flow back to you. With your wallet or your checkbook in front of you, draw the rune Feoh (Y) for prosperity that is earned and shared with the forefinger of your projective hand. Visualize the infinite flow of the universe that provides for you and guides you. State these or similar words:

> Universal abundance
>   infinitely flows.
> I live in your balance,
>   my abundance grows.

Be open to any messages or opportunities that reflect and influence your balance of abundance.

Karen Follett

Notes:

August 11
Thursday
Duck Fair

 1st ♎
𝄂 → ♏ 8:35 am

Color of the day: Purple
Incense of the day: Carnation

Moon Magic Spell

Ruled by Jupiter, Thursday oversees matters of money and security. This spell helps you make the most fruitful decisions. Find yourself Sacajawea dollar coin. You also need a gold candle and a bowl of shelled corn—the kind you feed to squirrels. Put the coin in the bowl, under the corn, and light the candle. Concentrate on your need for guidance and security, then say:

> Jupiter, god of all that
>   glitters,
> Father of what hopes we
>   hold,
> help me to make the
>   right decisions
>
> When I aim, let me
>   strike gold!

Reach into the bowl, stir the contents around, and pull out the gold coin. Give thanks to Jupiter, and blow out the candle. Keep the coin in your change purse, and it will bring you riches and confidence.

Elizabeth Barrette

Notes:

oliday lore: King Puck is a virile old goat who presides over the fair in Killorglin in Ireland. He watches the proceedings from a platform built in town, wearing a shiny gold crown and purple robes. Among the activities: gathering day, which includes a parade; fair day itself, and the buying and selling of livestock; and scattering day, when the goat is disrobed, dethroned, and sent back into the fields at sunset.

August 12
Friday

1st ♏

Second Quarter 10:38 pm

Color of the day: Pink
Incense of the day: Thyme

Wish on a Star Spell

Tonight is the peak of the Perseid meteor showers and it is also the Feast of the Lights of Isis. If you've ever thought about wishing on a star, tonight is definitely the night. Begin with an honoring of Isis. Light two candles for her—one pale gold and one sky-blue. Thank her for her gifts, and ask for her continued blessings on all of us. Ask that this great mistress of magic bless your wishing spells tonight. Take some time to clarify your wishes. Ask yourself if each dream and goal serves the highest good and contributes in some way to the betterment of all. Go outside around midnight, and bask in the glory of the night. Feel the presence of Isis as you open to the magic of starlight. With each meteor you see, visualize one wish manifesting with brilliance and beauty.

Kristin Madden

Notes:

August 13
Saturday

2nd ♏

☽ → ♐ 3:47 pm

Color of the day: Black
Incense of the day: Lilac

holiday of Diana Spell

Today is the day the ancient Romans set aside to honor one of their most respected deities—Diana. Diana was the powerful Moon goddess, protectress of the hunt, women, childbirth, forests, animals, and anyone in need. Her influence was widespread. Near Ephesus in present-day Turkey, her beehive-shaped temple was one of the seven wonders of the ancient world. Honor Diana by having a picnic in a wooded area. Leave her an offering such as a piece of bread spread with honey. Or, toast her with apple juice, and pour a bit onto the earth near a grove of trees. Speak words of power of your own devising to ask her help in your search for a home, or new career, or even a legal dilemma. Since rural areas are also sacred to Diana, end your day by stopping at a country market or a county fair and partaking in the sights and sounds and eating good country food. Give thanks to the goddess for all of her many blessings.

James Kambos

Notes:

August 14
Sunday

2nd ♐

Color of the day: Amber
Incense of the day: Sage

A Spell to Enhance Your Spells

The dog days of summer often leave us feeling sapped of energy. Spellworking takes much energy, so a good Witch knows that some "tools" can help increase the flow. To enhance our spellworking, use the properties of calcite. Write your spell on a piece of paper. Fold it, and place it on a mirror. Then place a piece of calcite on top of the paper. Enchant the mirror and the calcite by saying: "Mirror reflect, calcite enlarge—with your help, this spell I charge." Leave the stone in place for three days. Burn the paper, and clean the mirror with a soft cloth. Leave the calcite on a windowsill to recharge by sunlight for a few days. When the Sun goes down on the last day, it will be ready to use again.

Paniteowl

Notes:

August 15
Monday

 2nd ♐
☽ → ♑ 7:13 pm

Color of the day: Silver
Incense of the day: Chrysanthemum

hearth Protection Spell

The ancient Romans held their goddess of the hearth, Vesta, in such high esteem that in addition to Vestalia (on June 9), they also honored her with a second festival on this day. Modern Wiccans celebrate this festival by lighting six red candles and throwing herbs in the candle flames. It's also a time to bless and protect the home. Light a stick of raspberry incense. Raspberry is known for its protective qualities, in particular of the home. Walking through your home, use the incense stick to trace an invoking pentagram for protection on each window and external door. Visualize a pentagram of light at each entrance to your haven, continuously protecting you and your house as you say:

> With the smoke of
> incense
> I invoke protection for
> this place
> From unwanted energies
> Entering my sacred
> space.

Emely Flak

Notes:

August 16
Tuesday

2nd ♑
Color of the day: Red
Incense of the day: Honeysuckle

Jade, the Gardener's Friend

Tuesdays are days of the energy and protection of Mars, and

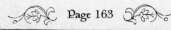

August is the height of the gardening season. To ensure good crops, potent herbs, and beautiful flowers, employ the magical powers of jade. Wear this gemstone while gardening to assist in your efforts for a fruitful harvest. Integrate jade's healing powers full-time into your green spaces by burying four small pieces of jade in the four directions. This will ensure healthy growth for your plants, and it will inspire prosperity for all those who enjoy your garden. After the harvest, place jade stones on your altar. Stroke them and gaze at them as you make plans for the next season.

Stephanie Rose Bird

Notes:

in her huntress aspect. Why not have a traditional hunter's feast for your Pagan friends this week? The main dish should be some form of meat, preferably venison if available, as deer are associated with Diana. Vegetarians could create a veggie loaf of grains and mushrooms. Serve seasonal vegetables and a good hearty soup such as mushroom or potato-leek, along with a full-bodied red wine like merlot. For dinner music, how about that Pagan classic "Songs from the Wood" by Jethro Tull? Or else play something suitably sylvan in tone. Such a meal served in summer reminds us of the coming winter, when we will eat hearty foods to stay warm.

Ruby Lavender

Notes:

August 17
Wednesday

 2nd ♑

☽ → ♒ 7:39 pm

Color of the day: Topaz
Incense of the day: Eucalyptus

hunter's feast Ritual

This day was traditionally a feast day for honoring Diana/Artemis

August 18
Thursday

 2nd ≈

Color of the day: Turquoise
Incense of the day: Geranium

Midweek Protection Spell

For some protection from mid-week demons and other such trials, gather together a pinch of cumin and salt today. Run your fingers through the herbs, thus allowing your energies to attune to each other. Say:

> Spirits of salt and cumin,
> I invite you to this place.
> I honor you and ask that
> you bless my spell with
> your protective energies.

In a glass bowl, combine the herbs with some warm water. Hold the bowl in your left hand, and hold your right hand open over the water, as you say:

> I ask the God and Goddess
> to bless this mixture.
> Guard us and guide us
> with love.

Visualize nurturing, protective energy filling the bowl. Anoint yourself at each chakra point with the liquid. Feel divine loving protection permeate your being. Anoint any others who share your home—including pets. Take the remaining liquid, and sprinkle it at each opening to your home.

Kristin Madden

Notes:

August 19
Friday

 2nd ≈

Full Moon 1:53 pm

☽ → ♓ 6:52 pm

Color of the day: Coral
Incense of the day: Sandalwood

Friendship Reconciliation Spell

The light of the Full Moon in friendship-loving Aquarius can help reconcile two pals who have argued. First of all, think on the reason you stopped seeing your friend, and if you genuinely wish to be friends again begin this spell with an open and loving heart. Place your friend's name on a piece of pink paper. Light a pink candle. Now write on another page the words that you want to say to your friend. For example, write something like: "I'm truly sorry that we quarreled, and I'd like us to be friends again." Hold the paper with the friend's name over your heart, and speak the written words as many times as you feel necessary. Close your eyes and envision yourself surrounded by pink light. See your friend stepping into the pink light with you and shaking hands or embracing you. Burn the candle a little each day. Imagine the anger between you waning as the Moon wanes. You are working on your own feelings here, so do not think this spell is manipulative. When you are ready, approach your friend and say what you wish to say. Be confident that you have been honest with your feelings.

Denise Dumars

Notes:

Sprite Guardian Spell

Ward sprites are natural guardians of settlements. They assemble each evening at crossroads near the center of a town. They pass along old fairy paths and hillsides warding off both seen and unseen bane. A sprite sentinel for the home is invoked by lighting a red candle during twilight hours. Put the candle in a secure holder facing the road outside. Wait till it is dark, and then take the candle to the front door. Open it and gently blow the candlelight outward. The candlelight will travel into the darkness and reach one of the earth guardians—who will respond by keeping watch over your home and its inhabitants each night. Arrange some quartz and other crystals in a corner of the garden. Regularly put some tiny pieces of bread and a small cup of mead near the crystals as a token of sincere thanks.

S. Y. Zenith

Notes:

August 20
Saturday

3rd ♓

Color of the day: Blue
Incense of the day: Juniper

August 21
Sunday

 3rd ♓

☽ → ♈ 7:01 pm

Color of the day: Yellow
Incense of the day: Clove

Revitalizing Light Spell

Breathe deeply and relax. Allow the worries of mundane life to flow away on the breath. Visualize the energy of the Earth flowing up though the soles of your feet. It fills your body gently and slowly, revitalizing you as it moves up past your legs into your torso and fills your arms, neck, and head. Now visualize the energy of the universe flowing down through the top of your head. It fills your body gently and slowly, revitalizing you as it moves down through your head and chest into your torso and fills your arms and legs. These energies merge in your heart and fill you nearly to overflowing. They pass through your skin, your eyes, your palms, and back out into the world at large. With each breath, you take in light and exhale it back out into the universe. The healing, invigorating energy of light fills you and in turn fills everything you encounter. The revitalizing aspect of the energy of light is well worth invoking when you need it.

Kristin Madden

Notes:

August 22
Monday

 3rd ♈

☉ → ♍ 8:45 pm

Color of the day: Ivory
Incense of the day: Frankincense

Rune Spell for Protection

Today marks the anniversary of the sixth day of Odin's ordeal. Odin, wounded by his own blade, hung upside-down from Yggdrasil for nine days to seek the knowledge of the World Tree. On the ninth night, the runic alphabet was revealed to him. With the waning Moon, it is an auspicious day to cast a runic spell for protection. Place two black feathers next to a black candle. Light the candle, and arrange from left to right three runes—beginning with Mann (ᛗ), the self. From your relationship to yourself flows your relationship with others. Next, place Tyr (ᛏ), warrior energy. Tyr counsels to look within to discover what your needs are and how to tap your inner resources. Finally, place Eohl (ᛦ), protection. Eohl counsels that correct conduct and timely action are the only true protection. This spell requires deep contemplation in order to be effective.

Lily Gardner-Butts

Notes:

front of a large group of people giving a fantastic speech. Release the ashes of the paper to the wind, or bury them. Release your fear. Recall the positive image each time you feel the fear.

Ember

Notes:

August 23
Tuesday

 3rd ♈︎
☽ → ♉︎ 9:58 pm

Color of the day: Scarlet
Incense of the day: Evergreen

Banish Fear Ritual

We each have a fear we'd like to conquer. Today, sketch a symbol of your fear or write it down in so many words. This is a burning ritual, so find a safe container and go outdoors. Think about the fear. Why do you have it? You may or may not know, but try to answer honestly. Imagine yourself without the fear. As you visualize, burn the paper. See yourself as confident and brave. For example, if your fear is public speaking, imagine yourself in

August 24
Wednesday

 3rd ♉︎
Color of the day: White
Incense of the day: Cedar

Fear of Success Spell

Is the fear of success holding you back either consciously or subconsciously? Call in the powers of earth and water to help you fight the fear. You will need paper, dirt, water, a wooden skewer, and an empty cardboard salt container. On the paper write or draw a representation of your fear. Now impale it on the skewer and place it in the cardboard container. Fill the container with dirt and soak it generously with water. Now go and bury the container. As the cardboard and paper break down, returning to the earth, you will win your fight against being successful.

Laurel Reufner

Notes:

in your ability to manifest heart. At the throat, have confidence in your communication. At the chakra of psychic vision, confidently visualize your goal. At the chakra of your higher self, ask for guidance in changing self-doubt into confidence.

Karen Follett

Notes:

August 25
Thursday

 3rd ♉

Color of the day: Crimson
Incense of the day: Musk

Seeking Confidence Spell

If there is an ingredient that is necessary in magic, that ingredient is confidence. Complete and certain confidence will make any spell work. While that's easy to speak and to intellectualize, sometimes it's more difficult to feel at a "heart and soul" level. Gather and light seven candles to represent the seven chakras. Focus on each candle as you direct "confidence" into each chakra. Pay attention to any feelings or "programmings" that turn confidence into self-doubt. At the root chakra, have confidence in your right to have and to be here. At the belly chakra, have confidence in your right to pleasure. At the solar plexus, have confidence

August 26
Friday

 3rd ♉
☽ → ♊ 4:43 am
Fourth Quarter 11:18 am

Color of the day: Rose
Incense of the day: Ylang-ylang

Ace Your Exam Spell

This is a time when many school and college students prepare for school to begin. Even if you are not a student, there are times when you wish for improved mental clarity, or the ability to communicate your needs more clearly. Wednesday, the day of Mercury, is aligned with learning, study, and communication, so here is a spell to help you today. On a handkerchief, dab some basil, lemongrass, and peppermint oils. If you only have one or two of these oils, that's okay. Inhale the invigorating scent of the handkerchief and recite:

> To my learning, I
>   dedicate this spell
> To help my memory to
>   serve me well.
> When I need to call
>   on you,
> I will find the scent of
>   clear thinking
> Will aid my mind.

Each time you need to think clearly, use the hanky and the oil blend.

Emely Flak

Notes:

yourself to a special home-cooked feast. Choose whatever foods you wish as long as you make them from scratch and use organic or locally grown and in-season ingredients. You need no other preparation. Let your table serve as your altar, your oven as a candle, and the smell of cooking food as incense. When you sit down to eat, say:

> Into my body's temple
> I take this food,
> Made with patience
>   and consumed with
>   gratitude.
> From these pure ingredients
> I build my health:
> The delight of my spirit,
> And the gods' wealth.

Focus your intent on serving as a temple, and enjoy the feast.

Elizabeth Barrette

Notes:

August 27
Saturday

 4th ♊
Color of the day: Brown
Incense of the day: Pine

Body Temple Spell

A wise saying advises that your body is your temple. Caring for your body therefore honors the gods. Promote your health today by treating

August 28
Sunday

 4th ♊
☽ → ♋ 2:57 pm

Color of the day: Gold
Incense of the day: Basil

Overcoming a Phobia Spell

Some people fear spiders, some fear bees or wasps. Overcoming these fears takes patience, though a little magical help wouldn't hurt! Get an old skeleton key today—the more ornate, the better. Clean the key with a soft cloth and a bit of silver polish. As you shine the key, enchant it by saying: "The more I know, the less I fear. Understanding is the key. I will unlock the secrets of this bothersome mystery." Tie a blue ribbon around the key, leaving a loop so that you can hang the key in a place you'll see every day. Research the subject that bothers you by going to the library or doing a search online. As you study, hold the key in your hand and picture it unlocking the truths about the subject.

Paniteowl

Notes:

A Sun Power Spell

The following spell uses the August Sun to empower a cord or ribbon. This can be used in knot magic later in the winter, when the Sun's strength has ebbed. Before the summer ends, obtain a yellow or gold-colored cord and offer it to the August Sun. Let it absorb the sunlight and say:

Before autumn leaves,
Protect me from winter's grief.
I thank the Lady;
I thank the Lord
For the power flowing through this cord.

To complete the spell, tie six knots in the cord. During winter, if you need some solar power to energize a ritual light an orange candle and untie one knot.

James Kambos

Notes:

August 29
Monday

 4th ♋

Color of the day: Gray
Incense of the day: Myrrh

August 30
Tuesday

 4th ♋

Color of the day: Maroon
Incense of the day: Sage

Summer Fast Ritual

In Chinese medicine, it is traditional to fast in late summer as preparation for winter. European traditions hold that fasting during the waning Moon is more effective than fasting during the waxing Moon. Fasting need not mean doing without food altogether, but eating lightly to cleanse the system. The Moon's power can help. One old spell recommends eating only "Moon-colored foods," such as potatoes, cauliflower, bread, and egg whites. What might be more effective is eliminating meat, cheese, white flour, sugar, and alcohol from your diet for a few days, and drinking plenty of water. Gaze on the waning Moon, and think of the coming shift of the tides at the equinox. You are preparing your body and mind for the time of dormancy.

Ruby Lavender

Notes:

Color of the day: Brown
Incense of the day: Maple

Amethyst Travel Spell

The amethyst is also known as the "come-home-safely" stone. Take an amethyst and anoint it with a protective oil. Place the stone on a piece of white cloth. Sprinkle honeysuckle, sage, and vervain on it. Tie the four corners together to make a little bag. Bless the bag, and place it in your pocket. Say: "Safe I travel to and fro, I will come home safely, this I know. By this rite, it is so." Forget about the stone. Replace the bag every three months. The same sachet can be used for protection during astral travel. Tuck it under your pillow, and replace it every three weeks.

Tammy Sullivan

Notes:

August 31
Wednesday

 4th ♋

☽ → ♌ 3:14 am

September

September is the ninth month of the year. Its name is derived from the Latin word *septum*, which means "seventh," as it was the seventh month of the Roman calendar. Its astrological sign is Virgo, the maiden (Aug 22-Sept 22), a mutable earth sign ruled by Mercury. Though September afternoons are warm, the days quickly shorten. Meadow grasses dry up as birds and monarch butterflies migrate southward. Leaves begin to fall from trees and bushes now, and though most of the harvests have been taken in, clusters of grapes hang dark and heavy on the vine. The wine harvest is most important now; it is best to begin this process by pouring a ritual libation into the soil and praying at an altar decorated with images of Bacchus and Dionysus. In ancient Germany, wine was considered sacred and placed into special stoneware jugs. Because wine is such a sacred fluid, the Full Moon of September was called the Wine Moon, though it is more commonly known as the Harvest Moon today. A ritual for this time involves dancing in a circle around some white wine in a silver cup with the Moon shining overhead. Corn, gourds, and squash play a part of the Autumnal Equinox celebrations, or Mabon. This celebration marks the time of the waning Sun, and the harvesting and storage of food for the coming winter.

September 1

Thursday

Greek New Year's Day

 4th ♌

Color of the day: White

Incense of the day: Jasmine

Banish Debt Spell

When money luck is stuck and debts are mounting up, light a purple candle and some incense. Sit down and write a list of sums you owe with a black pen on some parchment paper. Gaze at the candle flame for some minutes. Visualize yourself being debt-free and experiencing sensations of relief. Look at the list again, and sprinkle some salt upon it. Fold the paper, and put it into an envelope. Seal it up, and on the front of the envelope, write:

> Money, money, come to me,
> I desire to be debt-free,
> And as I will, so mote it be!

Dab some bayberry oil on each of the envelope's four corners, then pass the envelope over the incense seven times. Do the same over the candle flame before extinguishing it. Take the envelope to the nearest stream, and set it afloat along with a flower. Make a resolution never to become ridden with debt again.

S. Y. Zenith

Notes:

Holiday lore: Many Greeks consider this their New Year's Day. This day marks the beginning of the sowing season, a time of promise and hope. On this day, people fashion wreaths of pomegranates, quinces, grapes, and garlic bulbs—all traditional symbols of abundance. Just before dawn on September 1, children submerge the wreaths in the ocean waters for luck. They carry seawater and pebbles home with them in small jars to serve as protection in the coming year. Tradition calls for exactly forty pebbles and water from exactly forty waves.

September 2

Friday

 4th ♌

☽ → ♍ 3:56 pm

Color of the day: Pink

Incense of the day: Almond

Festival of the Grape Vines Ritual

In ancient Greece, today was the Festival of the Grape Vines. Visit the community gardens in your area and you'll notice a heady, intoxicating scent now—grapes ripening on the vine! In ancient times, wine was a sacred drink and aphrodisiac, as well as an everyday beverage. Many modern Pagans enjoy making their own wines from various fruits and herbs. When you make dinner tonight, serve a carefully chosen bottle of wine and offer a toast to the gods of the vine: Dionysus, Ariadne, and Bacchus. Ask their blessings of inspiration and ecstasy, saying:

> Great gods of the grape-
> vine, bless this cup and the
> wine contained within.
> Let it inspire me and
> bestow upon me health
> and wealth and strength
> and joy and peace. So
> mote it be!

Ruby Lavender

Notes:

September 3
Saturday

 4th ♍

New Moon 2:45 pm

Color of the day: Black
Incense of the day: Carnation

Gathering Herbs for Spellcraft

Herbs gathered under a particular phase of the Moon were supposed to be more efficacious in spell work and healing. Today, harvest, gather, or buy herbs that you would use in a waxing Moon context. Herbs of increase such as rosemary (sharpens mental faculties), basil (money), echinacea (boosts immunity), ginseng (sexuality) are some examples. If you grow your own herbs, cut them at dusk. If you are gathering wild herbs, give thanks to the earth for this "freebie" before harvesting. Do not cut any herbs on conserved or public lands where taking foliage is prohibited. If you buy herbs from a farmer's market, ask about the methods of growing, and buy organic if possible. Once your gathering is complete, at dusk take all your herbs and display them for the New Moon, feeling the power of the herbs increase. If you decide to dry the herbs rather than using them fresh, hang them in a warm, dry place, then place them in airtight containers in a dark pantry.

Denise Dumars

September 4
Sunday

 1st ♍

Color of the day: Orange
Incense of the day: Coriander

Sun Ra Tribute

Sunny days have helped you enjoy your summer so far, so why not pay tribute to the Sun god Ra for his blessings in the way he likes best. In ancient Egypt, myrrh was burned at high noon to please the Sun god Ra. Put a few small chunks of myrrh on a white charcoal block placed on a fire-proof surface outdoors. Use your hands to brush the smoke upwards toward the sky as you say:

> With honor and praise I
>   send this smoke to you.
> Thanks for the blessings
>   and the sunny days,
> Sun Ra, great god,
>   emblem of the Sun.
>
> I honor and praise you
>   for all that you've done.

Stephanie Rose Bird

September 5
Monday
Labor Day (observed)

1st ♍

☽ → ♎ 3:52 am

Color of the day: Lavender
Incense of the day: Rose

A Child's New School Ritual

If your child is anxious about the coming school year, try this spell with him or her. You will need a yellow candle, some ocean sand, a quartz crystal, and five pink stones. Find a safe space for the candle to burn once it is lit. Pour the sand into a glass container, and anchor the candle. Place the crystal point up in the sand in front of the candle. Arrange the five stones around the outside of the glass container. Have your child spend a few moments visualizing doing well in school, getting along with the kids and teachers, or specifically focusing on something her or she is having difficulties with. Let the child light the candle, helping younger children if necessary. Leave the candle to burn for a half hour, then allow the child to blow it out while picturing his or her problems leaving with the candle's smoke. This spell can be repeated.

Laurel Reufner

Notes:

brighter. When you are ready, draw a deep breath in and let it out, dispersing the red ball into space. This releases the energy. Use this technique to enhance any energy-raising activity or spell. Focus on your goal before releasing the energy, then release it.

Ember

Notes:

September 6
Tuesday

 1st ♍ ♎

Color of the day: Red
Incense of the day: Musk

Enhancing Energy Spell

Sit still in a comfortable position today. You can raise energy by using only your mind. Ground and connect with the Earth, and draw from the Earth's energy. Imagine you can see all the way to the core, feel the heat there, and pull it toward you. Visualize yourself in an energetic situation. See and feel yourself doing something exciting such as riding a roller coaster, dancing, or running. Quicken your breath. Transform the energy of the Earth and your body. Imagine it as a red sphere of gas glowing around you ever bigger and

September 7
Wednesday

 1st ♎

☽ → ♏ 6:50 pm

Color of the day: Yellow
Incense of the day: Pine

Breaking Destructive Ties Spell

To break the ties of a destructive relationship, prepare to handle phone calls from the person trying to manipulate or control you. Place a mirror on the wall behind your telephone. Place a drawing pad next to your phone. Look into the mirror and smile. Draw a picture of the person, with his or her head on the body of a toad. Practice taking a phone call from that person. Imagine some

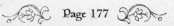

of the things he or she may say, and how it will affect you. Once again smile at yourself, and say: "I know you, and you know me. My life has changed, because I see. From ties that bound, I now am free. You have no power over me." When the call comes, take a deep breath and recite the words. Every time you hear a manipulative phrase, write "ribbit" on the note pad.

Paniteowl

Notes:

for a spell for abundance and success. On the candle, use a pin or needle to engrave the number 8 and a word or symbol that describes something you wish to attract. Light the candle and burn cinnamon incense to enhance the attraction of luck and success. While the candle and incense is burning, say these words:

> I look at symbols of
> abundance
> That will bless the
> energies required
> to attract this success.

Emely Flak

Notes:

September 8
Thursday

 1st ♏

Color of the day: Purple
Incense of the day: Chrysanthemum

The Number 8 Spell
The number 8 is a particularly lucky number for the Chinese, who will happily search for a home that features this number. In numerology, 8 is usually associated with material success. When turned on its side, this number is the infinity sign and represents continuity. Combine the vibrations of this auspicious number with a green candle

September 9
Friday

 1st ♏
☽ → ♐ 10:03 pm

Color of the day: Coral
Incense of the day: Nutmeg

Apple and Aster Love Spell
Two of September's loveliest symbols, the apple and aster, are quite magical; as such, they're key ingredients in this love spell. Combined

with rose petals, they make a potent love charm. Remember not to think of anyone specific as you perform this spell. Select a red apple, and place it beneath the increasing Moon near a window in a quiet room. After three days, rub the apple with a red cloth. Think of your wish, and eat this apple, saving the seeds. Combine the seeds with love herbs, such as aster and rose, saying: "Spirits red, spirits white, let this spell grow." Tie all in a crimson cloth, and place the sachet in a special place. Soon you should feel love's embrace.

James Kambos

Notes:

periodically, but it is vital that we first find our true strength within. Holding a purified tiger's-eye stone in your left hand, imagine a golden light surrounding you. In your center, see a golden ball of light providing you with inner love and a strong sense of self. These energies connect you with all of life, while at the same time intensifying your individuality. As you attune your energy to this stone, chant the following seven times.

> Sacred tiger's-eye,
> Let me see.
> Bring me confidence and
> clarity.
> Connect me now with all
> that is,
> And strengthen the
> power that is really me.

Kristin Madden

Notes:

September 10
Saturday

 1st ♐

Color of the day: Brown
Incense of the day: Jasmine

Eye of the Tiger Power Spell

With Saturn in Leo, this is the ideal time to clarify your personal boundaries and find love and confidence within your self. We all need approval from those around us

September 11
Sunday

 1st ♐

Second Quarter 7:37 am

Color of the day: Yellow
Incense of the day: Parsley

A Prayer for Peace

Historians have calculated that in the whole of human history there have been only twenty-nine years of global peace. The only way to achieve global peace is for each of us to practice peace individually. Light a black candle to remember the innocent people murdered on this day four years ago, and a blue candle for peace. Burn some cedar incense for protection. Wear or place a piece of malachite on your altar to promote tranquility and to deepen the spell. Center and say:

> I am protected and safe.
> I am happy and content.
> I enjoy good health. My
> life unfolds smoothly. I
> realize my higher self.

Say this same mantra for your family and friends, then say it for your adversaries and political figures that you disagree with or fear. You will feel the shift of energy immediately.

Lily Gardner-Butts

Notes:

September 12
Monday

2nd ♐

☽ → ♑ 5:16 pm

Color of the day: Gray
Incense of the day: Daffodil

Suit of Cups Dedication

By studying each suit in turn, you strengthen your connection, so that the tarot responds more readily to you. Devote today to the cups. Start this spell in the morning by removing the Ace of Cups from your deck and placing the card on your altar. Light incense with a cool watery scent such as amber, spearmint, or Blue Nile. Then say:

> Cup of wisdom,
> Cup of grace,
> Pour your blessings on
>   this place.
> Fill me up with what you
>   know.
> Teach me of the ebb and
>   flow.
> Let me taste the Moon
>   and rain,
> And all the magic you
>   contain.

Turn to your favorite tarot manual and read the part about the cups suit. Take some time to let the symbols and interpretations sink into your mind. Let the incense go out on its own. Throughout the day, watch for cup imagery and jot down what you see in your tarot notebook.

Elizabeth Barrette

Notes:

crystal up, and hold it with both hands. Take several deep breaths and relax in the bathtub while still holding it. After bathing, sit by the candles for a little while before dressing. Rinse the crystal with cool water, and put it in sunlight to dry. Repeat this bath whenever there is stress, exhaustion, nervous tension, and moodiness.

S. Y. Zenith

Notes:

September 13
Tuesday

 2nd ♑

Color of the day: Black

Incense of the day: Gardenia

Vitality Bath Ritual

When feeling low in spirits and physical strength, perform this spell to restore vitality. Concoct a mixture of the oils of bay, frankincense, and sandalwood. Obtain a handful of oak leaves, two red candles, and a piece of quartz crystal. Run a bath with the oak leaves and six drops of the essential oil mixture. Light both red candles and step into the bath. As you wash, close your eyes and visualize a rejuvenating force-field enveloping you. Feel it reinstating your waned energies and recharging your aura. Pick the

September 14
Wednesday

 2nd ♑

☽ → ♒ 5:02 am

Color of the day: White

Incense of the day: Neroli

Problem Solved Spell

Do you have a problem that, no matter what you have tried, seems to keep resurfacing? Write out the problem on a piece of paper. Take care to not word your problem in terms that are needy. The universe will manifest the intent of the words that you speak. So if you state, "I need money," the universe will tend to manifest the reality that you will continue to need money. Write instead something like: "Money will come to me as I need it." Light a candle and burn herbs or incense attuned to the resolution of your problem, and say: "Solutions revealed on this brilliant night, this problem is resolved in wisdom's light." Release the problem to the universal wisdom. Open yourself to the divine messages that will resolve your problem.

Karen Follett

Notes:

vastness of the ocean for extra prosperity. You will need a decorative glass jar, some shells and sand, and some ocean water. Fill the bottom of the jar with about an inch of sand. Begin filling the jar the rest of the way to the top with the shells while chanting the following:

> Mother, Mother,
> hear my plea.
> Send to me
> Prosperity.

Finish with "This is my will, so mote it be" as you gently pour the water into the jar. Seal the jar and set it where it can catch the Moon's light. Place it in a spot on your desk or near where you pay bills. One night a month set the jar in the light of the waxing Moon.

Laurel Reufner

Notes:

September 15
Thursday
Respect for the Aged Day

 2nd ♒︎

Color of the day: Rose
Incense of the day: Evergreen

Mother's Ocean Bounty Spell
The ocean seems infinite. Wave upon wave washes upon its shore, bringing offerings of her vast bounty in the form of shells. Call upon the

Holiday Lore: Keirou no Hí, or "Respect for the Aged Day," has been a national holiday in Japan since 1966. On this day, the Japanese show respect to elderly citizens, celebrate their longevity, and pray for their health. Although there are no traditional customs specifically associated with this day, cultural programs are usually held in various communities. School children draw pictures or make handicraft gifts for their grandparents and elderly family friends or neighbors. Some groups visit retirement or nursing homes to present gifts to residents.

is too heavy, the opposite occurs. Use Ma'at's magical tool to bring clarity and peacefulness into your life. Touch all of your ceremonial tools with an ostrich feather today. Then, touch your correspondence—particularly legal papers, judgments, or liens—with the feather of Ma'at so that people will deal with you in a fair and just manner, ensuring peace.

Stephanie Rose Bird

Notes:

September 16
Friday

 2nd ≈

☽ → ♓ 5:24 am

Color of the day: Rose
Incense of the day: Ginger

International Day of Peace Spell

The International Day of Peace invokes the spirit of the Egyptian goddess Ma'at, whose primary purpose is to ensure fairness, justice, and peace. Ma'at weighs the hearts of the gods and goddesses against an ostrich feather with a scale of equality. If equilibrium is struck between the feather and the heart, the god lived a good life and can pass on for a fruitful afterlife. However, if the heart

September 17
Saturday

 2nd ♓

Full Moon 10:01 pm

Color of the day: Blue
Incense of the day: Violet

Sacred Bathing Spell

In ancient times, when bathing in clean water was not something to take for granted, purifying oneself before a ritual or important activities was considered essential. Today prepare "Moon water" and take a sacred bath. Smudge your bathroom or light your favorite incense. Fill a silver or white china bowl with spring water. Place the moonstone you consecrated earlier in the year in the bowl as well. Place the bowl where the light of the Full Moon can "see" it for at least an hour. Light white candles in your bathroom. Draw a bath and add any cleansing herbs you like—including hyssop, lavender, cucumber, rose or jasmine petals. When the bath is ready, remove the moonstone from the Moon water and pour the water into the tub. Playing soothing meditational music or ocean sounds during your bath if you wish. Take this bath to prepare for ritual or a special evening event, or just to purify yourself, your aura, and your senses.

Denise Dumars

Notes:

Allergy Relief Spell

Allergy season is in full swing now, and many are miserable. But we need not miss communing with our Mother Earth because of allergy symptoms. Take a potato, and anoint it with eucalyptus oil. Cut the potato in half. Take a piece of paper, and write the words "Relief from allergy symptoms" on it. Roll up the paper, and stuff it in the potato. Use toothpicks to hold the potato together. Take it outside and bury it, saying: "I rid myself of allergy symptoms and return them to Mother Earth to be recycled and used for the good of all. As this potato rots, so does my suffering ease." Take a hot bath with healing oils and drink echinacea tea. It is done.

Tammy Sullivan

Notes:

September 18
Sunday

 3rd ♓

☽ → ♈ 5:43 am

Color of the day: Gold
Incense of the day: Poplar

September 19
Monday

 3rd ♈

Color of the day: White
Incense of the day: Peony

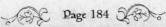

Persephone Returns Ritual

Heton Lampador Haera, the torch-lit procession of initiates of the Eleusinian Mysteries, represents grain goddess Demeter searching for her daughter Persephone. As we prepare for the season when Persephone returns to the underworld and the land becomes cold and dark, we give thanks for the gifts her mother has bestowed. A Demeter ritual is one that can solidify our appreciation of all that we have, and enhance the shift of the seasons. Dress in robes of autumn colors, and burn candles of red, orange, gold, and violet. Place autumn fruits and vegetables on the altar—especially apples, pumpkins, and corn. Display a pomegranate in a prominent spot. Pomegranates are sacred to Persephone, who after swallowing three of the seeds was taken into the underworld. Gaze upon the abundant gifts of the earth, and give thanks to Demeter for providing all the gifts you possess.

Ruby Lavender

Notes:

September 20
Tuesday

 3rd ♈

☽ → ♉ 7:47 am

Color of the day: Maroon
Incense of the day: Pine

Stress Management Spell

Do you have too much to do, and too little time? This is the catch-cry of our contemporary, time-poor lifestyle. Tonight, with a waning Moon, set aside some time to reduce some of that stress. Of course, we can't completely remove all the stress from our lives, but we can ease some of the pressure and minimize its impact. On a sheet of black or dark paper, with a dark-colored pen, write the things in your life that are currently causing you stress. Imagine the dark pigmentation of the paper absorbing the ink, drinking in your challenges, easing your anguish. Fold the paper three times, and burn it in the flame of a black candle, as you say:

> I will forgive
> I will let go
> Of those things
> That trouble me so!

As you breathe out, visualize your worries diminishing and floating away.

Emely Flak

September 21
Wednesday

 3rd ♉

Color of the day: Topaz
Incense of the day: Coriander

Air Meditation

Sit in a comfortable position where you can feel the movement of air—either outside or near an open window. Light an incense of your choice, and focus on the swirling smoke. Watch it curl into the air as you and consider the element of air. Play music if it helps you meditate, and breathe deeply. Think of the air we breathe. Think of wind and its power. Air is the element of the intellect and of communication, so consider all aspects of the mind as well. Imagine the air currents moving all around you. Do this for the length of time that it takes your incense to burn.

Ember

September 22
Thursday

Mabon – Fall Equinox

 3rd ♉
☽ → ♊ 1:07 pm
☉ → ♎ 6:23 pm

Color of the day: Green
Incense of the day: Dill

Hearth Warming Spell

The Fall Equinox gives us our second balancing point in the year. It also means the last of the harvest will soon be taken in. From this night onward the veil that separates our world from the spirit world grows ever thinner until, by Samhain, it will be open for all to pass through. In Welsh legends the land of the dead is in the western sea. To reach it you first had to pass several challengers along your path through Avalon, the vast orchard of

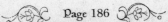

apples that guarded and guided travelers. Apples are a gift from the dead and the deities. Their orchard guards the pathway to the schools of magic and the land of the dead beyond. To make your home a happy place to be, take a big red apple and slice it crossways so you can see the the five-pointed star within. Remove the seeds and keep them away from children and pets. They contain trace amounts of cyanide, a deadly poison. Cover the entire white part of the apple by sticking cloves into it. Cloves are for protection and health. Place these in a 200-degree oven until they start to curl at the edges. Remove them from the heat and place them in a small glass bowl so their scent fills your home. Say:

> Bless'd be the apple tree.
> Protected with the
> cloves we be.

> Edain McCoy

Notes:

September 23
Friday

3rd ♊

Color of the day: Purple
Incense of the day: Cedar

Mask Spell

Today is the day that offerings were made to the Egyptian creator god, Atum. Atum is said to have risen from the waters to create the first land and command all the forces of nature. Atum is both male and female and represents total perfection and unity. On this day, consider how well you balance your masculine and feminine aspects and how this affects your relationships. Craft two masks for this exercise. One will embody your feminine side. The other should reflect your masculine side. Pour all your relevant feelings, memories, beliefs, and experiences into the respective masks. Afterward, talk to yourself through the masks and into the mirror—free-associating to explore how balanced and powerful is each of the two aspects of you. Ask each aspect of yourself how you can better integrate and balance this energy in your life. Use whatever information you obtain to create a more integrated and powerfully balanced version of you.

> Kristin Madden

Notes:

home. Light your candle and ask the salamanders to purify your home. Sprinkle holy water and ask blessings from the undines. Sprinkle salt and ask the gnomes for protection. Thank the elementals for their blessings. As an extra blessing, tie twigs of hazel together with a human hair and leave them on your mantle for protection from fire and storm.

Lily Gardner-Butts

Notes:

September 24
Saturday

 3rd ♊
☽ → ♋ 10:10 pm

Color of the day: Indigo
Incense of the day: Cedar

Fall Elemental Blessing

Fall housecleaning can be a spiritual practice when you believe that the physical is the end result of spiritual forces. As you clear away old clutter, visualize making room for new opportunities. When everything is clean, summon the elementals by saying:

> I call upon air the power
> to blow,
> I call upon fire, the
> power to glow,
> I call upon water, the
> power to flow,
> I call upon earth, the
> power to grow.

Light the stick of incense and carry it through each room asking the sylphs to purify and protect your

September 25
Sunday

 3rd ♋
Fourth Quarter 2:41 am

Color of the day: Amber
Incense of the day: Cinnamon

A Spell to heal Anger

To cleanse yourself of negative feelings today, this spell may help. Purchase some clay or other sculpting medium from an art supply store; it must be the type you can bake in a home oven. To begin the spell, work the clay vigorously. Feel the anger coming out of you, and channel it into the clay. Shape the clay into a small, flat, round shape. Inscribe it with the word "anger" and bake it. When your tablet is done, go into a garden or wooded area. Dig a small hole. Smash your tablet and crumble it into the hole. In a strong voice, say:

> Anger and sorrow be
>   gone!
> Back to the earth, back
>   to the ground.
> All of the anger, all of
>   the pain
> Dissolve to dust in this
>   earthly grave,
> Never to return again!

James Kambos

Notes:

When stressed at work, remind yourself to take a few minutes and breathe deeply. Go outside and look at the sky. If the sky is clear, say: "Clear of sky, and clear of eye, I see the way to spend my day." If the sky is stormy, say: "Storms of life may cause some strife, yet clear the way to a brighter day." Getting in touch with the elements will help enable you to accomplish tasks that formerly seemed overwhelming. When you return to your job, chant the affirmation and then center your attention on the task at hand.

Paniteowl

Notes:

September 26
Monday

 4th ♋

Color of the day: Ivory
Incense of the day: Lavender

Forgotten Energies Spell

Sometimes, we forget to use earth energies to rejuvenate ourselves.

September 27
Tuesday

 4th ♋
☽ → ♌ 10:03 am

Color of the day: White
Incense of the day: Juniper

Autumn Stone Protection Spell

Every home can benefit from protection. This spell employs one of nature's sturdiest objects, a stone.

Choose a plain rock at least as big as your fist. Set it on your altar between a bowl of salt and a bowl of water. Behind these, light a black candle. Sprinkle the stone with salt, saying: "I consecrate this stone with the purifying power of salt." Sprinkle it with water, saying: "I consecrate this stone with the cleansing power of water." Pass it over the flame, saying: "I consecrate this stone with the attraction of flame to moth." Finally, trace a pentagram on the stone with your finger, and say:

> To watch and guard
> around my home,
> I invoke the strength of
> stone.
> All evil thoughts be
> drawn within:
> Strike here and leave me
> alone!

Blow out the candle; empty the salt and water outside. Keep the rock near your door.

Elizabeth Barrette

Notes:

September 28
Wednesday

 4th ♌

Color of the day: Brown
Incense of the day: Sandalwood

Balance of Light and Shadow Spell

One of the main concepts in witchcraft is the duality of the universe. Nothing is purely good or purely bad. People bear these aspects of duality. We have the "light" traits of kindness and generosity and so on that we acknowledge and present to others. We also have our "dark" side as well. These are the traits (such as jealousy, anger, and greed) that we hold from public view and many times neglect to acknowledge. Again, nothing is purely good or bad. With that in mind, we can think of our dark traits as a power that balances our lives and promote positive change. Jealousy can be a motivator to strive for better. Anger can be the motivator to help change or prevent bad situations. Light a black and a white candle, and say:

> Goddess of darkness,
> Goddess of light,
> Balance of duality I
> accept as my right.

Focus on your traits, both in the light and dark realms. Focus on the positive messages that both have for you.

Karen Follett

Notes:

oil, and five ounces of your favorite talcum powder. Powder the herbs with a mortar and pestle before adding the oils and blending with a metal spoon. Add talcum powder to the combination and mix it thoroughly. Put the powder in a jar or other glass container. Take it to the altar and consecrate before use.

S. Y. Zenith

Notes:

September 29
Thursday

 4th ♌
☽ → ♍ 10:44 pm

Color of the day: Crimson
Incense of the day: Carnation

Money-Drawing Powder

When business is going through a slow period and income decreases, prepare a money-drawing powder. As a talcum powder for the body after bathing, it draws money toward you. Sprinkled on business documents and cash registers, it assists in generating improved activity and profits. Sprinkled on the floor around a shop, the powder attracts enthusiastic customers. Make this potent powder using one tablespoon of powdered cinquefoil (five-finger grass), one ounce of powdered sandalwood, a quarter teaspoon of powdered cinnamon, one teaspoon of powdered yellow dock, a quarter dram of patchouli oil, a half dram of frankincense oil, a quarter dram of myrrh

Holiday lore: The Feast Day of St. Michael the Archangel is celebrated in Western churches on September 29. In the Eastern (Orthodox) Church, it is observed on November 8. The cult of St. Michael first began in the Eastern Church during the fourth century. It spread to Western Christianity in the fifth century. St. Michael was the leader of the heavenly armies. Veneration of all angels was later incorporated into his cult. He was highly revered as a protector against dark forces. By Michaelmas, harvests were completed and fresh cycles of farming would begin. It was a time for beginning new projects, balancing accounts, and paying annual dues.

September 30
Friday

 4th ♏

Color of the day: White
Incense of the day: Ylang-ylang

Empowering your Personal Computer for Magic

Your computer may be charged and used as a magical tool. Cleanse the computer with a smudging of sage or sweet grass, then consecrate it to the four elements. Take a bit of sandalwood oil and anoint it in various spots. Charge a purple candle with intent of spirit, and light it directly in front of the monitor. Place clear quartz stones around your computer, and say it is to be used for magic. When you wish to use the computer, set your altar up directly in front of the monitor and set your screensaver to show the spell words repeatedly. Light a candle if the spell calls for it, and leave your computer to its assigned job.

Tammy Sullivan

Notes:

Notes:

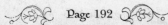

October

October is the tenth month of the year, its name derived from the Latin word *octo,* meaning "eight," as it was the eighth month of the Roman calendar. Its astrological sign is Libra, the scales (Sept 22–Oct 23), a cardinal air sign ruled by Venus. Colors are everywhere now, as trees burst into masses of red, orange, and yellow leaves. Our bodies begin to change in metabolism at this time of year, and our consciousness shifts from an active mental state to a more psychically receptive state appropriate to the dark half of the year. The biggest celebration of October, and one of the most magical nights of the year, is Samhain (or Halloween, which is used inter-changeably today). It is a time to decorate with signs symbolizing the out-ward manifestation of inward changes. Gourds and pumpkins decorate the porch or stoop; bundles of dried cornstalks sit by the front steps. As the day nears, the pumpkins change to jack-o'-lanterns that stare from the windows. Blood is common in Halloween costumes, and the Full Moon of October is known as the Blood Moon. Samhain is a celebration of death and is marked by several traditions—such as the Dumb Supper, in which dinner is served with places set for the dead; and the Samhain Circle, in which the living attempt to contact the dead to gain spiritual knowledge.

October 1

Saturday

The Godless Month

 4th ♏

Color of the day: Gray
Incense of the day: Patchouli

Recovery Spell

Do you still pine for an ex-lover? Or are you tormented with anger over something someone did or said to you long ago? You deserve to free yourself of any pain caused by another. Use the banishing vibrations of a waning Moon to diminish resentment or pain that is holding you back from realizing your full potential. Tonight, light a white candle and a blue candle. White is for protection, and blue is for healing. On a piece of blue paper, write that you now forgive this person for what they have done to you and declare your freedom to move on. After you have written your words, also say:

> I ask for courage with
> this spell
> To grant me the wisdom
> to dispel
> Pain, anger and residual
> tears,
> To banish and disappear!

After tonight, either burn or discard the note to symbolize your freedom.

Emely Flak

Notes:

Holiday lore: According to Shinto belief, during the month of October the gods gather to hold their annual convention. All of the *kami* converge on the great temple of Isumo in western Honshu, and there they relax, compare notes on crucial god business, and make decisions about humankind. At the end of this month, all over Japan, people make visits to their local Shinto shrines to welcome the regular resident gods back home. But until then, all through the month, the gods are missing—as a Japanese poet once wrote:

> The god is absent:
> the dead leaves are piling
> up,
> and all is deserted.

October 2
Sunday

 4th ♍
☽ → ♎ 10:24 am

Color of the day: Yellow
Incense of the day: Sage

Messages of the Otherworld

The ancient wise ones believed in maintaining the harmony and balance between humankind, earth, and the otherworld. When there is a readiness to listen and a willingness to understand, wisdom is bestowed. On a charcoal block, light a white candle. Burn sage for wisdom, oak for connection to the ancients, and mugwort to open your psychic eye. Focus on the candle through the smoke of the incense. State these or similar words:

> Voices of the otherworld
> speak to me.

> I long to hear your ageless
> messages from beyond,
> And your wisdom of
> harmony.

Let your mind open to the messages. The unconscious brain will receive the messages initially. Your conscious brain may interpret the messages over a period of time. Thank the ancients and leave an offering in their honor.

Karen Follett

October 3
Monday

 4th ♎
New Moon 6:28 am

Color of the day: White
Incense of the day: Maple

Durga Puja

Around this time of year in India is celebrated the goddess festival called Diwali. An important part of this sacred time is a Durga Puja, or worship service in honor of Durga the Demon-Slayer. She is portrayed as a beautiful woman wearing red clothing and sometimes armor, and riding a lion or tiger. She is an aspect of both Parvati and Kali, and combines traits of both. Let Durga know you want her help with difficult situations by creating an altar for her. Offer red flowers, candy, and nuts. Find an image of Durga to place on the altar, or wear a pendant featuring her image. (These can be found in Hindu shops and many New Age shops.) Greet Durga with the following:

> Great Mother Durga,
> Devi, Parvati, Kali,
> Divine guardian,
> Defender, lover,
> Bring peace and protection
> to this home.
>
> I honor you this day,
> your feast day.
> Namaste.

Stick with vegetarian food today and eat Indian cuisine if possible. Find out more about this splendid goddess, the patroness of Bengal, on the worldwide web.

Denise Dumars

Notes:

October 4
Tuesday
Rosh hashanah – Ramadan begins

 1st ♎
☽ → ♏ 8:03 pm

Color of the day: Silver
Incense of the day: Honeysuckle

Cleansing the Soul Spell

This year the New Moon of October will begin the holy month of Ramadan for Muslims, and it will begin the New Year, or Rosh Hashanah, for Jews. These two religions seem at first to have little in common except a desire to fight with one another. Yet both faiths—and Christianity too, in fact—begin with the book of Genesis, and all three claim descent from Abraham. This alone should tell us our mutual goal is to return to our creator, and that there are many paths that can take us there. On special holy days many religions—including Paganism—prescribe purification and cleansing rites to prepare for sacred rituals. Your soul cleansing can be as elaborate or as simple as you like, though it must be sincere and entered into with a sense of balance and a focused mind. You may shower, bathe, lie on the earth, climb a high hill, sit on your own bed, or stand on the bank of a river—any of these is appropriate. The imagery choose to process is most important now. Whichever method you choose, you should also use a chant or mantra to repeat over and over again while you visualize your soul's purification. Some suggestions include:

> heavenly parents,
> Make me a fitting vessel
> for you.

Lady Moon,
Shine through me and
banish the bane.

Lord of the Sun,
Burn from my spirit any
impurities.

Grandmother,
Know my sin and cleanse
my soul.

Lord and Lady,
Wash away the debris
that blocks me from you.

Edain McCoy

Notes:

would like to use for your tassel. Either pick colors that speak to you as being protective, or use colors that remind you of a particular deity. Cut seven two-foot lengths of ribbon in various colors and fold them in half. Tie them in the middle with a length of black ribbon, and hang them from your rear-view mirror. Feel free to dress up your tassel a bit by adding small charms, bells, or beads to the bottoms of the ribbons.

Laurel Reufner

Notes:

October 6
Thursday

 1st ♏

Color of the day: Purple
Incense of the day: Geranium

Legal Matters Spell

Use this spell when you have a legal issue you need assistance with. Find a symbol of the problem such as a copy of a ticket, court order, or other document, or write down the problem on a piece of paper. Fold

October 5
Wednesday

 1st ♏

Color of the day: Topaz
Incense of the day: Eucalyptus

Car Protection Tassel

Spend some time meditating on what colors of ribbon you

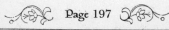

the paper in half again and again, making it as small as possible, and as you do this imagine making the issue itself as small and inexpensive as it can be. With each fold, envision the problem growing smaller and smaller, and easier to bear. If you have an altar or personal space, place the folded paper near the direction that corresponds with the elements of water or fire (west and south, respectively), and imagine the problem being burned away, its ashes washed away by the water. Allow the paper to remain in place until the issue is resolved, then say:

> This event is not the
> end, but a chance, to
> learn and mend.

Ember

Notes:

October 7
Friday

 1st ♏

☽ → ♐ 3:38 am

Color of the day: Pink
Incense of the day: Almond

Maple Leaf Love Spell

Maple trees are frequently used in love magic. Since maple trees are known for their strength, they're a good choice to use in spells where you want to strengthen an existing love. Perform this spell in the fall when the tree's leaves are burning with color—somewhat like love itself. Select three maple leaves, colored red if possible. They should be from the same tree. Next, find a book that you and your lover have both read. Open the book to a favorite passage and insert the leaves. Touch the leaves and say this charm.

> One leaf for our past,
> One for the present,
> And one for our future.
>
> May our love always be
> nurtured.
> Like these leaves we are
> from the same tree.
> We are its branches, you
> and me.
>
> Like these leaves,
> Our love is preserved.

Close the book so the leaves will be pressed and preserved. Return the book to its place and let the spell do its work.

James Kambos

Notes:

the heavens, and wait for your good fortune to manifest.

Lily Gardner-Butts

Notes:

October 8
Saturday

 1st ♐

Color of the day: Black
Incense of the day: Lilac

Kite Spell for Good Luck

The Chinese celebrate the Festival of High Places on this day by flying good-omen kites. Follow their example, and buy or make a simple box kite. Decorate the kite with symbols of the Sun, the Moon, and of your wishes. Use both pictures and words. Preparing your kite is part of the spell so remember to visualize your wish as you draw it on the kite. Go to a windy place, and call upon the sylphs, the elementals of air, to help you realize your goals. They rule thoughts and new beginnings. Let your kite soar up far into

October 9
Sunday

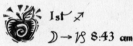 1st ♐
☽ → ♑ 8:43 am

Color of the day: Orange
Incense of the day: Clove

Celebrate Joy Spell

The Sun in Libra brings a feeling of balance and harmony to this day. Make today a celebration of joy and community. Upon awakening, turn your face to the rising Sun and breathe deeply, allowing a feeling of balance and happiness to fill you to overflowing. Repeat this exercise periodically throughout the day. Find something to be happy about all day. This may be a love or a success or it may be as simple as the Sun glinting on water or the feel of a gentle rain. As night falls, cut openings large enough to hold taper candles in the top of two shiny autumn apples. Place two pink, or one gold and one silver, candles in the apple holders. As you light them, remember all the joys of the day and of your life. Rejoice in the joy you have brought to others and give thanks for these gifts.

Kristin Madden

Notes:

October 10
Monday
Columbus Day (observed)

1st ♑
Second Quarter 3:01 pm

Color of the day: Lavender
Incense of the day: Chrysanthemum

Burning Wood Clean Spell

The end of the year draws near. The nights grow longer and colder, so now is the time to cut and store wood for fireplaces, stoves, and ritual bonfires. This spell helps the wood burn hot and clean. Take the stub of a red candle that you have used on your altar. Make sure the wax itself is red all the way through, not just colored red on the outside. With the red wax, draw the rune Sigil (ᛋ) on one end of each log. As its shape suggests, Sigil represents the Sun, magical will, and lightning success. While you work, chant:

> Red of fire,
> Brown of wood,
> Make this spell both
> strong and good.
>
> By the power of the Sun,
> Light and heat
> For everyone!

If any wax remains after you finish marking all of your firewood, bury the candle stub behind the woodpile.

Elizabeth Barrette

Notes:

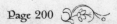

October 11
Tuesday

 2nd ♑
☽ → ♒ 9:32 am

Color of the day: White
Incense of the day: Evergreen

Waning Moon Spell

The birthstone for October is the opal. It is said to be unlucky for those not born in October to wear the stone. For those who were born in this month, it would be a good time to use the stone as your talisman for a variety of spellworking. If you have an opal already, you can use that. If you don't have an opal, now is the time to give yourself this beautiful stone as a gift. Place your opal on a chain, then hang it over a mirror. Gaze into the mirror, placing the opal on your forehead. Say: "Stone of birth is mine to own, and the fire of opal glows. My hidden beauty will be sought, as love within me grows." Wear your opal through the month of October to help your fondest wish come true.

Paniteowl

Notes:

October 12
Wednesday

 1st ♒

Color of the day: Yellow
Incense of the day: Cedar

Spell Bottle for Business Success

Take a small pair of lodestones and place them in a tall and thin green bottle. Add three drops of cinnamon oil, a pinch of ground nutmeg powder, and one whole clove. Shake the mixture nine times. Add two drops green food coloring to one-half cup of water, and pour this into a bottle. Add a pinch of blessed salt for protection and a shredded dollar bill. Cap the bottle and let it rest an hour. Before opening, shake it well. Allow the aroma to waft about the room. Sprinkle the oil where you wish to draw success, protection, and money. Bless the oil by saying: "Ye are as pure as Mother Earth and will draw success unto me. Wherever this potion flows, success I will know."

Tammy Sullivan

Notes:

October 13
Thursday
Yom Kippur

1st ≈

☽ → ♓ 2:05 pm

Color of the day: Turquoise
Incense of the day: Musk

healing the Past Spell

Yom Kippur is known as the Day of Atonement. More important than having others come to you to heal past hurts is your own willingness to forgive. It is unhealthy both physically and spiritually to harbor hatred in your heart. This hurts everyone who knows and cares about the warring factions. If there is an enemy in your life, letting the enmity fester interferes with your magical will and shuts down your chakra centers. If you are unable to go visit this person face to face, you can send mail, e-mail, or use the telephone. Chances are that the other party will be open to mending the fence, especially today. If your rift is with a family member or someone who was once a very close friend, they will be delighted to hear from you and as anxious to mend the tear as you. Apologizing is never easy, particularly when one is not sure how this reaching out will be taken. The night before the day you plan to seek a solution, light a small orange candle and sit in front of it thinking about what to say. Keep a pen handy to jot down ideas as they comes to you. Put a small violet or lavender flower in your pocket to help evoke a spirit of harmony, balance, and love. As you empower the herbs, chant:

> Betwixt and between,
> The chasm grew wide.
> Love for my friend
> Went out like the tide.
>
> I need words to heal,
> To help me in this bitter
>   endeavor.
> Though we've been at
>   odds,
> Our love lives forever.

Edain McCoy

Notes:

October 14
Friday

2nd ♓

Color of the day: Rose
Incense of the day: Nutmeg

The Good Luck You Need Spell

Try a different kind of love spell suited to the autumn season today. This one was a traditional form of divination in Europe and colonial America. It is especially good for those seeking a lover. You will need an apple and a sharp paring knife. Light some candles to create a calm atmosphere. Sit at a table and breathe deeply, meditating on the qualities you wish to find in your new lover. Then peel the apple, but do so very slowly and carefully so that it comes off in one long unbroken peel. Then, stand up and carefully toss the peel over your shoulder behind you so that it lands on the floor. The peel will fall into the shape of the first initial of the first or last name of your new love.

Ruby Lavender

Notes:

October 15
Saturday

2nd ♓

☽ → ♈ 3:39 pm

Color of the day: Indigo
Incense of the day: Juniper

Psychic Reconnection Spell

Gaining psychic perception involves practice, patience, and a reconnection of the preexisting psychic wiring that all people possess. Light a deep blue or purple candle. Burn mugwort on a charcoal block. State these or similar words:

> I'm open to the wisdom
>   beyond the veil,
> Of past, present, and
>   future,
> And the spiral flow.
>
> The words you speak,
> The visions you see,
> The sensations I feel,
> The knowledge of what
>   I know.
>
> I'm open as a channel
> To your wise words and
>   sights.
> Guide us through our
>   days
> And light up our nights.

Meditate to open your mind to the messages beyond the veil. Pay attention to the feelings, visions, sounds, and perceptions that you encounter.

Begin a journal of your perceptions, and examine carefully the outcomes.

Karen Follett

Notes:

October 16
Sunday

 2nd ♈

Color of the day: Amber
Incense of the day: Basil

Junk E-mail Graveyard Spell

The Moon is almost full. Work with her potency tonight with this ritual to banish bad vibes sent via the Internet. Use this powerful spell when hitting the Delete button is just not effective enough. To address the cowardly, hurtful letters from people who seek out this impersonal mode of communication to send insults and criticism, and to end relationships or zap energy, start by printing some of the offending e-mails. Bring them outside with some dried lavender, mullein, rosemary, and peppermint. Take the three most offensive letters,

place a few sprigs of each herb inside, and roll them up tightly. Light them, and let them burn completely. Repeat until all e-mail and herbs are burned. Set a few ashes aside, and bury the remaining ash. Pour rosewater over the earth mound. Put fresh flowers on top periodically. Realize that all the negative energies are now buried in the junk e-mail graveyard. They no longer affect or concern you. Touch your computer in each of the four directions with a smidgen of the ash. Repeat the ritual whenever you are so compelled. The flow of junk e-mail should decrease dramatically.

Stephanie Rose Bird

Notes:

October 17
Monday

 2nd ♈
Full Moon 8:14 am ♈
☽ → ♉ 6:04 pm

Color of the day: Ivory
Incense of the day: Frankincense

Cemetery Divination with Oya

This ritual is not for the squeamish! Work with the energy of Oya, the goddess of the cemetery, to help you use divination tools. Just don't be surprised at what your cards or crystals may reveal, however. Start by finding a quiet, secluded place to sit in the cemetery, preferably on a bench in a visitor's area. If you wish, however, do this at the grave of someone you love or who is famous and beloved. Bring some red grape juice for Oya and yourself, and dress in burgundy, burnt orange, or brown. Walk around a bit to orient yourself and become comfortable with the energy. If you do not feel comfortable, try this another time or at another cemetery. Drink some of the juice and pour a little into the earth near a tree or bush. Ask Oya for help in answering your question you have. Do your divination now if possible, focusing on one question only. Burn a candle in one of Oya's colors when you get home. You may do the actual divination at home after the cemetery visit if you prefer.

Denise Dumars

Notes:

October 18
Tuesday
Sukkot begins

3rd ♉

Color of the day: Gray
Incense of the day: Sage

Fire Meditation

Light as many candles as you desire, in any colors you wish. Place them all around you, and extinguish all other light sources if possible. If you are fortunate to have access to a fireplace, you may use this fire as your focus, or, better still, use a bonfire outside. Whichever method you choose, the idea is to focus your attention only on the flames. Listen for the crackling of the fire, or, if using candles, play whatever music helps you connect with the fire element. Consider the origin of fire and what it means to our life. We use it for warmth, light, and for cooking. Think of the heat of the Sun, and how this is one of the vital elements of life. Fire represents passion, creativity, and growth. Meditate on these aspects.

Ember

Notes:

·October 19
Wednesday

 3rd ♉
☽ → ♊ 10:44 pm

Color of the day: Brown
Incense of the day: Maple

Altar Purification Incense

Here is a good incense to purify and protect your sacred space.

Patchouli for earth
  protection,
Lavender for air
  purification,
Copal for fire purification,
And myrrh for water
  purification.

Grind the herbs and resins finely in a mortar and pestle, filling them with their desired intention. Burn the mixture over a hot charcoal, and let the smoke cleanse your space.

Laurel Reufner

Notes:

·October 20
Thursday

 3rd ♊

Color of the day: Green
Incense of the day: Jasmine

Unhappy at School Spell

Do you have a child, or know of someone else's child, who is unhappy at school because he or she is being bullied or teased? With their naive natures, children can be quite cruel to others without any understanding of the pain inflicted by words and behaviors. Without adult encouragement and empathy, teasing can destroy children's confidence and can affect their academic performance. On this waning Moon, offer your gift of magic to help a child banish this from his or her life. Write the words below on a piece of paper and fold it. Ensure that one of the folds is across the bully's name. Tie it up with black sewing thread or black ribbon. Place it in the freezer to "freeze" the bully's impact.

(Insert the bully's name.)

Your words no longer
  hurt me.
Your actions cause me
  less pain.

By trying to get my
  attention,

You have nothing more
to gain.

Emely Flak

Notes:

When you have dropped the last grain, observe the pattern the rice has made in the water. Be aware of any immediate impressions you receive. Then analyze the pattern and look for specific letters or images. The pattern will indicate the identity of your true love.

Kristin Madden

Notes:

October 21
Friday

 3rd ♊

Color of the day: White
Incense of the day: Ginger

Rice Divination

To gain insight into the identity of your true love, fill a small bowl with uncooked rice. Place a wide and shallow bowl, half full of water, on the floor, and stand with your back to it. Holding the rice in both hands, clear your mind of everything and let go of any hopes or expectations about the identity of this person. Pass the rice, grain by grain, over your left shoulder into the water. As you do so, chant the following to keep your mind open and the energy flowing:

> True love come to me.
> Let me see
> My true love's identity.

October 22
Saturday

 3rd ♊
☽ → ♋ 6:41 pm

Color of the day: Blue
Incense of the day: Pine

Wart Removal Charms

During the night, half fill a silver dish with spring water and some dandelions. Bathe the wart-afflicted body part in the dish. Rub the dandelions against the wart. Massage the sap of the dandelions into the wart, then pat dry gently with a towel. Discard the water and bury the dandelions in the earth. Before turning in for the night, dab some undiluted lemon essential oil onto the wart. There would be some easing of discomfort by the morning. Continue this treatment ritual for at least two weeks. Another charm for ridding warts is to rub them with a stone. When done, wrap the stone in several layers of tissue paper, and request a friend to bury it at a crossroads. Another folk remedy utilizes a potato for rubbing warts, which is then buried deep in soil. The wart will disappear as the potato disintegrates in the ground.

S. Y. Zenith

Notes:

October 23

Sunday

Swallows depart

 3rd ♋

☉ → ♏ 3:42 am

Color of the day: Gold
Incense of the day: Coriander

Winter Sunday Hazelnut Bread

Today is the Norse feast to celebrate the beginning of winter. One of the feasting foods is nuts. Hazelnuts are a prominent food during the month of October. They are used for charms and divination. To make hazelnut bread:

> 1 cup plus 1 tablespoon
> lukewarm water
> 3 teaspoons yeast
> 1 1/2 tablespoons butter
> 1 tablespoon sugar
> 1 teaspoon salt
> 1/2 cup toasted, chopped
> hazelnuts
> 1 cup whole wheat flour
> 1 1/2 cups white flour
> Cornmeal

Dissolve the yeast in the warm water. Add the butter, sugar, and salt. Mix until smooth. Add hazelnuts and both flours. Knead the mixture for ten minutes, then let the dough rest for fifteen minutes. Form the dough into a round loaf, and place it on a cookie sheet dusted with cornmeal. Let it rise until it is doubled in size. With a sharp knife cut a cross on top in honor of the four elements. Bake the bread in a 400-degree oven until it is nicely browned, about twenty to twenty-five minutes. String nine hazelnuts on a red cord, and hang it in your home for luck and money.

Lily Gardner-Butts

Notes:

Lore for an October day: Maples are among the most stunning trees in nature, often very brightly orange and red. In October, trees are in their full glory and natural beauty (as the green of chlorophyll fades from tree leaves, only the natural color of the leaves remains). Cadmium-colored sumac gathers on roadsides and riverbanks, and provides contrast to the still-green grass and clear blue skies. The first fires have now been kindled inside to fight the coming chill at night, and days suddenly seem very short. Quilts have been pulled from cupboards to warm cold beds; our bodies begin to change in metabolism at this time of year, and our consciousness shifts from an actively mental state to a psychically receptive state appropriate to the dark half of the year. This is the time of the apple harvest; and apples fill fruit bowls or are stored in the root cellar. The house is scented with applesauce laced with cinnamon. Apples have always been magically important—playing a key role in the "wassailing" ceremonies meant to ensure a bountiful harvest

in the coming year. Wassail was traditionally made with hard cider heated with spices and fruit—and a ritual imbibing of this drink was likely performed at Halloween and Samhain, and at Yule. Candy apples are a modern treat celebrating the magic of the apple harvest—these treats are eaten often at Halloween even today. Bobbing for apples, too, has a long tradition as a celebratory ritual. Apples have ancient associations with healing (thus the phrase "An apple a day . . ."), and were said to be useful for curing warts. The interior of an apple, sliced horizontally, reveals a five-pointed star. The final harvest of the year is the hazelnut harvest. Gather the nuts in wickerwork baskets to cure until they can be stored properly. The hazel tree was long held sacret and is symbolic of secret knowledge and divination. Forked hazel rods are useful for dowsing for sources of water or for underground minerals, and hazel is a traditional wood for magical wands.

October 24

Monday

United Nations Day – Sukkot ends

3rd ♋
☽ → ♌ 5:48 pm
Fourth Quarter 9:17 pm

Color of the day: Silver
Incense of the day: Myrrh

Call-of-the-Ocean Fertility Spell

This spell draws upon the primordial womb of the ocean to increase your fertility and to dispel some of the hindrances standing in your way. Place an iron nail in a bottle of ocean water while saying: "As this iron decreases, so do the obstacles in my path." Place the bottle somewhere out of the way and forget about it. To make a substitute if there is no ocean water available, take some spring water and add a good amount of sea salt and some sand to it.

Laurel Reufner

Notes:

October 25
Tuesday

Color of the day: Scarlet
Incense of the day: Musk

A Blessing for an Autumn Fire

When the hills of my valley blaze with autumn color, I know it's time to ready my woodstove for the winter season. If you have a fireplace or wood stove, it's a good idea to perform a blessing ritual as you light the season's first fire, especially if you perform fire magic. Ready the wood and ignite the fire using the flame of a white or orange candle as you recite this blessing:

> Ancient fire,
> Burn safely and bright.
> Favor me with warmth
>   and light.
>
> Creator of the magical
>   Jinn,
> Welcome to my hearth
>   again.
> Outside nature dies,
> And the world grows
>   dark.
> Warm me forever with
>   your spark.

As a purifying offering, sprinkle a bit of salt on the flames. Sit by the fire and meditate or divine by the flames. Most of all enjoy the season's first fire.

James Kambos

Notes:

October 26
Wednesday

 4th ♌

Color of the day: White
Incense of the day: Neroli

Clearing Your Home Spell

Samhain is almost upon us. The indoor season will soon follow. To prepare for this we should do a clearing, so that stagnant energies cannot build up during the dormant time of the year. Set up a tray with a censer containing sage incense, a bell, and a small bowl with blessed water containing basil. You will also need your besom. Walk through your home in a clockwise manner beginning at the front door and ending at the back. Enter the first room and waft the sage smoke everywhere. Dip your fingers in the water and sprinkle it about. Next, walk the room in a clockwise fashion ringing the bell. Take your besom and sweep any leftover energy to the door saying: "I sweep the bad out, and good remains throughout."

Tammy Sullivan

Notes:

October 27
Thursday

 4th ♌
☽ → ♍ 6:28 am

Color of the day: Purple
Incense of the day: Carnation

Clean Divination Ritual

The season of Halloween is a special time of year. The veil between the worlds is thin now, and divination possibilities are strongest. Now is the time to bring out the tarot cards or the runes so you can see what the future holds for you. Place a piece of soapstone in the bag that holds your cards or runes, and gently shake the bag to cleanse them. Then enchant your cards or runes by saying: "Cards (or runes) of fortune, this is what I ask of you—a glimpse of what will come to me, a hint of how my life may be." If you read for others, be sure to cleanse the cards or runes with the soapstone between readings.

Paniteowl

Notes:

October 28
Friday

 4th ♏

Color of the day: Coral
Incense of the day: Parsley

Love Maintenance Spell

Ruled by Venus, Friday oversees matters of love and relationships. This includes long-term ones, as well as new flings. Take some time today to nurture yours. First find two pictures—one of yourself and one of a person you love. You also need a red candle, a red apple, and a paring knife. Put the two photos on the altar, and light the candle. Carefully cut the peel off the apple in one piece. Lay the peel around the pictures in the shape of a heart, and say:

> As the apple unto the tree,
> My heart to you,
> your heart to me.

Meditate on the love you share for as long as it takes you to eat the apple. Let the candle burn down on its own. When the spell is complete, take the peel and core outside for the birds, who are sacred to Venus.

Elizabeth Barrette

Notes:

October 29
Saturday
Lost-in-the-Dark Bells

 4th ♏

☽ → ♎ 6:15 pm

Color of the day: Black
Incense of the day: Lavender

Pendulum Divination

The pendulum is a focusing tool that opens the user to messages of the higher self. Purchase or create a necklace to use as your pendulum. While often used in matters that require "yes" or "no" answers, there are many wonderful uses for your pendulum. To use it, support your elbow on a firm surface and hold it with your thumb and forefinger. Relax and open your mind. Direct your pendulum to swing between two options. These answers are usually exhibited by a back-and-forth or a side-to-side motion. Pose your question or concerns, observe the motion that indicates your answer. Thank the energies of the higher self. Wear your pendulum, or store it in a safe place.

Karen Follett

Notes:

oliday lore: Many villages in the English countryside share the tradition of "lost-in-the-dark bells." Legend tells of a person lost in the dark or fog, and heading for disaster, who at the last moment was guided to safety by the sound of church bells. The lucky and grateful survivor always leaves money in his or her will for the preservation of the bells. This day commemorates one particular such case, a man named Pecket in the village of Kidderminster, in Worcestershire, who was saved from plummeting over a ravine by the bells of the local church of St. Mary's. In honor of this event, the bells still ring every October 29.

October 30
Sunday
Daylight Saving Time ends 2 am

 4th ♎

Color of the day: Orange
Incense of the day: Poplar

Persephone, Mistress of Keys Invocation

he Greek goddess Persephone is the mistress of keys, especially the keys to the underworld. Just as an iron key may unlock the door of a house, a computer keyboard unlocks the doors of cyberspace. So by extension, the mistress of keys also becomes the mistress of keyboards. Persephone guards all passages into numinous realms. To protect your keyboard and computer from mishap, simply invoke Persephone. First, touch two traditional iron keys to your keyboard, saying: "Like calls to like." Place the keys on your altar and light some myrrh incense. Tie a black ribbon to the keys, and say:

> hail, Persephone,
> Keeper of keys!
> heed my magic and
>   hearken my pleas.
>
> Grant your protection
>   over all these.

Leaving the keys attached to the black ribbon, hang them in a safe place within sight of your keyboard.

Elizabeth Barrette

Notes:

October 31

Monday

halloween – Samhain

 4th ♏

Color of the day: Orange
Incense of the day: Rose

A Janus Samhain Spell

Thousands of rituals and spells have been composed for Samhain. On this night when the boundaries of life and death are blurred we honor our ancestors, and we remember others who have passed over that we never knew. What has been part of our past shapes our future. This Samhain we might also want to look forward. Someday we will be the past that helped shape someone else's future. Janus was the two-faced Roman god for whom January is named. One face looks to the past, the other to the future. Turn to face the west, the land of the dead and the deities, saying:

> Janus, who looks into the
> night toward the place
> where spirits seek light,
> bless all souls who come
> now as they hear it, and
> dance in the circle of spirit.

Turn to face the east, the point of the rising Sun, away from death and into the promise of a new day, saying:

> Janus, who into the day
> at dawn's first glow and
> Sun's first ray, bless this

circle without hesitation, and fear not the past nor times not yet here.

Edain McCoy

Notes:

November

November is the eleventh month of the year. Its name is derived from the Latin word *novem*, meaning "nine," as it was the ninth month of the Roman calendar. Its astrological sign is Scorpio, the scorpion (Oct 23-Nov 22), a fixed water sign ruled by Pluto. The golden and ruddy leaves of October now lie brown on the ground, and bare tree branches stand out against a bleak gray sky. It is cold outside, and dark, and home hearths glow now with warmth. This is the time of year for psychic, as opposed to physical, activity, and for quiet. Use candles of various magical colors inscribed with runes for magical purposes at this time. It is a good time for nurturing your shamanistic instincts, or for consulting a shaman. As the first snows begin to dust the ground, there are many indoor chores to be done. Celebrate your circle of fire now, knowing that the dark months of the year are what lie ahead. Be thankful for the warmth of your oven, bulging with turkey, pheasant, mincemeat and pumpkin pie. The main holiday of November, Thanksgiving, was originally designed to celebrate the first harvest of Indian corn by the Pilgrims in 1621. The original holiday was not much different from ours today—a large feast, games and contests, with all the community gathered around to look forward to winter months.

November 1

Tuesday

Day of the Dead – All Saints' Day – Election Day

 4th ♎

D → ♏ 2:29 am

New Moon 8:25 pm

Color of the day: Gray
Incense of the day: Gardenia

Letter to the Deceased Ritual

This was one of the days the ancient Romans set aside to communicate with the dead. During November, the spirit world is drawn closer to us, making it easier to contact those who have departed this earth. One way is to write a letter to the deceased. This is a very loving and solemn act which shouldn't be taken lightly. Begin the ritual in the evening at dusk. On a bare-wood table place the following: three candles, (one black, two white), one white feather, a piece of white paper, a black-ink pen, and a photograph of the deceased. Light all the candles and say: "You who have passed through heaven's gate, you who I mourn— receive this letter I'm about to write." Write your message using whatever words are on your mind. End the letter by wishing the spirit peace and rest. Extinguish the candles and fan the smoke toward heaven with the feather. Bury the letter facing the west. Your letter has been received.

James Kambos

Notes:

Holiday lore: The time between sundown on Samhain to sundown today, the Day of the Dead, was considered a transition time, or "thin place," in Celtic lore. It was a time between the worlds where deep insights could pass more easily to those open to them. Through the portals could also pass beings of wisdom, of play, and of fun. And while in time these beings took on a feeling of otherness and evil, as our modern relationship between the realms has been muddled, today can be a day to tap into the magic and wonder of other worlds.

November 2

Wednesday

All Souls Day

 1st ♏

Color of the day: Yellow
Incense of the day: Coriander

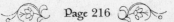

Letter Spell

To express your need, try writing a letter as though you were writing to a dear friend. This is good practice for communicating with others and for knowing yourself. Choose paper and ink color that best corresponds to your need. Decorate the paper, making it as visually attractive as possible. Use paint, markers, stickers, colored pencils, drawings, pictures, or use a computer and add clip art. Take the letter outside and read it to the universe or to the deity of your choice. Know that someone is listening and hearing your plea. End with this statement: "I will take action necessary to support my desire. For the good of all and harm to none, so mote it be." To add extra energy, mail the letter to yourself. After you receive it, place it on your altar until the spell manifests.

Ember

Notes:

Holiday Lore: All Souls Day is an official holiday of the Catholic calendar following All Saints' Day.

November 2 is traditionally attributed to St. Odilo, the fifth abbot of Cluny. The day was intended to honor the faithfully departed with offerings and Masses that would assist their souls' transit successfully from purgatory to heaven. It is believed that the Aztecs had an important role in the development of this tradition, though their history is complex with varied interpretations. For example, when a person dies the soul is said to pass through nine realms before arriving at Mictlan, the place of the dead. Once there, according to the Aztecs, the soul awaits transformation, or its next destiny.

November 3
Thursday

1st ♏

☽ → ♐ 8:55 am

Color of the day: Turquoise
Incense of the day: Sandalwood

harvest Is In Ritual

The harvest is in, and the cold winds of November blow sleet and rain against the windowpanes. A warm home is security against the winter weather to come. Now is the time to set a soup to simmer on the stove. As you gather the ingredients, think about the health and welfare of your loved ones. When the stock is ready, stir deosil (clock-

 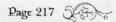

wise) and add vegetables, one at a time. Enchant the soup as you stir by saying, "I stir this brew with loving care to keep my family well. The gifts of the earth will keep us strong."

Paniteowl

Notes:

with your favorite oils. After your bath, in the candlelight and slowly massage your body with lotion or oil as you imagine yourself being prepared as a temple goddess. Look in a mirror and admire your body. Think about a person you would like to share your passion with. Imagine that person coming closer to you, joined to you by a pink thread of light, as you say:

> As the candle of passion burns,
> You will think of me,
> But only if your free will
> Wants this to be.

Emely Flak

Notes:

November 4
Friday
Mischief Night

 1st ♐

Color of the day: White
Incense of the day: Dill

Venus' Day Spell

Friday is the day dedicated to Venus, goddess of love and beauty. This is the day to attract a special person, or to get a special person you know to think of you. Tonight, arouse your inner goddess and celebrate your body. Your body has been designed for the divine gift of physical pleasure. Light a red candle while you take a long bath

November 5
Saturday

 1st ♐
☽ → ♑ 8:55 am

Color of the day: Blue
Incense of the day: Jasmine

Remembrance Garland

This is the time when the veil that separates the living from

 Page 218

the dead is at its thinnest. Pagans around the world embrace these rare days by remembering their ancestors now. Garlands are an ancient decoration, made of botanical items, that capture the magic of the seasons. To create a remembrance garland, string pieces of cockscomb, bay leaves, cranberries, orange peels, dried lemon slices, cinnamon stick and allspice. Begin tonight by soaking the bay, cranberries, cinnamon, allspice, and orange in Florida water or Kananga water (substitute plain water if these specialty waters are unavailable). As soon as you have time on the next day, cut a suitable length of waxed linen or hemp string. Begin the strand (and end it) with cranberries, and create your own pattern with the remaining botanicals. Place it in the entrance-way to your home. A remembrance garland is a fragrant invitation to your ancestors and departed loved ones.

Stephanie Rose Bird

Notes:

November 6
Sunday

 1st ♑
☽ → ♏ 10:00 am

Color of the day: Amber
Incense of the day: Clove

Autumn halfway Point Ritual

This day marks the halfway point of autumn. It is also known as the birch month, symbolic of new beginnings. Some pagans believe the Celtic New Year occurs on October 31, the day on which we traditionally celebrate Samhain. Today might be more appropriate for a new-year celebration. It is a fine time for making resolutions, because in the approaching "down time" of winter we can make plans for projects and things we'd like to work on. Make a list of things you'd like to accomplish this winter, and decide what categories they fit under—such as "practical" (i.e. organize closets, fix gutters), or "magical" (make a new tool, write a new ritual), or "somewhere in between" (learn French cooking). Then, get out your calendar and write in tips to get you started.

Ruby Lavender

Notes:

November 7
Monday

1st ♐

☽ → ♒ 4:31 pm

Color of the day: Lavender
Incense of the day: Peony

The Power of Pink Spell

Pink is a happy color—the color of harmony, peace, and love. To ease household tensions or strife, try the following exercise. Visualize everyone in the home encased in a big pink bubble. This bubble stretches to reach all rooms in the house. It grows larger and larger until it encases the home completely. It looks like a bubble gum bubble, but it is as strong as a steel-belted tire. The bubble is light as air and nice and cool to the touch. If you listen, you can hear it contains the sound of laughter and joy. Visualize everyone in the bubble laughing and smiling. When they leave the home, the bubble goes with them wherever they go. Hold this vision as long as you can. Try to keep it in the back of your mind all day.

Tammy Sullivan

Notes:

November 8
Tuesday
Election Day

1st ♒

Second Quarter 8:57 pm

Color of the day: White
Incense of the day: Ginger

Election Day Spell

Today is Election Day in the U.S., the day you will be using the wisdom of all the ancestors, the presidents who have passed on, and the goddess Athena to help elect wise men and women to lead the country. For this, place an image of Athena on your altar. Place a few photos of loved ones who have passed on and whose opinions you would trust, along with a few photos of deceased presidents (such as those in your wallet). Burn a blue candle and some rosemary incense, saying:

> Wise Athena,
> Trusted ancestors
> Revered presidents,
> Bless us with wisdom
>   to elect the finest men
>   and women today.
>
> Let us be strong
> And have the courage of
>   our convictions.
>
> Let those who are elected
> Tread the path of honest
>   and true leadership.

Let my words be heard
by the gods
And the honored dead.
As my will, so mote it be.

Look into the candle flame and meditate on honesty and integrity. Write a few words about what you would like your elected officials to accomplish. Place the paper under the candle, and burn the candle a little each day while meditating on the idea of truth.

Denise Dumars

Notes:

the short end of situations? Are you beginning to feel stagnant? This spell can be the catalyst that begins your transformation—the one that allows you to live the life that you want to live. One word of caution though: Asking for growth and change is just the beginning. Accepting growth and change is a more difficult and lengthy process. Choose candles and herbs that represent the desired change. Write the change that you are going to manifest, and be specific. Write the actions that you will enlist to manifest this change, and be specific. Place the list, candles, and herbs on your altar. Focus your mind, and say: "Currents of change, flow through me—transforming me. So mote it be!" State daily affirmations to yourself to reinforce your wonderful transformation.

Karen Follett

Notes:

November 9
Wednesday

 1st ≈
☽ → ♓ 7:22 pm

Color of the day: Brown
Incense of the day: Eucalyptus

Catalyst for Transformation Spell

Does your current method of operation seem to be leaving you on

November 10
Thursday

 2nd ♓
Color of the day: Purple
Incense of the day: Chrysanthemum

Reason and Liberty Celebration Ritual

In revolutionary France, people honored reason and liberty as two aspects of the same goddess. They held fabulous processions through Paris in celebration of her holiday on this day. They chose a French woman and garbed her in a dress of white, a mantle of blue, and a cap of red. Her worshippers wore crowns of oak leaves. Today, celebrate reason and liberty by dressing in red, white, and blue. Get together with some friends and hold a debate. Focus on making logical arguments even if dealing with emotionally charged issues. Give a reading of inspirational passages about freedom, or attend a lecture on history. Instead of casting any spells, practice honing your will. Focus your attention on just one thing and see how long you can hold it. Visualize reshaping reality to your own particular specifications. Thought is power—treat yours with care.

Elizabeth Barrette

Notes:

November 11
Friday
Veterans Day

 2nd ♓

☽ → ♈ 10:22 pm

Color of the day: Coral
Incense of the day: Thyme

Martinmas Day Spell

Some Christians will tell you that St. Martin, whose feast day is celebrated today, was a saint famous for his acts of charity. He was said to have cut his coat in half in order to clothe a naked beggar. But the sad truth is Martin was behind the destruction of many of the Druidic groves and responsible for the murder of Druidic priests. Celebrate this day by planting a sacred tree: birch, rowan, ash, alder, willow, hawthorn, oak, holly or hazel. Say as you work:

> Sacred tree I plant thee,
> So your roots will reach
>   deep within the earth
> And your branches reach
>   high toward the highest
>   heavens.
>
> May you shelter and
>   inspire me
> For all the years to come.

Leave a crystal at the base of your tree as a gift to the tree spirits.

Lily Gardner-Butts

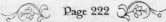

Notes:

November 12
Saturday

 2nd ♈

Color of the day: Indigo
Incense of the day: Violet

The Power Within Spell

Correspondences, incantations, and the like are wonderful adjuncts to the art of magic. But all magic begins and ends with the practitioner. The magical practitioner is the one who charges the universal energy that creates magic. The mere act of reciting words at a particular phase of the Moon really does little to influence outcome. This working is not one of attracting power to you. Rather, your power has to come from within. This working therefore is one of inner growth, intended to help you learn what power you possess and how to recognize any blocks to that power. To start, sit in a relaxed position. State your intent to gain wisdom regarding your personal power. Beginning with the root, focus a stream of energy to each chakra. Focus on the emotional aspect of the chakra—on the feelings and on any blocks or negative messaging clogging these power centers. Here is a list of associations for each of the seven chakras:

> Root chakra: "I am."
> Belly: Creation and pleasure.

Historical lore: Veterans Day commemorates the armistice that ended the Great War in 1918. Oddly enough, this war ended on this day, November 11, at 11 am (the 11th hour of the 11th day of the 11th month). Though Congress changed Veterans Day to another date in October at one point during this century, in 1968 they returned the holiday to November 11, where it stands today. The number 11 is significant. In numerology, it is one of the master numbers that cannot be reduced. The number 11 life path has the connotation of illumination and is associated with spiritual awareness and idealism—particularly regarding humanity. It makes sense then that this collection of 11s commemorates the end of an event that was hoped to be the War to End All Wars. Unfortunately, it wasn't the last such great war, but we can at least set aside this day to ruminate on notions of peace to humankind.

Solar plexus: Ability to manifest.

heart: Emotions and perceptions; the link between the mundane and spiritual planes.

Throat: Speaking the truth.

Brow: Perceptions of the future.

Crown: Connections to a higher self.

Listen to the messages from your higher self. Ground any excess energy. Journal your perceptions.

Karen Follett

Notes:

Before falling asleep, count down from ten to one and go into total relaxation. Imagine that you and the person you are in conflict with are walking through a beautiful garden of roses and daisies. As you cross a small bridge over a crystal-clear stream, stop to release your fears into the cleansing stream. Tell yourself that you will continue this healing walk in your dreams. Set an intent that both of you will be able to speak clearly, without the interference of ego, and be understood with love. Ask your spirit allies to help resolve this conflict for the best of all concerned. Allow yourself to fall asleep.

Kristin Madden

Notes:

November 13
Sunday

 2nd ♈

Color of the day: Orange

Incense of the day: Sage

Dreaming Away Conflict Spell

Dreaming is a wonderful method to use to work out any personal conflicts. Sprinkle a small amount of mugwort or thyme under your pillow.

November 14
Monday

 2nd ♈

☽ → ♉ 2:02 am

Color of the day: Silver

Incense of the day: Lavender

Radiant Light for the home Spell

A home without much natural light during the day is considered a "yin" abode according to feng shui. Inhabitants of such homes are prone to ailments and depression, especially if they have a lot of stagnant clutter. A "yang" home is one where there is ample sunlight from morning till afternoon. To balance yin and yang for a dark dwelling and to ensure a healthy flow of chi, perform this energizing spell in the morning or at noon. Gather a bunch of fresh orange or yellow flowers, and arrange them in a few vases, one for each room. Hold a length of golden ribbon and walk through every room with the ribbon trailing behind you. Put a vase of flowers in each room, and in the evening light a golden dinner candle at the altar and visualize radiance, stability, happiness, good health, and fortune positively manifesting in the home.

S. Y. Zenith

Notes:

November 15
Tuesday

 2nd ♉
Full Moon 7:58 pm

Color of the day: Black
Incense of the day: Poplar

heed My Words Spell

If you feel your suggestions or desires have been unheard or ignored, use the Full Moon in Taurus to get your point across effectively. Go outside when the Moon rises, and imagine it as a spotlight. Walk around and concentrate on feeling comfortable while in the "spotlight." Now imagine an actual bull, head lowered, ready to make a big impression on his opponent! Laugh if this image is funny to you, but do not let go of the image. Now go indoors and stand beneath the brightest light in the house. Visualize the last person who ignored you or who acted against your wishes. Imagine the expression on the person's face if he or she saw the bull. Let your anger dissolve into giggles as you imagine him or her fleeing from the bull. Now see the bull fade from view and replaced by an image of yourself. See the person who has ignored your wishes look on you with new respect and attention. Speak your mind positively and resolutely the next time you need to get your point across.

Denise Dumars

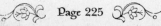

Notes:

the flame burns. Tomorrow, before entering work, dab some of the oil on your wrists and inhale the aroma. Let it remind you of your enjoyable workplace. Burn the candle each night until the following Friday. Wear the oil until you no longer need it. In the future, if you feel things beginning to grow tense once more, you can always start wearing the oil again.

Laurel Reufner

Notes:

November 16
Wednesday

 3rd ♉
☽ → ♊ 7:10 am

Color of the day: White
Incense of the day: Cedar

Calming the Workforce Beast Ritual

For this ritual, you'll need a brown candle, salt, and one or more of the following oils: lavender, myrrh, sandalwood, or ylang-ylang. We've all experienced distress and heavy negativity in the workplace. Whatever the cause, this ritual should help alleviate it. Dress the candle with the oil. Draw a circle of salt around the candle and its holder. Light the candle. Ground and center yourself. Focus your thoughts on a happy workplace—a place you enjoy going to each day. Hold the bottle of oil in your hands, pouring all of those images into it. Set the oil near the candle, and leave it there as

November 17
Thursday

 3rd ♊

Color of the day: Crimson
Incense of the day: Evergreen

Leonid Prosperity Spell

Every year on this day the Leonid meteor shower is visible in the sky close to the constellation of Leo. Pick a spot outside where you will not be disturbed and light prosperity incense. Watch the skies for a bit. Align yourself with a gently drifting energy. Visualize the meteors falling softly to earth and bringing good fortune with them. See them as green and gold for money and pink for love. Visualize that they are landing all around you in a shower of prosperous energy. Feel this energy building within you. Hold the energy. When you can no longer bear it, slowly let the energy stream from your right index finger back into the heavens. Say: "I accept the gifts rained upon me. I return my blessings and love."

Tammy Sullivan

Notes:

November 18
Friday

 3rd ♊
☽ → ♋ 2:42 pm

Color of the day: Pink
Incense of the day: Sandalwood

Elder Flower Footbath

The theme of this month is the remembrance of elders, community, stability, and wisdom. Honor an elderly friend or family member by utilizing the gifts of the elder tree as a tribute to the elder Moon. Elder flowers (*Sambucus nigra*) ease depression and are a relaxant and treatment for puffy eyes and rheumatism. Steep one cup of elder flowers in four cups of water. Dip two cotton squares in the elder tea, put them in a bowl, and place the bowl in the freezer. Strain one cup of the infusion and set it aside. Pour the remaining tea and flowers into a basin. Have your elder put his or her feet up, relaxing and drinking the tea with a bit of honey and lemon. Test the temperature of the elder infusion in the basin, and when it is not too hot add one teaspoon of lavender flowers. Have your elder place his or her feet into the floral infusion, then put cotton squares on his or her eyes. Let him or her relax as long as he or she would like, then gently towel-dry his or her feet and offer a pair of comfortable slippers.

Stephanie Rose Bird

Notes:

November 19
Saturday

 3rd ♋

Color of the day: Gray
Incense of the day: Patchouli

Day of Reckoning Spell

Saturday is named after Saturn, the Roman god of planning and the harvest. This day has also been identified as "the day of reckoning," making it a favorable time to summon energy for knowledge, wisdom, and self-improvement. With a purple candle burning, write down on a piece of paper one thing you wish to improve about yourself. It should be something simple like:

> By the end of five or six weeks, I will improve my well—being by drinking two liters of water per day and much less coffee.

Make it specific, achievable, and measurable, and remember to include a time frame. Put your note away. Make a diary note to retrieve it by the end of your nominated time frame, or if that won't work for you ask a friend to send it to you via mail or e-mail. Remember: This is a contract with yourself, and should be treated seriously as an important and effective tool for growth and self-empowerment.

Emely Flak

Notes:

November 20
Sunday

 3rd ♋

Color of the day: Yellow
Incense of the day: Clove

Soothing Bath Ritual

This fragrant bath is conducive to healing, meditation, and the soothing of the blues. It also calms the nerves and restores inner equilibrium after a hectic day. Gather one cup of lavender flowers, one cup of carnation, one cup of chamomile, half a cup of valerian root, and six bay leaves. If possible, use fresh flowers. If they are not available, substitute with dried ones. When flowers are in season, pluck and store them in the freezer for future use. Put all the ingredients into a white cotton bag and tie it with a piece of string. Attach the string to the tap, and run the bath water over the bag. Two drops of geranium essential oil in the warm bath will benefit those with dry and flaky skin conditions. Visualize yourself washing

away all of your troubles and your
worldly burdens.

S. Y. Zenith

Notes:

With no worries and no
pain.

Ember

Notes:

November 21
Monday

 3rd ♋
☽ → ♌ 1:10 am

Color of the day: Ivory
Incense of the day: Maple

Bath Relaxation Spell

To your bath add your desired
bath salts, some dried peppermint
leaves, and chamomile flowers tied
in a bundle of cheesecloth, and some
lavender essential oil. Light candles
in the room, and extinguish all other
light. Play music if you like. Try
to remain undisturbed and visualize
the water drawing the tension from
your body. Feel your muscles relax,
and close your eyes and say:

> Water wash away my
> worries.
> Take them down the
> drain.
> Leave me rested and in
> peace,

November 22
Tuesday

 3rd ♌
☉ → ♐ 12:15 pm

Color of the day: Maroon
Incense of the day: Pine

Enchanted Gift Spell

Anyone can give a gift by going
to a store and buying something
nice. Enchanting a gift makes the
gesture much more meaningful. To
do this, think of the person you
intend to gift. Select something you
know will be appreciated. As you
wrap the gift, visualize all the things
you'd like to see come true for that
person. Tie a ribbon, or a length of
yarn, around the gift. Use red for
passion, green for healing, or yellow
for prosperity. As you tie the ribbon,
say: "Ties that bind us will remind
us of the love we have to share.
May your life be filled with kindness,

and all your days be free of care."
For a birthday gift, add a small
birthstone to the ribbon in the center of your bow.

Paniteowl

Notes:

been in your way. Write each obstacle on a small strip of paper. Focus
on actions and thoughts that will help
you overcome the obstacles and write
these on the paper with your goal.
Visualize the obstacle disappearing
as you burn the "obstacle strip" on
the charcoal. Repeat with each obstacle. Acting on your goals can now be
your recipe for achieving goals that
are "full-flavor nice."

Karen Follett

Notes:

November 23
Wednesday

3rd ♌
☽ → ♍ 1:41 pm
Fourth Quarter 5:11 pm

Color of the day: Topaz
Incense of the day: Neroli

Full Flavor Goals Spell

During a mead-tasting contest, I
recently learned that the full-
flavored meads were called "nice," and
the meads that didn't achieve full
flavor were called "not quite." With
those terms in mind, how would
you define the final flavor of your
goals for yourself? Are they turning
out "nice," or are they leaning toward
"not quite"? Burn incense attuned
to your goal on a charcoal block. Write
your goal on paper. Visualize your
goal. Visualize the obstacles that have

November 24
Thursday
Thanksgiving

4th ♍
Color of the day: Green
Incense of the day: Dill

Harvest Wishbone Spell

The autumn feast we now refer
to as Thanksgiving has roots
that go far deeper into the past than
a presidential decree. The feast of
thanks grew out of the old European
harvest home festivals that were
Pagan in origin, and that retained

their Pagan character. Many of the Puritans in the Massachusetts Bay Colony proposed this feast of thanks to their god for helping them prepare for the harsh winter ahead, and to the presence of the local Native American tribes that were critical players in the Colony's survival. You can make your own Thanksgiving feast special by inviting some that are less fortunate to join you. A warm house and a special meal will make a memorable day for all. As various dishes are passed clockwise around the table, have people tell not only what they are thankful for, but what they wish for themselves in the year to come. After everyone's plate is filled, take the wishbone from the turkey—or a makeshift one from a broken tree limb if you are vegetarian—and say:

> The lord and lady have
> heard all our chatter,
> Your god, my god, the
> source does not matter.
> In peace and hope we
> share this meal,
> With gratitude and zeal.

Edain McCoy

Notes:

November 25
Friday

 4th ♏

Color of the day: Rose
Incense of the day: Ylang-ylang

St. Catherine's Day Ritual

St. Catherine, saint of unmarried women, is the matron of this day. Even in this age, there is a lot of pressure for women to marry and have families by a certain age. Women who are happily single and childless still face societal expectations that can be hard to deal with. On this day, try a spell for self-love and acceptance. Wear robes of pale pink, blue, or green. Light candles and decorate the altar with flowers. Have cakes and wine ready. Meditate upon your life: your accomplishments, your dreams, and all the friends and loved ones whose company you enjoy. Drink the wine, saying: "I toast my independence and celebrate my choice to be solitary." Eat the cakes, saying: "I nurture myself, and within me I can find everything I need." Then recite in a bold voice:

> As I drink this wine and
> eat these cakes,
> I celebrate companionship
> and loyalty
> Of many friends and
> loved ones.

Ruby Lavender

Notes:

"I turn back the look of hate."

Cast the cloves onto the fire, and this will destroy the evil stare. Let the fire die, as it does the curse will break. Pour the water mixture onto the ground outside your home.

James Kambos

Notes:

November 26
Saturday

 4th ♏

☽ → ♎ 1:58 am

Color of the day: Black
Incense of the day: Lilac

Evil Eye Curse~Breaking Spell

The belief in the evil eye is taken quite seriously in many parts of the world. To break the curse of the evil eye, read the following spell.

> In the evening before you
>   retire,
> Sit before a crackling
>   fire.
> At your side gather an
>   earthen bowl
> Filled with water and a
>   drop of olive oil,
> Nine whole cloves
>   (Jupiter's incense)
> That will break the hex.
> Scry into the bowl to
>   reveal the curse.
> Gaze until you see a face.
> Then say: "By the powers
>   of heaven and fate,

November 27
Sunday

 4th ♎

Color of the day: Gold
Incense of the day: Basil

Nature Communion Spell

This is a wonderful day to commune with nature. Go for a walk, taking full advantage of the healing benefits of reconnecting with earth energies, even in the middle of a crowded city. If you cannot go to a park, focus your attention on the plants, trees, stones, and creatures you see as you walk. Breathe deeply until you feel connected with each thing. Imagine how it must feel to be this object. Thank it for sharing this space with you, and allow yourself to be led to whatever natural object calls to you. Continue to give thanks and move on to the next thing until you a kinship with the natural world. Thank the earth for sharing its essence with you.

Kristin Madden

Notes:

someone about to embark on a tricky challenge give a potted chrysanthemum to embolden the heart. The Chinese say that if you drink from a stream bordered by chrysanthemum blooms, you will live for a hundred years. Chrysanthemum imagery appears frequently in temples. Consider decorating your altar with a chrysanthemum.

Elizabeth Barrette

Notes:

November 28
Monday

 4th ♎
☽ → ♏ 11:33 am

Color of the day: Gray
Incense of the day: Frankincense

Warmth and Wellness Ritual

The chrysanthemum is the quintessential flower of fall, bringing particular luck to people born in November. Although its name means "golden flower" in Greek, it also comes in fiery autumn shades of red, orange, and bronze. It represents longevity and perfection. During the Chrysanthemum War in 1357, the Japanese wore this flower as an emblem of courage. Today, the Order of the Chrysanthemum ranks as the highest honor Japan can bestow. If you know

November 29
Tuesday

4th ♏
Color of the day: Red
Incense of the day: Juniper

St. Andrew's Eve Divination

For centuries, people have practiced various divination and love spells on this night. Melt wax in a pot and pour it through the hole of a key into a vat of cold water. When the wax is hardened, pull it from the water and place it between a burning candle and a piece of paper. The shadow it throws should suggest something to you. If you wish to marry in the upcoming year, snip a branch from a cherry tree and plant it in wet soil. Keep the ground moist. If it flowers before Christmas, you will marry in 2006.

Lily Gardner-Butts

Notes:

of prosperity and fertility. To invoke the blessings of Lakshmi during Diwali infuse one cup basil leaves in four cups of water, and strain. Add one-half teaspoon of peppermint and basil essential oils. Wash floors and walls with Lakshmi's spiritual wash.

Stephanie Rose Bird

Notes:

November 30
Wednesday

4ħ ♏

☽ → ♐ 5:32 pm

Color of the day: Brown
Incense of the day: Coriander

Diwali Celebration

Diwali is a two-week long celebration of the Hindu people that teaches people to vanquish ignorance by driving away the darkness that engulfs the light of knowledge. Diwali is a festival of lights, and the word is derived from the Sanskrit words *deepa*, meaning "light," and *avali* meaning "row." Set up hanging lamps or as many candles in a row as possible to encourage the presence of Diwali. Welcome Lakshmi, goddess of prosperity, who is linked to this celebration. Lakshmi is embodied by basil, rice, coins, and other symbols

December

December is the twelfth month of the year, its name derived from the Latin word *decem,* meaning "ten," as it was the tenth month of the Roman calendar. Its astrological sign is Sagittarius, the archer (Nov 22–Dec 21), a mutable fire sign ruled by Jupiter. This month is buried under blankets of snow. In the evenings, holiday lights twinkle for the Yule season. Back porches are stacked with firewood. Ovens bake confections for serving around a decorated table. Sweets have a particularly ancient history at this time; they are made and eaten to ensure that one has "sweetness" in the coming year. The Full Moon of December is the Oak Moon. It is a time when the waxing Sun overcomes the waning Sun, and days begin to grow longer again. In some Pagan traditions, this struggle is symbolized by the Oak King overcoming the Holly King; rebirth triumphing over death. It is no coincidence that Christians chose this month to celebrate the birth of Jesus. The Winter Solstice is a solar festival and is celebrated with fire in the form of the Yule log. New Year's Eve is another important celebration during December. The old dying year is symbolized at this time by an old man with a long white beard carrying a scythe. The new year is seen appropriately as a newborn child.

December 1
Thursday

 4th ♐
New Moon 10:01 am

Color of the day: Purple
Incense of the day: Carnation

health and Athleticism Spells

Most of us could use more exercise and could stand to pay more attention to our health and fitness. Sagittarius the Archer can help us keep on track with our exercise and help us avoid the holiday weight gain. Find a statue or image of the Archer and also a statue of Diana with her bow and arrow for your altar. Write down your fitness goals. Buy some rosemary or black pepper essential oil and place the bottle of oil in your gym bag. Go to your altar, and place your fitness goals by the statue of Diana. Ask her to inspire you as you exercise and then leave her a copy of your goals. At the gym, sniff the essential oil when you feel the need for more energy, and then visualize the goals that you wrote down earlier. As the Moon waxes, see yourself working toward your goal. Talk to Diana or to the Archer as you work, and allow them to act as your be your exercise coaches throughout this season.

Denise Dumars

Notes:

December 2
Friday

 1st ♐
☽ → ♑ 8:42 pm

Color of the day: Coral
Incense of the day: Nutmeg

hari Kugo festival Spell

Each year on this day, in Tokyo, the Hari Kugo festival takes place. This celebration, which translates as "broken needles," honors women's crafts. It's dedicated to the patron goddesses of Japanese craftswomen. You can also tap into the energies of this celebration by identifying one skill that you excel in, and then congratulating yourself for that talent. This can be any craft such as herb growing, cooking a special dish, or incense making. Or perhaps your gift is of a more intellectual nature—writing, finance, or teaching. Think about how others benefit from your talent and be proud of your gift. Think of one way to

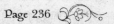

share your craft or help someone with your skill as you state this short affirmation, adapting it to your own special talent:

> Beginning today, I will write a special poem (or other act) for my niece on her birthday.

Emely Flak

Notes:

Now say:

> This gift holds more than meets the eye, for I send love and joy, laughter and peace. Delight and harmony that lift your spirit high. I send you contentment and well wishes to follow you through the next year. With good for all and harm to none, as I say it, so it is done.

Tammy Sullivan

Notes:

December 3
Saturday

 1st ♑

Color of the day: Brown
Incense of the day: Pine

Gift-giving Spell

The time of year for shopping and gift-giving is upon us. We can magically charge the wrapping paper in such a way that when the gift is unwrapped, the opener receives a jolt of warm wishes and very happy thoughts. Spread the paper under the present as you normally would. Lay your right hand on the present and send vibrations of warmth and love.

December 4
Sunday

 1st ♑
☽ → ♒ 10:36 pm

Color of the day: Yellow
Incense of the day: Parsley

Rowan Protection Lore

This is the Rowan month in the Celtic tree calendar. Rowan, also known as mountain ash, is a hardy tree associated with magic and Witches.

Its folk names include witchwood, witchbane, and quickbane. The folk lore concerning the rowan tree is vast and sometimes confusing. In some cases, rowan is thought to be useful for protection from witchcraft, but the tree is also used by Witches for enchantment. Its bright red berries were used throughout the British Isles as protection against evil forces, and the branches were tied over the doorways of houses and barns. Scottish cows were considered vulnerable to evil magic or, worse, to having their milk "stolen" by Witches and fairies. To prevent this theft, cows were given garlands of rowan branches and berries tied with red thread to wear for protection from such attacks.

Ruby Lavender

Notes:

this on your own on behalf of both family and friends. Locate photos or items that remind you of each person you wish to remember and honor. They can be living or deceased, close or far away. Use any objects that belong to the person: jewelry, clothing, photos. If you don't have an item, simply write the person's name on a piece of paper or use something that reminds you of them, or you can create a collage of photos. The "altar" can be a table, dresser, or fireplace mantle. Keep the altar up for the holiday season to remind you of your emotional ties and connections.

Ember

Notes:

December 5
Monday

 1st ≈

Color of the day: Silver
Incense of the day: Myrrh

Create a Family Altar Spell

Invite everyone in your home to participate in this spell, or do

December 6
Tuesday

1st ≈

Color of the day: Black
Incense of the day: Honeysuckle

Holiday Bliss Spell

For a bit of extra holiday bliss at this time of year, you will need at least four large vanilla-scented candles. The holidays are a good time to become frazzled and then just stay that way. This simple spell relies on both the scent of the candles and the ambience they create. Place candles in the living room, kitchen, your bedroom, and the bathroom. Feel free to put them in other rooms as well. Make sure your candles are in areas that are safe for burning—that they won't scorch the surface they are resting on and they won't set alight anything that is hanging nearby. Each evening, burn your candle for a half hour or so, take a few deep breaths, and let the stress melt away.

Laurel Reufner

Notes:

Nutcrack Divination

There are two versions of this fun divination exercise. If you have a fireplace, take two whole walnuts and set them in front of your fire as it burns brightly. As you watch the fire, hold the question you want answered in your mind. When the fire has died down, place the walnuts in the glowing embers. If one or both crack loudly, this is a sign you will be successful. If they just burn, you may have a brief success but it will not last. If you are unable to divine by fire, crack a bag of walnuts with a nutcracker while holding your question in mind. If the majority of the shells break into complete halves, your dreams will be realized. If most of the shells shatter when cracked, you will need to reevaluate your goals.

Kristin Madden

Notes:

December 7
Wednesday
Burning the Devil

 1st ♒

☽ → ♓ 12:44 am

Color of the day: White
Incense of the day: Sandalwood

Holiday lore: Cultures around the world have shared a penchant for the ritual burning of scapegoats, enemies, and devils. There is something primal about the roar of a large bonfire and its ability to bring purging light to a community. Today is such a day in the highland towns of Guatemala. Men dress in devil costumes during the season leading up to Christmas, and children chase the men through the streets. On December 7, people light bonfires in front of their homes, and into the fires they toss garbage and other debris to purify their lives. At night, fireworks fill the air.

ancient practice is to build a box shrine containing holly, ivy, and an image of Mary called a Milly box. ("Milly" is a doggerel version of "My Lady.") When you offer friends and family a leaf of greenery from the box, they must pay you a coin to receive good luck for the new year.

Lily Gardner-Butts

Notes:

December 8
Thursday

 1st ♓
Second Quarter 4:36 am

Color of the day: Turquoise
Incense of the day: Geranium

Immaculate Conception Meditation

Mary worship has always been synonymous with Demeter worship. For instance, Mary's feast days follow the major Eleusinian festivals. In particular, today marks the day when Kore, the virgin goddess, was conceived. Coincidentally, on this same day the holy virgin, Mary, was said to be conceived. An

December 9
Friday

 2nd ♓
☽ → ♈ 4:02 am

Color of the day: White
Incense of the day: Ginger

Cranberry Garland Love Spell

To create an enduring love between you and your mate, perform this "crafty" spell. First, light two red candles. Between them place a bowl of cranberries, about seven feet of strong thread, a sewing needle, and a few drops of sweet red wine in a small glass. Also have a plain pine wreath on hand. Anoint the thread with the wine as you say: "Wine, crimson red. Red as love, bless this thread." Thread the needle, knot one end and begin stringing the cranberries. As you add each berry, think of your love growing stronger. Add berries until you have about a foot of thread left, then securely knot the end several times. Decoratively wrap the garland around the wreath as you speak this charm:

> Like the wreath, always
>   round,
> We are also bound.
> And like the magical
>   evergreen
> Our enduring love has
>   no end.

James Kambos

Notes:

December 10
Saturday

 2nd ♓

Color of the day: Gray
Incense of the day: Lavender

Fast Cash Spell

This time of year can be taxing on both our physical and financial resources. To find opportunities to gain fast cash, anoint a green candle with patchouli essential oil. Write your financial desires on a piece of paper that has also been anointed with the oil. State these or similar words: "Energy builds, and money flows to me. This spell I cast, so mote it be!" Focus on your desires, visualizing that you have obtained them. Light the paper in the flame of the candle, and allow it to burn in a fire-proof container. State these or similar words: "My energy is released on wings of fire. Bring back to me my visualized desires!" Relax your mind. Listen for any messages from the universe. Be alert for any money-making opportunities that arise.

Karen Follett

Notes:

December 11
Sunday

 2nd ♓

☽ → ♉ 8:46 am

Color of the day: Orange
Incense of the day: Poplar

Cartouche healing Talismans

Cartouche is sometimes referred to as an "Oracle of Ancient Egyptian Magic." The symbols of several cartouche cards may be used to effect self-healing or to send healing to someone in need. The three main deities of cartouche that can be invoked for healing purposes are Horus, Bast, and Thoth. Horus, the son of Isis and Osiris, is worshiped by all as the redeemer and patron of homes and families. He is also the "All-Seeing Eye," who deals with troubling physical ailments and eye conditions. Bast, the twin sister of Horus and also the patroness of cats, takes care of all those who suffer from mental problems and psychological setbacks. Thoth, the lord of time and the patron of healers, looks after any imbalances that can cause disease in people or society. He is petitioned by many to look after the overall healing of the soul or spirit. Use your intuition as a guide when invoking gods and praying to them for the restoration of good health.

S. Y. Zenith

Notes:

December 12
Monday

 2nd ♉

Color of the day: Lavender
Incense of the day: Rose

Final Suit Spell

The final suit in the tarot is pentacles, which completes your yearlong study of the suits. Spend the day examining the cards of the suit of pentacles, and gain a solid grounding in this divinatory system. First, find the Ace of Pentacles in your deck. Set the card on your altar. Burn some incense with a rich, earthy aroma such as patchouli or oakmoss. Then say:

Pentacle, emblem of the
    earth below,
Teach me whatever I
    need to know.
Weave a connection
    from me to the land.

> Pentacle, symbol of
>   strength and wealth,
> Bring to me courage,
>   success, and health.
> Let me wield wisely the
>   power at hand.

In your tarot guide book, read the section on pentacles. Consider the imagery as you let the incense burn down. For the rest of the day, pay attention to any pentacle imagery you encounter. Write about what you see and keep it with your other tarot notes.

Elizabeth Barrette

Notes:

Snowman Making Spell

Making a snowman can be much more than just child's play. The snowman can also be a guardian and protector for your household during this season of colds and flus. If you have snow where you live, use it. If not, a small snowman made of Styrofoam balls will be just as effective. Use bits of charcoal for the eyes, and old buttons for the nose and mouth. Be creative, and be sure to give him personality as you sculpt the face. Add evergreen boughs for the arms, and a small evergreen wreath for his hat. Wrap a scarf around his neck, and enchant him by saying:

> Man of snow,
> While cold winds blow,
> Protect our home from
>   care and woe.
> Health and comfort come
>   to me,
> And our home will
>   blessed be.

Paniteowl

Notes:

December 13
Tuesday

2nd ♉
☽ → ♊ 2:59 pm

Color of the day: Maroon
Incense of the day: Evergreen

December 14
Wednesday

2nd ♊

Color of the day: Brown
Incense of the day: Eucalyptus

Martian Shield to Keep from harm
This day is acknowledged as the sacred day for the goddesses of wisdom—Athena, Minerva, Maat, and Sophia. It's a day to open your mind to all possibilities and to make yourself receptive to your inner wisdom by increasing your awareness of the synchronistic events that occur in your life. Events that may seem like random occurrences are often meaningful coincidences that serve a divine purpose, offering you special and timely lessons and messages. Repeat this affirmation three times before you leave your home:

> I accept that all events
> in life occur for a higher
> purpose. There are no
> mistakes, only lessons.

Instead of punishing yourself with guilt for doing "silly" things, accept that hindsight is part of the journey.

Emely Flak

Notes:

December 15
Thursday

2nd ♊
Full Moon 11:16 am
☽ → ♋ 11:01 pm

Color of the day: Green
Incense of the day: Musk

Both Sides Now Spell
The Full Moon in Gemini can help us see ourselves in more than one aspect. How do you usually describe yourself—as a "brain," or as a "jock"? Now is the time to strip away any stereotypical images we have of ourselves and see another side of our nature. Take a cleansing bath with lavender or your favorite herb. Dress in white and imagine yourself as a clean slate. Sit and visualize what you would like to see written on that slate. Imagine yourself doing activities that you would like to do but haven't yet attempted. See yourself as a well-rounded person, and congratulate yourself on your accomplishments—no matter how they may come across to others. Promise yourself that you will not judge yourself by others' yardsticks. Make a list of areas of your life that need more attention. Now see yourself as twins doing two separate activities— for example, reading a book alone and charming friends at a party. Slowly visualize the two persons

becoming one complete individual. Review this visualization whenever you feel the need for more balance in your life.

Denise Dumars

Notes:

December 16
Friday

 3rd ♋

Color of the day: Pink
Incense of the day: Almond

Witches holiday Survival Spell

Are you completely swept up in the holiday hustle and bustle? Witches can easily get caught up in the fray. We care deeply for friends, family, and community. In the midst of all the chaos, remember to illuminate the dark season with candles. Choose red for energy, green to symbolize the renewal of life, blue for healing, and white for the sacred. Remember: Witches hunt and gather. Hunt for magical objects with history and good karma as gifts. Gather a cornucopia of seasonal spices, flowers, fruits, and vegetables, and put them near your hearth and at your altar.

Create a sachet filled with lavender and borage leaves. Squeeze it on bad days to relieve tension. Rejoice in nature. Acknowledge the winter birds by spreading seed or suet for them. Listen for messages emitted by the trees. Dance in the snow, and bring snow inside. Put it in a metal bowl on your altar. Sing with spirit. Play inspirational music. Recognize the gifts of the harvest. Praise the earth. Above all else, rejoice!

Stephanie Rose Bird

Notes:

December 17
Saturday
Saturnalia

 3rd ♋
☽ → ♌ 11:01 pm

Color of the day: Blue
Incense of the day: Coriander

Mocha Cocoa Recipe

To make a cold winter night warm, whip up this heavenly mix and then brew yourself a cup of mocha cocoa. Then sit back and contemplate the nature of things.

> 1 1/2 cups instant nonfat
>   dry milk powder
> 1 1/2 cups powdered non-
>   dairy creamer
> 1 1/2 cups brown sugar
> 1/2 cup cocoa
> 1/2 cup, plus 2 tablespoons,
>   instant coffee
> 1 2/3 cups miniature
>   marshmallows

Mix all ingredients except for the marshmallows, stirring well to combine them thoroughly. Then add the marshmallows, and store the mixture in an airtight container. To make the cocoa, mix three or four tablespoons with one cup of boiling water.

Laurel Reufner

Notes:

Holiday lore: Saturnalia was the Roman midwinter celebration of the solstice, and the greatest of the Roman festivals. It was traditional to decorate halls with laurels, green trees, lamps, and candles. These symbols of life and light were intended to dispel the darkness of the season of cold. The festival began with the cry of "Io Saturnalia!" Young pigs were sacrificed at the temple of Saturn and then were served the next day. Masters gave slaves the day off and waited on them for dinner. Merrymaking followed, as wine flowed and horseplay commenced. Dice were used to select one diner as the honorary "Saturnalian King." Merrymakers obeyed absurd commands to dance, sing, and perform ridiculous feats. It was also a tradition to carry gifts of clay dolls and symbolic candles on the person to give to friends met on the streets.

December 18
Sunday

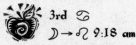 3rd ♋
☽ → ♌ 9:18 am

Color of the day: Amber
Incense of the day: Cinnamon

Epona Feast Day Lore

Epona was the horse goddess of the Celts and Romans. From Epona we get our word "pony." She is the goddess believed to watch over draft animals—such as horses, donkeys and oxen—and also of the war horse. She was the only Celtic goddess whose feast day was also celebrated by the Romans. Deposits of Roman coins and other artifacts have been found buried near the large Paleolithic-era chalk hill figure in Uffington, England known as the White Horse. The figure is thought to be dedicated to Epona. This area is also known as White Horse Hill, and horses are still grazed in the many fertile pastures nearby. It is believed that the well-known British aversion to eating horsemeat during wartime food shortages and rationing comes from a deep-seated reverence and worship of the horse as practiced by their Celtic ancestors.

Ruby Lavender

Notes:

December 19
Monday

 3rd ♌

Color of the day: Gray
Incense of the day: Peony

Home Blessing to Prepare for the Holidays

Many homes celebrate more than one winter season holiday. Bless and cleanse your home to prepare for the celebrations. Burn sage throughout your home by carrying a sage wand or censer from room to room. This waning Moon phase is a good time to banish all negative energies. Follow by ringing bells and sprinkling consecrated water as you chant:

Bless this home for joy
to come,
Singing praise for
everyone,
Peace and love will
hereby reign.

Lift any cause of hurt
or pain.
Cleanse this space of
hearth and home,
For loved ones near and
those that roam.

Unite us in this sacred
time,
By these words our
kindred bind.

Ember

Notes:

Mother Goddess and Father God. Blessed are those who reside here. So it is from this day forward." You may also empower a mistletoe wreath for additional protection.

Tammy Sullivan

Notes:

December 20
Tuesday

 3rd ♌
☽ → ♍ 9:39 pm

Color of the day: Red
Incense of the day: Sage

Mistletoe Magic

Mistletoe has long been used for protection and for love magic. Burning mistletoe banishes evil. Take a bottle of rubbing alcohol and drop fresh mistletoe sprigs in it. Let this set for a few hours. The longer it rests, the more potent will be the potion. When ready, pour the alcohol in your cauldron and light it. If you do not have time to allow the potion to rest, instead burn some sprigs of mistletoe. As you burn the potion or sprigs, say: "Evil may not reside or visit this happy and healthy home—not in any form, nor at any time. This home is protected by the

December 21
Wednesday
Yule – Winter Solstice

 3rd ♍
☉ → ♑ 1:35 pm

Color of the day: Yellow
Incense of the day: Cedar

Turning the Wheel Spell

Over the last fifty years, television has provided us with many game shows in which the fate of contestants rests on the random outcome of a spinning wheel. This wheel of fortune concept dates back to the ancient Middle East. On this cold Yule night, light some candles and pull out an old board game that has a spinning wheel, or else devise one for yourself out of poster board and appropriate items from a craft store. Mark what each section of the poster board wheel means. Keep it simple with sections such as "yes," "no," "perhaps," "get a life," "listen to your inner voice," "not in this lifetime," and any other category you wish. Take turns with friends and family asking questions as they take turns spinning the wheel. As the needle spins around, the spinner should speak one of the following statements, depending on what they want the answer to be.

> Please say yes, this is my
> wish come true.

Or:

> Please, kind wheel, I
> need help from you.

Or, if you want a negative answer:

> Please say no,
> O Fortune's Wheel.

Or:

> You know my heart and
> what I feel.

Edain McCoy

Notes:

Holiday lore: The Yule season is a festival of lights, and a solar festival, and is celebrated by fire in the form of the Yule log—a log decorated with fir needles, yew needles, birch branches, holly sprigs, and trailing vines of ivy. Back porches are stacked with firewood for burning, and the air is scented with pine and wood smoke. When the Yule log has burned out, save a piece for use as a powerful amulet of protection through the new year. Now is a good time to light your oven for baking bread and confections to serve around a decorated table; sweets have an ancient history. They are made and eaten to ensure that one would have "sweetness" in the coming year. Along these lines, mistletoe hangs over doorways to ensure a year of love. Kissing under the mistletoe is a tradition that comes down from the Druids, who considered the plant sacred. They gathered mistletoe from the high branches of sacred oak with golden sickles. It is no coincidence that Christians chose this month to celebrate the birth of their savior Jesus. Now is the time when the waxing Sun overcomes the waning Sun, and days finally begin to grow longer again. In some Pagan traditions, this struggle is symbolized by the Oak King overcoming the Holly King—that is, rebirth once again triumphing over death. And so the holly tree has come to be seen as a symbol of the season. It is used in many Yuletide decorations. For instance, wreaths are made of holly, the circle of which symbolized the wheel of the year—and the completed cycle. (*Yule* means "wheel" in old Anglo-Saxon.)

December 22
Thursday

 3rd ♏

Color of the day: Crimson
Incense of the day: Vanilla

Jade Prosperity Restoration Spell

Jade is attributed various magnificent virtues, and it is highly prized by the Chinese since time immemorial. Among the desires that jade can fulfill are love, money, prosperity, longevity, wisdom, protection, and healing. When going through difficult financial times, charge a piece of jade, a ring, pendant, or bangle with money-attracting energies. Wear it and develop a confident and positive attitude toward money. Visualize yourself being restored with prosperity lost prior to owning or charging the piece of jade. When pondering business matters, hold a piece of jade in your hand and be receptive to its prosperous vibrations. Then hold it against your "third eye," and close your eyes for a few minutes. Be open to the wisdom

it will bestow in making decisions about money matters. When prosperity returns to you, remember to donate something to charity and use the rest of your money with conscientious intent.

S. Y. Zenith

Notes:

December 23
Friday

 3rd ♏
☽ → ♎ 10:26 am

Fourth Quarter 2:36 pm

Color of the day: Coral
Incense of the day: Dill

Ghosts of Christmas Spell

It is appropriate that Larentia, the Roman mother goddess of friendly ghosts, was honored today. Traditionally, December is a time when ghosts are active. All we have to do is think of Charles Dickens' *A Christmas Carol* to understand this. As the year draws to a close, it is time to honor our ancestral spirits and any friendly spirits that have taken up residence with us. Prepare the following sachet to protect your home and to welcome friendly spirits. In an attractive scrap of fabric tie up a pinch of nutmeg, clove, cinnamon, one crushed bay leaf, and a tablespoon of dried orange peel. Tie it up with a green ribbon, and leave it near a window, or put a pinch in an old shoe and leave on your porch—a place where house spirits frequently dwell. End by lighting a green candle and saying: "Friendly spirits alone are welcome in this place. Come in peace, or come not at all. As I will, so mote it be."

James Kambos

Notes:

 4th ♎

Color of the day: Indigo
Incense of the day: Violet

Witch's Ladder Spell

Give yourself this wonderful Christmas present and see how good you feel afterward. Braid a cord the length of your body with black, red, and white ribbons. Prepare the braid before Christmas Eve. Make a list of thirty-one wishes that you want to see manifest this coming year. On Christmas Eve, light a red candle. Say each wish and knot your cord. Visualize how it will feel as each wish comes true. When you are finished, make nine additional knots to bind the spell, and say:

> By knot of one, the spell's begun.
> By knot of two, it cometh true.
> By knot of three, thus shall it be.
> By knot of four, 'tis strengthened more.
> By knot of five, so may it thrive.
> By knot of six, the spell we fix.

By knot of seven, the
stars in heaven.
By knot of eight, the
hands of fate.
By knot of nine, it shall
be mine!

Goddess, bless this gift I
give.
May it bring joy and love
to my loved one.

Lily Gardner-Butts

Notes:

through city streets with evergreens strapped to the roof, non-Christians get a bit tense. And why not? The accoutrements of this Christian holiday all originated from Pagan practices. But this is an argument we'll never win, so heavily is the culture infused with the symbols and spirit of traditional Christmas. So it's probably best to stop fighting it, and just think of Christmas as a second Yule. Who wouldn't want two major festivals in one week? We'll all be avoiding our scales after all the celebrating has ended, but what a way to go! Take time now to go alone, or with your family or a group, to the place in your town that has the largest concentration of garish decorations, and simply bask in the glow of all the holiday hoopla.

Edain McCoy

Notes:

December 25

Sunday

Christmas

 4th ♎

☽ → ♏ 9:04 pm

Color of the day: Gold
Incense of the day: Sage

Second Yule Spell

When the first red and green lights start appearing on rooftops, and when cars begin to meander

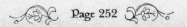

December 26
Monday

Kwanzaa begins – hanukkah begins

 4th ♏

Color of the day: Scarlet
Incense of the day: Chrysanthemum

Future Dreams Spell

The darkened Moon at this close of the calendar year is a good time for rest and reflection. On this night, draw an herbal bath of lavender and jasmine. Surround the tub with candles and flowers. Reflect on the past year—its opportunities for growth, for joy, and even the difficulties. Reflect on all that you have learned this past year. Allow the tub to drain, visualizing any excess negativity draining away with the water. Prepare a pouch of lavender and jasmine to place on your pillow. Before drifting off to sleep, say these words:

> The future calls
> The continuous turn of
> the wheel.
>
> All inspirations of hope
> and renewal
> My dreams reveal.

Upon awakening and prior to rising from your bed, journal any perceptions or dream memories that you have had.

Karen Follett

December 27
Tuesday

 4th ♏

Color of the day: Scarlet
Incense of the day: Gardenia

Let No Evil In Spell

The long nights of winter provide ample opportunity for mischievous spirits. If you find yourself bothered, fear not! Tradition also provides a means of guarding your home through the night. Start by obtaining a handful of whole mustard seed at a health food store or in your supermarket spice aisle. Pour it into a bowl on your altar to charge overnight. The next night, sprinkle the mustard outside the door to your home, saying:

> Mustard hot and mustard
> hard,
> By my home stand watch
> and guard.
> Bar the door with
> discipline;
> Guard! and let no evil in.

All malicious entities will be bound to stop and count each tiny seed before they can go another step. They will still be stuck outside your door at dawn, when the Sun will banish or destroy them.

Elizabeth Barrette

Notes:

tie it with a purple ribbon. Light a purple candle, and rub it with oil of rosemary. Enchant the candle by saying: "As this year draws to an end, I have counted up each friend. I bless each one in memory, for they have shared their lives with me." Let the candle burn out by itself. Place the list in a safe place, and next year add the names of new friends you've met. Count yourself lucky in the richness of your friendships.

Paniteowl

Notes:

December 28
Wednesday

 4th ♏
☽ → ♐ 3:43 am

Color of the day: Topaz
Incense of the day: Neroli

Old and New Friends Listing Ritual

The end of the calendar year is a time of reflection, and a time to consider the future. We should take time to think about our friends and relations who make our lives richer by their presence. Make a list of old friends and new. Think about how they have affected your life during the past year. Roll the list up, and

December 29
Thursday

 4th ♐

Color of the day: White
Incense of the day: Chrysanthemum

Wet Fire Wish Spell

For this wish spell, you will need to make a small boat of heavy paper or light wood. It only needs to be large enough to stay afloat holding a tea candle or votive. It is a good idea to cover the bottom and sides with tape to waterproof it. On the bottom of the boat, just under where the candle will sit, write your wishes in your favorite color ink. Take the boat to a pond or fill your bathtub with water. Sprinkle a small amount of sage on the water. Place a tea candle or yellow votive in the boat and light it. Call upon the energies of the elements and ask them to help manifest your wishes. Float your boat out onto the water, imagining your dreams coming true as it floats away.

Kristin Madden

Notes:

New Love in the New Year Spell

Are you looking to meet someone new in the new year? Maybe you just want a last-minute New Year's Eve date? Try this New Moon divination: Get out your tarot cards and a statue of Bast or a picture of a cat. Bast is the goddess of joy, and cats are also sacred to Freya, whose day is Friday. Ask the cards to tell you how to meet this new person. Explain your wishes and ask for guidance. Now do a three-card spread. Read the cards intuitively. What do they tell you to do? Do they indicate action on your part or are they telling you to let the universe bring the one you want? If the cards seem negative, wait and take the latter approach. If they seem positive, ask Bast if you are going to be meeting just a fun date or a possible long-term partner. Pull one more card for the answer. Whatever cards you pull, be positive about your romantic future when the new year arrives and the Moon waxes.

Denise Dumars

Notes:

December 30
Friday

4th ♐

☽ → ♑ 6:35 am

New Moon 10:12 pm

Color of the day: Purple
Incense of the day: Nutmeg

December 31

Saturday

New Year's Eve

1st ♑

Color of the day: Black
Incense of the day: Lavender

hope for Freedom Spell

As we end another year, it is good to recognize the great blessing of freedom. If there are bonds tying you down—such as debt, addictions, or unwanted relationships—create a list that marks out a strategy that leads toward freedom. Wear white today—it is the color of spirituality strength. For dinner, cook your favorite food using fire in the over or on the stove—fire is a symbol of freedom. As the fire is gaining heat for cooking, and as the Sun begins to set, burn old unnecessary papers. Set yourself free from the past. Later, when you go to bed, slip a High John the Conqueror root into your pillowcase. High John is the herb of freedom. Sleep with High John and dream of your life of freedom.

Stephanie Rose Bird

Notes:

Notes:

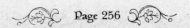

A Guide to Witches' Spell-A-Day Icons

 New Moon Spells   Full Moon Spells

 New Year's Eve, Day   Jewish Holidays

 Imbolc   Samhain, Halloween

 Valentine's Day   Thanksgiving

 Ostara, Easter   Yule, Christmas

 April Fool's Day   Sunday Health Spells

 Earth Day   Monday Home Spells

 Beltane   Tuesday Protection Spells

 Mother's Day   Wednesday Travel Spells

 Father's Day   Thursday Money Spells

 Litha   Friday Love Spells

 Lammas   Saturday Grab Bag

 Mabon

Daily Magical Influences

Each day is ruled by a planet that possesses specific magical influences:

Monday (Moon): peace, healing, caring, psychic awareness, and purification.

Tuesday (Mars): passion, sex, courage, aggression, and protection.

Wednesday (Mercury): conscious mind, study, travel, divination, and wisdom.

Thursday (Jupiter): expansion, money, prosperity, and generosity.

Friday (Venus): love, friendship, reconciliation, and beauty.

Saturday (Saturn): longevity, exorcism, endings, homes, and houses.

Sunday (Sun): healing, spirituality, success, strength, and protection.

Lunar Phases

The lunar phase is important in determining best times for magic. Times are Eastern Standard Time.

The waxing Moon (from the New Moon to the Full Moon) is the ideal time for magic to draw things toward you.

The Full Moon is the time of greatest power.

The waning Moon (from the Full Moon to the New Moon) is a time for study, meditation, and little magical work (except magic designed to banish harmful energies).

Astrological Symbols

The Sun	☉		Aries	♈
The Moon	☽		Taurus	♉
Mercury	☿		Gemini	♊
Venus	♀		Cancer	♋
Mars	♂		Leo	♌
Jupiter	♃		Virgo	♍
Saturn	♄		Libra	♎
Uranus	♅		Scorpio	♏
Neptune	♆		Sagittarius	♐
Pluto	♇		Capricorn	♑
			Aquarius	♒
			Pisces	♓

The Moon's Sign

The Moon's sign is a traditional consideration for astrologers. The Moon continuously moves through each sign in the zodiac, from Aries to Pisces. The Moon influences the sign it inhabits, creating different energies that affect our daily lives.

Aries: Good for starting things, but lacks staying power. Things occur rapidly, but quickly pass. People tend to be argumentative and assertive.

Taurus: Things begun now do last, tend to increase in value, and become hard to alter. Brings out an appreciation for beauty and sensory experience.

Gemini: Things begun now are easily changed by outside influence. Time for shortcuts, communications, games, and fun.

Cancer: Stimulates emotional rapport between people. Pinpoints need, supports growth and nurturance. Tend to domestic concerns.

Leo: Draws emphasis to the self, to central ideas or institutions, away from connections with others and emotional needs. People tend to be melodramatic.

Virgo: Favors accomplishment of details and commands from higher up. Focus on health, hygiene, and daily schedules.

Libra: Favors cooperation, compromise, social activities, beautification of surroundings, balance, and partnership.

Scorpio: Increases awareness of psychic power. Precipitates psychic crises and ends connections thoroughly. People tend to brood and become secretive under this Moon sign.

Sagittarius: Encourages flights of imagination and confidence. This Moon sign is adventurous, philosophical, and athletic. Favors expansion and growth.

Capricorn: Develops strong structure. Focus on traditions, responsibilities, and obligations. A good time to set boundaries and rules.

Aquarius: Rebellious energy. Time to break habits and make abrupt change. Personal freedom and individuality is the focus.

Pisces: The focus is on dreaming, nostalgia, intuition, and psychic impressions. A good time for spiritual or philanthropic activities.

Glossary of Magical Terms

Altar: a low table that holds magical tools as a focus for spell workings.

Athame: a ritual knife used to direct personal power during workings or to symbolically draw diagrams in a spell. It is rarely, if ever, used for actual physical cutting.

Aura: an invisible energy field surrounding a person. The aura can change color depending upon the state of the individual.

Balefire: a fire lit for magical purposes, usually outdoors.

Casting a circle: the process of drawing a circle around oneself to seal out unfriendly influences and raise magical power. It is the first step in a spell.

Censer: an incense burner. Traditionally, a censer is a metal container, filled with incense, that is swung on the end of a chain.

Censing: the process of burning incense to spiritually cleanse an object.

Centering yourself: to prepare for a magical rite by calming and centering all of your personal energy.

Chakra: one of the seven centers of spiritual energy in the human body, according to the philosophy of yoga.

Charging: to infuse an object with magical power.

Circle of protection: a circle cast to protect oneself from unfriendly influences.

Crystals: quartz or other stones that store cleansing or protective energies.

Deosil: clockwise movement, symbolic of life and positive energies.

Deva: a divine being according to Hindu beliefs; a devil or evil spirit according to Zoroastrianism.

Direct/Retrograde: refers to the motions of the planets when seen from the Earth. A planet is "direct" when it appears to be moving forward from the point of view of a person on the Earth. It is "retrograde" when it appears to be moving backward.

Dowsing: to use a divining rod to search for a thing, usually water or minerals.

Dowsing pendulum: a long cord with a coin or gem at one end. The pattern of its swing is used to predict the future.

Dryad: a tree spirit or forest guardian.

Fey: an archaic term for a magical spirit or a fairylike being.

Gris-gris: a small bag containing charms, herbs, stones, and other items to draw energy, luck, love, or prosperity to the wearer.

Mantra: a sacred chant used in Hindu tradition to embody the divinity invoked; it is said to possess deep magical power.

Needfire: a ceremonial fire kindled at dawn on major Wiccan holidays. It was traditionally used to light all other household fires.

Pentagram: a symbolically protective five-pointed star with one point upward.

Power hand: the dominant hand, the hand used most often.

Scry: to predict the future by gazing at or into an object such as a crystal ball or pool of water.

Second sight: the psychic power or ability to forsee the future.

Sigil: a personal seal or symbol.

Smudge/Smudge stick: to spiritually cleanse an object by waving incense over and around it. A smudge stick is a bundle of several incense sticks.

Wand: a stick or rod used for casting circles and as a focus for magical power.

Widdershins: counterclockwise movement, symbolic of negative magical purposes, and sometimes used to disperse negative energies.

Norse Runes

Feoh:	money, wealth	ᚠ
Ur:	strength, physicality	ᚢ
Thorn:	destruction, power	ᚦ
Os:	wisdom, insight	ᚠ
Rad:	travel, change	ᚱ
Ken:	energy, creativity, change	ᚲ
Gyfu:	gift, sacrifice	ᚷ
Wynn:	joy, harmony	ᚹ
Haegl:	union, completion	ᚻ
Nyd:	need, deliverance	ᚾ
Is:	ice, barrenness	ᛁ
Jera:	bounty, fruition, reward	ᛃ

Eoh:	resilience, endurance	ᛇ
Peordh:	change, evolution	ᛈ
Eolh:	luck, protection	ᛉ
Sigil:	success, honor	ᛋ
Tyr:	courage, victory, justice	ᛏ
Beorc:	healing, renewal	ᛒ
Eh:	journeys, work	ᛖ
Mann:	man, self, intelligence	ᛗ
Lagu:	healing, protection, life	ᛚ
Ing:	fertility, energy	ᛝ
Daeg:	opportunity, change	ᛞ
Ethel:	land, prosperity, power	ᛟ

Call for Submissions

We are looking for magical daily lore for next year's *Witches' Spell-A-Day Almanac.* If you have lore or history to share about a day or holiday, we'd like to hear about it.

Writers: Daily lore pieces should be 100 to 150 words long, and focus on the folklore, historical information, or trivia particular to a calendar day or holiday. We are looking for unique and interesting lore that is timely, revealing, and intriguing.

Submissions should be sent to: annualssubmissions@llewellyn.com

or

Witches' Spell-A-Day Submissions
Llewellyn Worldwide
P.O. Box 64383
St. Paul, MN   55164

(Please include your address, phone number, and e-mail address if applicable.)

If you are under the age of 18, you will need parental permission to have your writing published. We are unable to return any submissions. Writers and artists whose submissions are chosen for publication will be published in the 2006 edition of the *Witches' Spell-A-Day Almanac* and will receive a free copy of the book.